CLASSIC MOTORCYCLE MADNESS

PHILLIP ISLAND CLASSIC

CLASSIC MOTORCYCLE MADNESS

DUNCAN COUTTS

Photo Credits
Darren Begg
Darin Fitzgerald

Credit
Thanks – Michelle Elvy, my editor.
Many thanks for her work and patience with me.
Michelle is challenged by my difficulty with the dangling modifier.
A dangling modifier, to me, is to be handled like a hanging dag.

Published 2025
by Duncan Coutts

ISBN 978-0-473-76280-3 (International Edition)

© Copyright Duncan Coutts 2025

All rights reserved.

Except for the purpose of fair reviewing, no part of this publication may be reproduced or transmitted in any form or by any means, electronic or mechanical, including photocopying, recording or any information storage and retrieval system, without prior written permission from the publisher.

COPYPRESS

Designed and distributed in New Zealand by CopyPress, Nelson, New Zealand.

www.copypress.co.nz

Do not go gentle into that good night, Old age should burn and rave at close of day; Rage, rage against the dying of the light.
> *Dylan Thomas (1914–1953)*

To Fletcher Coutts – who has been smart enough to stay away from motorcycles; early on he recognised their danger. However, each to their own. He's more than happy to have a cricket ball bounced at his head at 80 mph.

To Frances Coutts (my wife) who has basically funded my disease – Secretly I believe she may have a life insurance policy on me

CONTENTS

Part one	**Arrival**	1
Part two	**Dinner with men**	57
Part three	**Race days**	81
Part four	**The heat goes on**	135
Part five	**The business end**	163

LIST OF CHARACTERS

DC: Duncan   narrator, New Zealand team captain

Simon   ex-copper, shaven head, bulk muscle, Chucky's minder

Andy   nearly Yorkshireman (emigrated to NZ), CEO engineering co, clean freak

Matt   Yorkshireman, émigré, 6'4", plagued by performance anxiety

Campbell   truck/digger contractor from Christchurch, understated

Spotty Dave   mirror man, operates on the edge of reality

Brendan   Irish member of Kiwi team, ball of energy, Russian wife,

Rastus   lobster fisherman from Bluff, ruddy-cheeked, larger than life

Poppa Smurf   dude with long white beard

Chucky   doll

PART ONE

ARRIVAL

GOD HELP ME — ME – AND CAMPBELL

'Hey pal.' It was a small, quiet voice.

'Yes, God.' I smiled serenely.

'I thought you might be on this plane.'

I nodded. 'You are the all-seeing one, your omnipresence.'

'Ha, you've never called me that before,' the voice giggled softly. 'But I like it. Are you on something?'

'God, I'm on you… but you know that.' Perhaps this trip was going to be alright.

'Hey pal, did Andy and Matt make it on?

'You know they did, invisible one.' I frowned slightly, then smiled again. 'Let's get back to me.'

'Not always about you, pal. I'm up the back.'

I eased opened my aisle-side eye. There he was: not God. Campbell.

Campbell's face was at eye level. I opened my eye fully. Campbell was crouched in the aisle, his blue eyes sparkling with amusement. He was from Christchurch and an enthusiastic Post Classic and Bears class rider. Campbell ran an earth moving operation. Diggers, trucks and other assorted equipment. He specialised in building horse arenas even though he wouldn't know one end from the other – of a horse, that is.

'What the hell are you doing here?' I asked, opening both eyes and pulling myself upright in the seat. 'For a moment there, I thought I was talking to God.'

'I've been called worse,' chuckled Campbell. 'Anyway, I'm down the last row if you need me.'

'What are you doing on this plane?' I asked. 'Why aren't you with Simon on the South Island flight, on the earlier one?'

'Got my flights a little mixed up. Ended up in Auckland – yesterday.

Stayed at the Ibis last night.'

The air hostess arrived and made shooing motions at Campbell.

'I'm down the back row,' said Campbell, conspiratorially lowering his mouth to my ear. 'It's like the school bus. That's where all the fingering happens.' He chuckled happily and moved away.

I shook my head, *God help me*.

HIGH HEELS AND YORKSHIREMEN

We had stumbled onto the airport shuttle bus that morning at 4.30 am and I had eyed up the driver who was wearing a black cowboy shirt with silver sequins, black jeans with a wide diamante belt and a platinum blonde wig that fell to his waist.

I could have taken it as a sign that all was not going to go well on this trip – not going to be regular. But it was very early and my sign warning defence system had not been activated. In hindsight I should have turned around and stepped off the bus.

I had bumbled my way to a seat. *Too early, I'm not going to engage my brain in figuring this dude out.* Besides I had more pressing problems – namely the fellas with whom I was travelling. I was about to hop aboard a plane in Auckland, New Zealand, with two Englishmen, worse still, bloody-minded Yorkshiremen, who had somehow made the Kiwi motorcycle team despite their broad northern accents and stubborn, sometimes sullen, attitudes.

Cheap airline tickets dictated the time of departure from New Zealand and arrival in Australia: either you left at the crack of dawn and arrived at a decent time, or you left later and arrived in the night. *Night owl or an udder squeezer?*

The International Island Classic (IC) was a dream event if your fix was racing classic motorcycles, especially big ones. The Phillip Island track near Melbourne was very fast, yet wide and forgiving, like a good mum. You could butcher a corner, make all kinds of mistakes, fire out all sorts of amateur lines and apexes but still exit leaving a big blackie and looking like the legend Mick Doohan.

The bus had lurched away from the kerb – difficult to drive smooth in high heels. I briefly squinted out the window. Was that a hint of dawn or just a flash from a neon billboard? I was still resisting opening my eyes fully and slid further down in my seat. By rights, I should still have been asleep like most normal people.

THE FLYING MOLE ....ANDY

One of the Yorkshiremen, Andy, was afraid of flying. Andy had spent 13 years underground in a coal mine in Yorkshire; it was certainly unnatural for a mole to fly. Andy was from a town called Clowne – technically in Derbyshire. Clowne even got a mention in the Doomsday Book – *there were some wags out there.*

Andy had needed to pee a lot this morning. He'd undergone psychological damage control courses to overcome his flying phobia. But he wasn't relying solely on mind control, I noted, as I had watched Andy slide some anti-depressant and anti-anxiety pills into his gob.

Andy was the CEO of a huge engineering company. He had many men under his control and he had his work cut out trying to keep them safe while progressing the many jobs at hand. Shutdowns and maintenance were their specialties. Andy was big on systems and protocol. He carried this over into his racing. He had little understanding of someone who could turn up with a bike that was poorly turned out. It made no sense and wasn't

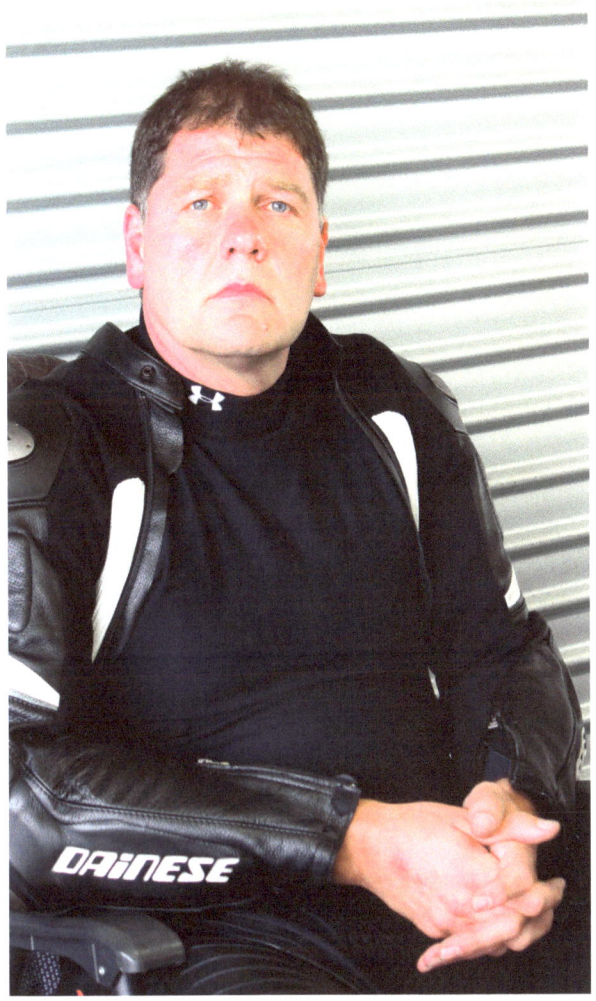

floor so as not to dirty it: to leave children foot smudges on the mats. If it rained while out for a Sunday ride, which it often did in Auckland, Andy would find an overbridge to park under until the shower had passed. Rain equalled water, add dirt and it meant marks.

Andy was certainly on the spectrum. Hell, every fella I knew, including me, was on the spectrum. For sure, he would be turning the toilet rolls right way round in the plane dunny.

He struggled with the turnout of my bikes, I could tell, but he had come to realise that he needed to accept this; knowing me had benefits, me being the organiser of outings and motorcycle trips. One had to sometimes put up with less-than-ideal situations for the greater good. He also suspected that sometimes I would turn out a bike that was a little grubby just to annoy him. I practiced a form of wabi-sabi (a celebration of imperfection).

Andy had a larger brain than me and didn't appreciate that small things amused small minds – but he knew it was a thing. Andy was big on rules.

I was a Kiwi of Scottish/Irish pedigree and by nature had a problem with rules and a difficulty with authority, which wasn't uncommon amongst motorcyclists. I was of the school of thought where the ref was there to blow the whistle for kick off and then to get the hell out of the way. I didn't watch much rugby since it had turned professional; they now even announced the name of the bloody ref!

proper. Do it properly or not at all, was Andy's ethos. Andy's bikes were immaculate. And shiny. He kept Pledge in business.

His was a constant battle of trying to be more chill; of trying to be more Kiwi. When he had first shifted from the UK to NZ, Andy had bought a new car. He had been in a full-on anal-clean phase. His kids were occasionally allowed in the car but they had to ride with their feet suspended off the

FAIR T' MIDDLIN .... MATT

The other Yorkshire lad, Matt, had been busy quoting statistics on the chances of crashing. This was obviously very disturbing for Andy who had gone white-eyed and headed off for another pee.

Andy had missed the premise that Matt was not talking plane Armageddon but was focussing on Phillip Island where he hadn't raced before. Matt figured if he didn't crash then he would likely be the slowest guy out there. Either way it would be shite.

Matt had been around motor racing for a long time, having been involved in the World Rally Championship. He was something of an electronics whizz. A really great time was summed up by Matt: 'Yeah, it was okay'. An average show: 'Fair t'middlin'. A shitshow: 'Mingin' – meaning disgusting.

Gotta love that northern English glass-half-empty approach, I thought. I had my work cut out just understanding their dialect. This was an international meeting so there would be much strange lingo to interpret.

Matt, being a tech geek, was very useful when dealing with bikes with full electronic packages: quick shifter, launch control, anti-wheelie, anti-slide, traction control, abs, engine braking, blipper, shapeshifter. The bikes we rode had none

of those. We rode classic bikes. Dinosaurs, like their owners. Classic bikes were piloted by stick and rudder pilots.

PATHETIC .... ME

We had checked our bags in. Mine weighed 23.8 kg; as usual pushing the limit. I always, always resented Air New Zealand only allowing passengers 23 kg per piece. The American airlines allowed 30 kg – and, they were already carrying bigger people. *Perhaps American planes had bigger engines.* Qantas allowed 30 kg. I had wanted to book with Qantas but Andy, with his phobia, would have none of it. He had chosen to live in NZ 'because I trust Kiwis' and he wanted to fly Air NZ. I knew that was a load of bollocks as Andy had never trusted me.

Also, Andy's wife, Mel, said they migrated because the UK had become 'un-English' – plus former World Superbike racer Aaron Slight came from NZ, and she had a thing for him.

My favourite airline was Emirates – *the UN airline*. The pilot would come on the mic and boast about the number of different nationalities working the plane. I was intoxicated by the exotic aromas swirling about the cabin. Frankincense, myrrh and Bvlgari Au the Noir cologne.

It was proving increasingly tough for me to get away on these motorcycle trips. Lord knew it was difficult for virtually any motorcycle racer to

get away to chase his forlorn and pitiful passion. Many wives and/or girlfriends didn't understand the need for speed. A motorcycle trip often came with the knowledge that a reciprocal obligation of some form would be required – a credit owed; the haunted look of a pussy-whipped man.

I had broached the subject of this latest trip, one morning, a couple of months back. I had shuffled my worn slippers into the bedroom.

"I'm dying," I said, stopping by the bed, shoulders slumped.

"Yes, you are," replied my wife.

"No, really, I am." I coughed weakly for emphasis.

"We all are. It's just a matter of when," soothed my wife. "You're fine.

We are getting older."

My wife was in bed, her back propped up with pillows, a book on her lap and a coffee on the bedside table. She glanced briefly up, pulled her reading glasses down a notch and considered me. 'Why are you wearing sunglasses inside?'

'Because I'm dying,' I exhaled. 'People don't want to see the eyes of dying people. Yellowing, or worse still, blood leaking out of them.'

My wife sighed, withdrew the glasses from her ears and placed them on the bed cover. She couldn't be accused of not having endurance.

'What's brought this on?' she asked, her tone reasonable, maintaining self-control.

'A visit to the doctor. Yesterday. She said I could have a year. Maybe longer if I had treatment.'

My wife was still in self-control mode but her voice thought she had moved into early-annoyance mode and went up a notch. 'Did she also say you should have a holiday? Maybe get away overseas? Perhaps something that involved racing motorcycles?'

'Yes. That's exactly what she said.' I squinted, 'How did you know?'

'You are pathetic.'

'Yes I am.' I shrugged, feeling slightly dickless. 'I'm pathetic … and dying.'

'Go. Just go.' Her self-control mode was trying to amp up – *what an opportunity to let rip*. But no, *she* was not the one with the problem. She pressed her reading glasses back on and picked up her book. 'Go on whatever pathetic motorcycle racing trip you've planned. I don't know why you even try these feeble acts anymore. I've seen them all.'

She was right: it had been feeble. Perhaps even more feeble than the other poor role plays I had dreamt up. There had been the one about needing to check out Melbourne to see if it was a suitable place for our eldest daughter to shift to, to undertake an osteopathic equine course. At least my wife had laughed at that. I was going on about the stables of the well-to-do of Victoria: seeing if the horse shit was of a texture fit to stick to the bottom of Bianca's gumboots. It just so happened that Phillip Island Circuit was just down the way in the state of Victoria and that's where the infamous Island Classic was held each January.

I considered that it may be time to get an agent to negotiate these trips with my wife. I was, after all, a Motorcycle Man.

MOTORCYCLE MAN

I slung my helmet bag over my shoulder. We had kept our helmets as carry-ons. This could be considered a little unnerving for the other passengers. The reason for doing so being that helmets were the most treasured part of the kit and you didn't want some mushroom-head in cargo using them as footballs, and heaven forbid, you didn't want them being lost in transit. Helmets are very particular to a rider: the fit, the feel, and mostly, the smell. You sweat a lot when you're racing, despite the fact you're basically just sitting on your fat arse twisting the throttle.

But to the horde at an airport, a helmet was a sign that you were different to Joe Public. You inhabited a different hemisphere. Most people in the modern world had become so integrated into the so-called norms of society that unknowingly they were operating on only one

Photo: D Begg

plane; their lives had increasingly become constricted, fearful and conservative to the point where anything different did not compute, was to be avoided, was risky even. Every spare moment was fixated on a device screen and the small void it sucked the user into. The arrival of a motorcyclist near that insular sphere created a disturbance – a ripple. It brought out that universal first-world, buried but occasionally nagging doubt that there could be another way to live your life. Joe Public would rather have a conversation with an Artificial Intelligence chatbot than a motorcyclist; at least the AI bot would be speaking the same language as them.

Joe Public had no real comprehension of what portal a rider took for his or her habit but they suspected it was like doing drugs: barely legal – a fringe activity, and Joe Public kept well away from the fringe; you could fall off a fringe.

PRE-FLIGHT RITUALS .... THE BOYS

The boys hadn't sat together on the plane. Matt was furthest towards the front. He was 6' 4", a full head taller than the people beside him. Andy was a few rows behind Matt. I was sat further back and across at an angle from Andy. I had regarded Andy, sitting motionless, his eyes staring ahead but blank and unseeing. The drugs had kicked in. Passengers were busy fidgeting and fossicking with their carry on and preparing for the flight. Tissues in, tissues out. Personal devices out, or in. Ear buds in. Scrolling madly through the in-flight screen choices. Poking the screen with a hard digit to get a response. Jamming the seat pocket with throat lozenges, moisturisers, books and magazines. Andy was frozen in time. He was a wax figure. I had observed Andy on planes before. He was a living form of rigor mortis: immobile, staring fixedly straight ahead but without vision. You could wave a hand in front of his eyes and there wouldn't be a flicker. He wouldn't even respond to the hostess when it was meal or drink orders time. He was in his own drugged frozen dimension and there was no breaking into it. Some kind of weird zombie zone. The hostess was busy with her pre-flight ritual, shutting overhead lockers, checking seatbelts, keeping her butt away from the happy hand passengers – but not too busy to cast the occasional worrying glance at the rigid passenger in 22B. She would eventually be quietly thankful. Heaven knows, if only all the passengers were birdbrains, cinched tight in an enforced cryogenic sleep, how easy her life would be. She would be able to go back to the galley, pull the curtain, let her hair out, slam a quick gin and tonic, and do a line. *Hang on,* she did that anyway.

I was seated in 26D, near the back of the plane. I had selected an aisle seat, I always did. It gave one options: toilet, walkies, easy signalling to the hostess for a brandy and Heineken. You could keep an eye on passengers; early detection of onboard freak about to go berserk. I settled back in the chair and closed my eyes for a few minutes, stilling the excitement and worry of another trip – finding calm. Around me, passengers were still making last minute preparations before belting themselves in. The safety video came on instructing us to obey all crew instructions. *Good luck getting rigor-Andy to the life-raft*, I thought. Return to your seat if the seatbelt sign lights up. Put valuables under the seat in front of you – that would be the crash helmet;

plane; their lives had increasingly become constricted, fearful and conservative to the point where anything different did not compute, was to be avoided, was risky even. Every spare moment was fixated on a device screen and the small void it sucked the user into. The arrival of a motorcyclist near that insular sphere created a disturbance – a ripple. It brought out that universal first-world, buried but occasionally nagging doubt that there could be another way to live your life. Joe Public would rather have a conversation with an Artificial Intelligence chatbot than a motorcyclist; at least the AI bot would be speaking the same language as them.

Joe Public had no real comprehension of what portal a rider took for his or her habit but they suspected it was like doing drugs: barely legal – a fringe activity, and Joe Public kept well away from the fringe; you could fall off a fringe.

PRE-FLIGHT RITUALS .... THE BOYS

The boys hadn't sat together on the plane. Matt was furthest towards the front. He was 6' 4", a full head taller than the people beside him. Andy was a few rows behind Matt. I was sat further back and across at an angle from Andy. I had regarded Andy, sitting motionless, his eyes staring ahead but blank and unseeing. The drugs had kicked in. Passengers were busy fidgeting and fossicking with their carry on and preparing for the flight. Tissues in, tissues out. Personal devices out, or in. Ear buds in. Scrolling madly through the in-flight screen choices. Poking the screen with a hard digit to get a response. Jamming the seat pocket with throat lozenges, moisturisers, books and magazines. Andy was frozen in time. He was a wax figure. I had observed Andy on planes before. He was a living form of rigor mortis: immobile, staring fixedly straight ahead but without vision. You could wave a hand in front of his eyes and there wouldn't be a flicker. He wouldn't even respond to the hostess when it was meal or drink orders time. He was in his own drugged frozen dimension and there was no breaking into it. Some kind of weird zombie zone. The hostess was busy with her pre-flight ritual, shutting overhead lockers, checking seatbelts, keeping her butt away from the happy hand passengers – but not too busy to cast the occasional worrying glance at the rigid passenger in 22B. She would eventually be quietly thankful. Heaven knows, if only all the passengers were birdbrains, cinched tight in an enforced cryogenic sleep, how easy her life would be. She would be able to go back to the galley, pull the curtain, let her hair out, slam a quick gin and tonic, and do a line. *Hang on,* she did that anyway.

I was seated in 26D, near the back of the plane. I had selected an aisle seat, I always did. It gave one options: toilet, walkies, easy signalling to the hostess for a brandy and Heineken. You could keep an eye on passengers; early detection of onboard freak about to go berserk. I settled back in the chair and closed my eyes for a few minutes, stilling the excitement and worry of another trip – finding calm. Around me, passengers were still making last minute preparations before belting themselves in. The safety video came on instructing us to obey all crew instructions. *Good luck getting rigor-Andy to the life-raft*, I thought. Return to your seat if the seatbelt sign lights up. Put valuables under the seat in front of you – that would be the crash helmet;

that piece of bodywear could become gold in the right circumstance. If there's a mishap during take-off or landing, brace yourself on the seat in front of you. Or put your hands on either side of your head, your elbows on either side of your legs and your feet flat on the floor. The video went on to talk about life jackets but every passenger knew that by the life jacket stage you were well and truly fucked. I would far rather there'd be a hot hostess fronting with bon-voyage tequila shots as we were going down.

MOTORCYCLE MAN

I contemplated that perhaps I was getting a little old for this racing lark. I'd started late in the racing game at 50 and I'd had 10 good years. I had been fastish right off the bat. My crash ratio worked out roughly at three crashes per season and one of them would put me in hospital. So, 10 years would be 30 crashes and 10 hospital visits - give or take. Not bad, not good. That didn't include my idiotic misadventures on my dirt bike.

I had broken ribs a few times, scapula twice, collar bones a few times and high-sided high enough to feel like I'd broken everything in my body when I returned to earth, only to discover that I may not have broken anything: the x-rays on my heels showed no breaks; the blue and black bruising was impressive, as it was on my tailbone.

A DC crash.

I had a small odd love affair with pain. I would be slow to admit it, but if prodded, I would admit that it may well be worth hurting yourself for a hit of morphine. Morphine was like many good things, it was illegal in everyday life.

My most painful injury had occurred in the rain when I was sliding down the track on my back and used my chest as a battering ram on a competitor's rear wheel – hard enough to knock the dude off. Torn rib cartilages was the diagnosis. Chest protectors became mandatory shortly after that. There was the chap who turned up to the Greymouth Street Races with a wooden chest protector, but that's another story.

My biggest crash was the 200 kph one at Manfield but the list of injuries from that was too long to remember.

I also had an odd affair with suffering and pushing myself. It wasn't necessarily something I wanted; it was something I *needed*.

However, I was now over 60 so perhaps it was time to start listening to myself, my inner voice, to try for some reason. *Whatever*.

VROOM VROOM .... CAMPBELL

A couple of hours into the flight and I was disturbed from the movie.

There was an intrusion, an irregular vibe to the normal noises of a flight. I detected a small commotion at the back of the plane. I glanced around. An air hostess was knocking softly on a lavatory door. She was muttering to a steward beside her. I eased out of my chair and moved to the back of the plane, sliding past the crew who were huddled beside the toilet door. I did some stretches in front of an escape door. Hamstrings and a quad pull. Stretching was a good way to keep away deep vein thrombosis. At least, I thought it was – something I'd read in a magazine. I looked out the door's window into blue space. Had DB Cooper had a similar view in November of 1971 before flinging himself out the door of the plane at 30,000 feet above Reno, USA – albeit with a parachute and a satchel of ransom money? Those escapades were no longer possible with the modern airliner. You couldn't open the door willy-nilly anymore and pretty much everyone thought that was a good idea.

I was just behind the crew and could hear the hostess muttering. I edged a little closer to listen better.

'He's been in there for ages,' she said.

'Well, what's ages?' asked the stout steward.

'More than 30 minutes.'

'Oh. That's not good.'

'Excuse me sir,' she tried again, knocking lightly. She didn't want to arouse suspicion, curiosity or questioning from the other passengers. That could quickly turn to fear and then bedlam. There was no answer to her knock. She nodded in silent confirmation to the steward. He picked up a phone nearby and had an urgent but brief conversation.

I took a couple of paces back into the cabin and peered around the corner. Campbell's seat was empty. I padded in my socks back to the escape exit and took another glimpse out the window at the big blue. So serene. So tranquil.

The Air NZ captain came down the aisle, smiling assuredly at those who glanced up. She got to the back and went into a brief and hushed conference with the attendants.

'How long?' asked the captain.

'More than half an hour.'

'Can he hear you? Is it a he?'

'Yes,' said the hostess, consulting her iPad. 'A Mr Campbell Stevenson.'

The captain pursed her lips. 'Is he a crazy?'

'Don't think so.'

'Not like that one they had the other day on the LA run?' The captain rubbed her neck. 'Fella was in the john and started barking.'

The steward and hostess stared at the captain in wrapped astonishment.

'Yeah, barking like a border collie.'

'What happened?' they asked, in unison.

'They, through trial and error, found that using commands on him seemed to work. It was the only thing he responded to. They could hear him panting. He would bark, when ordered to sit. Like he was obeying the command.'

'How did that end?' asked the steward.

The hostess and steward had forgotten Campbell for a minute, so engrossed were they in the story. I too, wanted to know how it ended.

'The captain said, "Paw" and they could hear him scratching on the door. Then he said, "Paw – Door" and the man pulled the door handle open with his paw.' The captain whistled quietly. 'He was on all fours with his tongue hanging out.'

They stood silently for a moment imagining the scene. The captain broke the spell: 'Anyway, this guy's not nuts – as far as we know?'

'No,' replied the hostess. 'He's a contractor from Christchurch. Owns his own business. Employs a few workers. Builds horse arenas. Digs a bunch of swimming pool holes. Builds pads for sheds. Unremarkable. No criminal past. Has a wife and two kids – a boy and a girl.' She paused, glanced more closely at the iPad and scrolled down. 'He's hardly travelled. This would only be his second time out of the country.'

'Perhaps he's just nervous,' offered the steward. 'Air sickness.'

'It's been a smooth as flight,' said the captain. 'This guy drives diggers for a living. He will have guts of steel.'

'He occasionally makes strange sounds,' said the hostess.

'What kind of strange sounds?' asked the captain.

'Like a "vroom, vroom". Then, "didoom, didoom".'

'Didoom?'

'Excuse me,' I said. I had moved to stand behind the three crew. 'I couldn't help noticing, but you seem to have a problem.'

'Just a minor, sir,' said the captain. 'Nothing to bother you. If you would just move back to your seat.'

'I think I can help,' I offered.

'Why. Are you a doctor?'

'Yes, of sorts.' I inclined my head towards the captain. 'I'm a psychiatrist.'

'Oh. Are you?' The captain looked hard at me, then she glanced briefly at the steward and hostess. She made a quick judgement call. 'Look, we do have a small situation here. It's nothing to cause concern. But there's a fella in here,' she indicated with her head. 'He's been in there for quite some time.'

'I understand he's making some noises,' I said.

'Have you been listening in?' said the captain, her voice taking on a sterner note. Perhaps she shouldn't be including this passenger; she knew nothing about him.

'I couldn't help hearing a little. I've been back here doing some stretches. For the thrombosis,' I said. I smiled at the captain. 'I have an interest in the human condition.'

The captain regarded me again. I looked normal. I had a black cap on with the words MotoGP embroidered on it. I was wearing a hoodie with a pocket logo: Mad Cow Racing Disease. *What the hell did that mean?* Doubt was creeping in again. It was never good to hand control of a situation, at 30,000 feet, to a passenger. But she was paid to use her smarts and make decisions.

'Can I just put my ear to the door?' I said. 'I think I can identify the noises the man is making. I'm sure I've heard them before.'

The captain paused. 'Very well. As you are a psychiatrist, you might have some ideas.'

The crew shuffled aside slightly, like a small herd, to give me access to the door. Then, like a small herd, they regrouped around me; not wanting to miss any action.

'Vroom, vroom, vroom … vahh, vahh.' The sounds were soft but clear.

'What …' the captain went to speak. I put my hand up, asking for silence.

'Didoom….vahh. Didoom, didoom. Vroom, didoom, vahh.'

'I'm pretty sure I know what's going on,' I said, confidently. 'The sounds are quite clear.'

'It's like motor noises,' interjected the steward.

'Yes, exactly like motor noises,' I confirmed. 'I'm thinking a GS1000.

It's a Suzuki motorcycle – a Post Classic race bike.'

'Well, that's good,' said the captain, smiling crookedly. She felt like she had lost a little control of the situation. 'Is that good?'

'Yes, it is good.' I nodded my head. 'Very good. We have the bike and model. We just need to know which track it is on.'

'What do you mean, "track"?' asked the captain, hooking a finger between her collar and neck, loosening her tie – it had suddenly gotten very warm.

'I will need quiet for the next one minute and 12 seconds,' I cautioned. 'I think he's just gone across the start/finish line.'

'What the …'

I raised my hand. 'Sshh.'

The group stood huddled around the toilet door, their ears pressed to the plastic, trying to hear the soft sounds.

'Vahh…vahh.'

'Wait for it,' I said, smiling quietly. 'He's on the back straight. Tight left coming up. A fast one.'

'Didoom. Vaaah…'

'What, he only goes down one there,' I said, frowning in consternation. 'I always go down two.'

'What do you mean!' exclaimed the captain, trying to regain some control. The situation seemed to be going into a spiral. Spiral wasn't a good word at 30,000 feet.

'He's nearly done,' I soothed. 'I'm 99 percent sure he's at Levels Racetrack – Timaru.'

The crew were no longer concentrating on the toilet door. Their attention was now fully fixed on me, although the steward and hostess were also surreptitiously checking their captain for signs of unease. She had a light sheen of sweat on her upper lip.

'Campbell, last lap,' I said, through the door frame. 'White flag is out.'

I straightened up and turned to the crew, smiling broadly. 'He will be out in a minute and a quarter, plus probably another minute for the warm down; they use an exit path at Levels. Anyway, just over two minutes.'

The captain began smiling with relief, then her face went cold. 'Are you with this fella? How do you know so much?'

'No, relax,' I clucked. 'As I said, I'm a doctor of the human condition. 'Interesting, isn't it?' I drifted smoothly away to my aisle seat. I sat, fastened the belt and reclined the seat a few notches. I gazed confidently at the rear toilet light monitor. It went from red to green.

I slowly swivelled my head to look back down the aisle. Campbell emerged from the toilet, wearing his helmet. He had the tinted visor pulled down. He nodded once at the captain, hostess and steward, then he slid sideways into the back row and regained his seat.

An hour later, the plane touched down with a bump. I shook hands with the steward and hostess as I was departing the aircraft. I told them they had done well in what could have become a tricky situation. 'It's always good to let them finish the race,' I confided. 'Pulling them out early, unless it's a mechanical, it's never a good idea.'

SHOTGUN .... SIMON

Simon was waiting at the Hertz desk. He had also been up in the wee hours to drive from Dunedin to Christchurch to catch the flight to Melbourne. It had landed 30 minutes before the Auckland flight – the one Campbell should have been on.

'All good?' enquired Simon, as we shook hands all around. Simon was the big fella in our team. Working out in the gym and a steady diet of junk food on the couch in front of the telly had built him into a powerful unit. He had calf muscles the size of baby heads. His noggin was shaven and he could produce a 'don't fuck with me' stare.

'Yes, top flight,' I said. 'Couldn't have been easier.'

The rental van was a 10-seater with not much room in the back for luggage. Somehow we got our mountain of bags into it; helmets went on the

laps. It was a lot of luggage considering most of us had packed our riding gear in the shipping crates with the bikes. The crates had gone into a shipping container and were hopefully waiting at the PI track.

Matt was nominated as driver and didn't seem to mind. Simon rode shotgun. Andy was still in a semi-zombie state; the drugs were wearing off slowly. He was manoeuvred onto a back seat for the three-hour drive. Campbell took the back seat; of course.

LEAP BEFORE YOU LOOK .... THE BOYS

Phillip Island was only 125 kilometres southeast of Melbourne but the motorways were busy and the Victorian police notoriously vicious. The traffic thinned as we headed further south and the natural urge was to speed up. Staying at the speed limit on an open road always felt wrong to a racer. Sayings like 'pedal to the metal' didn't come from thin air. And that was why Matt was driving. He was a man of restraint; possibly the only one in that van that looked before he leaped. I sure as hell was an impulsive leaper.

Phillip Island formed a natural breakwater for the shallow waters of the Western Port. At only 26km long and 9km wide, it wasn't large but it did offer a large variety of activities. It had been a place of interest to humans for centuries.

The first skirmishes on the island occurred in the early-1800s when sealers from Tasmania visited and didn't see eye to eye with the indigenous Bunurong people.

The island was connected to the mainland by a concrete bridge. The population was only about 10,000 but in the summer it quadrupled. Put on a MotoGP race and 90,000 hooligans would arrive for the weekend.

HALL OF MIRRORS .... SPOTTY DAVE

'The hall is perfect,' grinned Spotty Dave. Spotty Dave was standing on a chair in the hallway with a drill in his hand. There were framed mirrors lined side by side, leaning against the wall like resting soldiers, all the way down the hallway. Each mirror was about 500mm by 300 and each one had a thin wooden frame.

He grinned again at me. 'I thought you'd let me down, but no. The hall is 10-metres long, even a little more. This should do nicely.'

Spotty Dave had arrived sometime during the night. His mode of transport to the rental house was a mystery: he could have arrived by teleport, for all anyone knew: he was both an expert appearer and a disappearer. He had taken the lower bunk opposite Campbell. He was full of his usual bonhomie and enthusiasm. Spotty Dave was nuggety.

He was from Paraparaumu, just up the coast from Wellington. Paraparaumu had an 'oceanic climate' whatever that was a euphemism for. You needed some grit to live there. Constant wind battered the coastline and a sprinkle of fortitude was taken with the cornies each morning. Spotty Dave wore shorts all year round. He had a steady constitution; his lowest point was above a Yorkshire high point. He had arrived in the night with two massive suitcases. He didn't have a vehicle and mentioned cryptically that he'd been dropped off. Campbell hadn't heard him arrive but Campbell's hearing wasn't the best: he drove large, noisy machines for a living.

Spotty Dave was standing on a chair so he could reach the ceiling. There was a line of screw eye hooks in the ceiling, running the length of it. Pencil marks indicated he had taken some care in measuring and positioning the hooks.

'Don't worry, guv. I have spackle and a small tin of ceiling paint.' Spotty

Dave laughed wickedly. 'No one will ever know I've been here.'

I suspected that had been the modus operandi for much of Spotty Dave's life.

'Should I ask what you are doing?'

'You should,' agreed Spotty Dave. 'But wait till I'm finished.'

I shuffled sideways to get past Dave and the mirrors.

GALAHS AND HAIRY POPCORN .... THE BOYS

The rental house I had sorted was in Cowes, the main town of Phillip Island. It was a bland, horizontal weatherboards, single-storey affair. Gum trees towered over and around it; they grew like weeds on the island. The boys had departed the van to the screaming of galahs.

Rental houses all over Cowes were filling up with bike racing enthusiasts. They came from around the globe; much like a United Nations conference.

This year there was a team from the United States of America, United Kingdom, Ireland, Australia and New Zealand. That put several hundred foreigners into Aussie baches. You paid a lot for a lot of bedrooms but once the cost was split, it was cheap accommodation. The sting could be in the condition the rental was left in so it paid to consider who to have as temporary flatmates. The cleaning cost could blow out the deal. My flatmates fit into the better class of grub.

I had first choice of the rooms, being the organiser – and team captain. My room had the luxury of an ensuite, and it was the only one. I knew I might have to share it, but if I put enough gear in front of its door and spread my undies around, it could become my territory; that was the theory. I was happy with my room. It would be my place of peace on the island, an island within an island.

Simon, Matt and Andy also had their own rooms.

Andy and Matt were snapping jibes at one another across the hall.

'Aye up, sunshine, ow do with your room?' asked Andy.

'It's not 20 yakkers of farmland but I could swing a cat in it,' replied Matt.

'It's better than a cracked cup, an' all.'

'Oh, we never had a cup, we used to drink out of a rolled-up newspaper.'

'Ha, you were lucky, the best we could do was to suck on a piece of damp cloth.'

'But you know, we were happy in those days, though we was poor.'

'Aye, was right.'

'Aye.'

The Monty Python act showed the numbing airline tonic had finally worn out of Andy. Their Yorkshire accents were pretty funny, especially during a slanging match. I figured this was a good sign. I was no Tonto but I did know that when a Yorkshireman went quiet, it wasn't a good sign. I was also no psychiatrist – except when I was at 30,000 feet – but I did have a good feel for how to handle most motorcycle racers. Many of them were bullshit and hairy popcorn on the surface but that was just to cover the insecurities swirling beneath. The quiet ones needed closer attention; but the quietest ones were often the fastest ones.

THE BUNKROOM .... CAMPBELL, SPOTTY DAVE, BRENDAN

The bunkroom was set aside for Campbell, Brendan and Spotty Dave. Brendan was driving down from Melbourne the next day. The rooms were connected by an especially long hallway. That had been the one request from Spotty Dave: 'It must have a long hallway – nothing less than 10-metres.' Try entering that onto the online booking form as the main demand. I had to wing it as I could find no mention of halls. I had to go on the photos and house layout. I tried e-mailing the owners of a couple of the rentals to get them to do a measure. Strangely, those rentals suddenly became unavailable to me for that week.

I found Campbell sitting alone in the bunkroom at the end of the hall.

He was on a lower bunk, his suitcase opened on the floor in front of him. He was staring into it. I sat on the bunk opposite. There was one pair of underwear in the suitcase, nothing else. I looked calmly about for signs of other clothes. There were none.

'I see you're travelling light,' I observed.

'Yes,' sniffed Campbell, considering the inside of the large suitcase. 'People pack way too much. You never end up wearing half the bloody stuff. But, I must admit, I thought I had packed a little more.'

'True that,' I agreed, nodding my head. 'At least you won't waste energy on having to decide.'

'I may have more luggage on the return flight,' said Campbell, enigmatically. 'I fancy something comfortable. Perhaps a 900 bevel.'

I grinned. 'The Lord works in mysterious ways.'

PAMPERED BLOKES... THE BOYS

The crew assembled in the lounge. 'Matt, you're driving, we're going up to the supermarket,' I commanded. 'Food, water, air and shelter: the three necessities of life. Then my work with you peasants is done.'

'Aye, fair enough,' said Matt. 'And it appens your maths is off.'

Phillip Island had a beach feel to it. Most of the houses and baches were owned by Melbourne residents who saw it as a good long-term investment. However, many people were now seeing it as a good retirement patch; an oasis from the rat-race.

It was the end of a beautiful day and still 25 degrees. The boys grabbed individual trolleys and split up. We only needed breakfast and something to snack on during the day. Water was the most important item. Slabs of cling-wrapped bottles were in the supermarket foyer – very environmentally unfriendly.

You could tell who didn't keep house back in NZ. The more pampered the bloke, the more he bought, half of it being useless crap that wouldn't be eaten – muesli bars and rice crackers and other items promising energy and vitality. I bought some tea, honey, muesli, milk, and water and headed next door to the bottle store: no booze for sale in the supermarket. New country, new rules. The groceries were cheaper than NZ but the beer was a lot more expensive.

Andy and Matt were excited as they had found some Yorkshire Gold. Tea, but extra strong.

I observed the two poms huddled together in their food bubble.

Photo: D Begg

'I spect this is as close as will get to God's food,' commented Matt. 'Nowt chance of a sly pie or even cheese savoury sandies. Die for a Chorley cake.'

'Way,' agreed Andy. 'Pot pie and mushy peas.'

I smiled to myself. Mushy peas; grey-green like the back of a Klingon's hand. Hideous.

'Nae a proper chippy even,' muttered Andy, as the two of them clanged their trolleys merrily together like two old fisherwomen and shuffled away down the supermarket aisle.

We got Thai takeaways and settled into our rental. The Australian Open was in its second week- a nice distraction on the telly. Nadal, Federer and Djokovic were all on 20 grand slam wins and vying to be the most winningest player in history. A couple of quiets and early to bed.

MOTORCYCLE MAN

I was working on yet another theory: I figured that the older you got the *more dangerous* the activity you should participate in. I had friends, non-motorcycle racers, who thought my pastime was silly, foolish and at my age I should probably grow up. I also had friends that had died from cancer or were dying from cancer. *Surely blowing oneself off a road or track at 200 kph was preferable to rotting away with the rust.* Of course, I realised, a problem with that concept was that by the time the rust had you, it had been at your insides for a while and you were perhaps in no shape to even ride a bike. However, there was usually a window of opportunity: a difficult discussion with the family about your wish to be strapped to a large missile and fired off into oblivion. Euthanasia with a bang.

The Isle of Man TT entry level event, the Manx Gran Prix, had a minimum entry age of 18 and a recent change to give it a maximum age. It never had a maximum age before and it had been at the discretion of the IOM stewards. Now it was a maximum age of 45. I reckoned that was bunkum.

To this point 265 riders had died racing the IOM course. When a 20-year-old killed himself on the mountain course it was an appalling thing. The funeral was inevitably tragic and there was little joy to be found in *celebrating* his life; he'd barely begun it. The common platitude was that 'he died doing what he loved'. But anyone who's been around that scene knows how hollow that rings for one so young.

Perhaps if you were 20 in 1917, lying sodden and wretched in the bottom of a trench in Flanders Fields, then death may in fact have been a welcome release.

'I am young, I am twenty years old; yet I know nothing of life but despair, death, fear, and fatuous superficiality cast over an abyss of sorrow.' Erich Maria Remarque, All Quiet on the Western Front.

I figured the minimum entry age for the IOM should be 55, or even 60. There could even be a class for 80-year-olds; of course, they would get free entry. The gold class. This would bring in a whole new dimension of spectator – voyeur, more correctly – who would find joy and hilarity in just watching the riders trying to find their bikes: myopically bumping into one another, milling about like old mutton at the abattoir – let alone watching them propel themselves at death-defying/inducing speeds on open roads.

Competitors currently needed insurance cover to the tune of 25,000 euros for death, 50,000 for temporary partial disablement, 185,000 for medical treatment and 75,000 for repatriation costs. I wasn't exactly sure what temporary partial disablement meant. Could it be when your head separated from your body but by some stroke of luck managed to come back down and land perfectly back on your neck?!

Having an older gent, or lady, entry limit would do away with that need for insurances, saving everyone a lot of headaches. There would obviously be a box to be ticked on the entry form saying the rider wasn't to be revived in the event of a crash. In fact, the whole funeral thing could be done away with, saving thousands for the left-behind family. You could just dig a hole in the nearest field on the Isle, gather the leftover pieces of the rider, and bury them right then and there. Much tidier, so to speak, and a chance for some crowd participation. Hand some shovels around and everyone can be at it, digging a racer's grave.

Then go ahead and say, 'He died doing what he loved'; he was 75 years old. And everyone could have a bit of a giggle: *The silly old scallywag.*

BORN READY .... THE KIWIS AND THE POMS

The house awoke to the smell of bacon cooking. Campbell was in the kitchen making a proper job of breakfast. He was a contractor and used to being up at the crack of dawn. The rest of the crew gradually stumbled through to the kitchen and we settled into our cereals and toast.

It wasn't a problem being up early with the state of Victoria being two hours behind NZ time. We got away smartish – early bird gets the worm – but when we arrived at the Phillip Island circuit, vehicles were already well backed up in the field leading to the track.

The early morning light was hard and flat in the lucky country. The ground was sunburnt bare. There were plenty of rental cars, interspersed with vans and utes towing large, covered trailers. Security was tight at the gate and slowing the entry process.

There was an Irishman running the entry booth. He carefully ticked off our names on the Kiwi team list. 'You boys ready for a good week?'

'Aye. Born ready,' said Matt.

The Irishman raised an eyebrow, 'Were you now?' He let us through with a quiet smile.

There was a track day in progress: $300 a pop and limited to 160 riders. PI track days were booked out months in advance – good income for PI; owning a racetrack was no fast track to wealth. You had to be a racing enthusiast as well as a business person.

The Poms had somehow got some track time on the Wednesday. They were already one step ahead of the game. *It's who you know, not what you know.*

The Kiwis had been allocated some pit garages between team USA and

Ireland. The UK team was on the other side of the Americans and the Aussies were spread all over the place. The trick was to cajole the forkhoist driver into unloading your team's container before the others. The laconic fork driver wasn't much fussed about who he did in which order, he was paid by the week. He had a fag in his mouth and his cap pulled back on his head. The Poms were already unloaded. *It's who you know, not what you know.*

The Americans had their container unloaded before the Kiwi's. The Kiwis weren't surprised to be unloaded last. Americans strutted like the most powerful nation on the planet; Kiwis, were used to being Tail End Charlie.

Kevin McDonald, from Rogers Motorcycles, Invercargill, took charge of the Kiwi unloading. He was probably the most sensible guy on the team – well, as much as any motorcycle racer could be called sensible.

Kev surveyed the crates in the container with a distant eye. He was a McDonald and had built-in genes for surveying craggy situations that could prove troublesome. His kind came originally from Islay and were suspicious of anything or anyone who didn't have a tang of venerability about them. Kev was there to race; and mechanic as he owned a two-stroke.

EEH BA GUM .... MATT

Riders milled about anxiously, anticipation high. It was a little like a hospital delivery room. Composure was the key but never in abundance when motorcycle racers were concerned. The bikes were individually crated so it made for easy handling without too many tears.

Matt was still muttering about the freight company in Auckland and its handling of his precious cargo, a Suzuki GSX1100. He had a small van with a rear door that swung upwards. Matt had ramped his bike up into the van and then assembled his crate around it: inside the van. At the freight yard they couldn't get the forks to his crate as the rear door barred the forkhoist. The answer they, along with Matt, came up with was to put a rope around the crate and drag it out partway and then try and get the forks under it.

The Onehunga forkhoist driver was a good one. He was paid by the week. He wasn't paid to be sworn at by a big fella with a northern English accent. He had single-handedly unloaded all of the Kiwi bikes as they arrived at the Onehunga warehouse from all parts of Aotearoa. It had gone well. *But there was always one.*

Matt's van was scratched as the crate was dragged out. Increasingly large utterances followed – and it was probably 'Fockin' twat' that caused the fork driver to shut the hoist down. He considered belting the 'Pommy git', but he liked his job. He left the crate, still unloaded, and went away to an early smoko. The boss of the freight forwarding company took over the forkhoist. Unfortunately, he pulled the crate a little too far out and it went over the tipping point. Matt's hands went to his head in disbelief. 'Jesus wept.'

'Whoops,' said the boss. 'But should be able to get the forks to it now.'

Photo: D Begg

MOTORCYCLE MAN

A motorcycle racer is generally a nice person but stay out of his way when a race motorcycle is the centre of his attention. The cruisiest laidback dude can become an uncharitable, boorish, egocentric prick in the track pits. He will want his bike just so and all his bits just so.

Fortunately, classic racing brings out the best in people and age helps dull the sharp competitive urge – a little. The International Challenge (IC) races were the pinnacle of the programme at the Island Classic and as such, there was pressure on riders to perform. There had been the creep of 'hired guns' there to up the ante. It was cool having a McGuinness, or McWilliams, a Corser, brought onboard as they were older former world-class riders and happy to get into the vibe of the gathering. It was the younger, current racers, who put a few noses out of joint. I had a problem with the hiring of young guns to ride classic bikes. I had a theory that you should have to be older than the bike you're racing.

Many of the older racers shared my view – thought you should have to own the bike you raced, or at least, to have been born when it was manufactured. Come the end of the race and you pull the sweaty helmet off your 55-year-old head, you don't want to see the guy you've just been bashing bars with – and eventually losing to – pull the helmet off a 20-year-old head.

VIM AND VIGOUR .... THE KIWIS

The Kiwis had four pit garages made available to us. These were the same pits used by the MotoGP teams when they hit the island every October and World Superbikes in February. I could have been standing on the very same spot that Valentino Rossi had occupied. If only I could breathe in a bit of the great man's vim and vigour.

MotoGP was the biggest drawcard at Phillip Island in the motorcycle racing world. World Superbikes was next, and the Island Classic was third. 90,000 people for the GP, 50k for WSBK and 20k for the Island Classic. The main difference was that spectators were welcome at the Classic to wander – not to touch, mind – and to get amongst the riders and machines.

The Kiwis set to unbolting our crates and freeing our babies. There were some very pretty babies, mostly Japanese. Two-strokers congregated naturally into one pit garage; Castrol R was strong DNA. They might be stinky but they were exotic; and expensive. A couple of TZ 750s were popped onto their stands beside an RG500. That was a cool few hundred thousand bucks right there. A plethora of TZ350s lined a wall in speedblock yellows and reds. Ready to do their magic slipstream conga down the front straight.

Campbell's GS1000. Photo: D Begg

XR69 — SIMON AND CHUCKY

Simon got the last of the packaging off his CMR-framed XR69. I helped him angle the big Suzuki onto its rear stand. It was a work of beauty; grown men would show little embarrassment in wetting themselves lavishly at the sight of it. The CMR frame was designed by Denis Curtis. Denis was English but had lived in Canada for many years and had put his love for the Harris frame into action. His frames were made from chrome-moly and looked similar to the Harris in shape. However, the Harris frames had tig braising and a gorgeous aluminium swingarm which made them easy to differentiate. Simon's was a CMR replica frame made of chrome moly steel, including the swingarm. It was a work of art but the swingarm was not as beautiful as a Harris alloy one.

Simon's XR69 hadn't proved to be a lucky bike to this stage. The GSX 1100 engine had a knifed crankshaft, Carillo rods, JE forged pistons, Webb hi-lift cams, a ported and planed head. It breathed gas and air through Keihin FCR round-slide carbies. It blew the spent fire out a full titanium Yoshimura exhaust system. There was no space in that fuel/air chain event for a product called luck; in racing there's usually only one sort of luck. The GSX had been built the summer before but never ran right. There were gremlins. The bike would run great in the workshop and on the dyno. In trial runs, usually at Levels Raceway, it would run great for a while. Then the gremlins would take over.

Simon had a cunning plan for Phillip Island. He had brought his Chucky doll to the event.

Harris frame beauty. Photo: D Begg

Chucky's usual place of residence was in Simon's kitchen, above the shelves, perched with his bloody knife. Simon didn't have children but he did have Chucky. And he did have a snaggle-toothed small dog called Milt. Milt was Simon's mate and the two were nearly inseparable. Milt was small but fierce; *it's not the size of the dog in the fight but the size of the fight in the dog.* He would hide in the bushes inside the fence at the front of the property: Milt, not Simon. If a person should walk by, Milt would launch himself with ferocity. The fence kept him in. Simon would tut tut approvingly on Milt's triumphant trot back to his side. Another trick Milt had been taught, was to take a dump on the neighbour's verge; but then who hadn't encouraged their dog to do that?

Milt wasn't allowed at PI but Simon figured that having Chucky in the pits would keep the motorcycle gremlins at bay. This was a dangerous game as anyone who had seen the horror films knew Chucky had a low boredom threshold. He needed action – usually of the mayhem kind. He may have been Simon's other little mate, but surely that relationship could only be tenuous at best.

FECKER ARRIVES..BRENDAN

'He's *great* isn't he?' declared Simon, standing Chucky on the tank of his XR69.

'Not the word I would use,' I said, arms folded beside Simon.

'You and yer man keep that little *fecker* away from my bike,' came a voice. Brendan had arrived. The Irish member of the Kiwi team had just driven down from his home in Melbourne, where he lived with his Russian wife – a newish interracial marriage. Brendan was Irish. The jury was out on how an Irish/Russian marriage would run. Potatoes and borscht. Potatoes had the variety: mashed, boiled, baked, roasted, fries. Borscht, a sour soup made with beetroot – not so much.

Brendan came from a line of Irish racers and had two brothers who also raced. His Russian wife hadn't come on the trip; she didn't like motorcycles. He was the last of the flatmates to arrive. He got to share the room with Spotty Dave and Campbell.

'Welcome aboard,' I said, warmly shaking Brendan's hand. 'Good to have a bit of the luck of the Irish in our team.'

Brendan danced about from foot to foot; he had a lot of kinetic energy:

ADHD would have been the diagnosis if he would stay still long enough. 'I may be here for my luck, and a bit of craic, but that little fecker isn't lucky,' he said, pointing a stubby finger at Chucky.

'Come on, brother, you Irish have fairies and leprechauns,' chuckled Simon.

'Yeah, but they don't go around knifing folk in the middle of the night.' Brendan clucked. 'Well, it's never been proven.' He moved forward and back, light on his feet like a boxer, thrusting his finger at Chucky.

'Everyone has done something in their past they are not proud of,' soothed Simon. 'Those movies were a long time ago. Chuck's a chilled dude these days.'

Like Simon, Brendan also had an XR 69, but his was the Harris-framed model – it had the beautiful aluminium swingarm.

'Well Chucky's one thing, but I have the force,' I said, brandishing a camshaft like it was a light sabre.

'Careful,' warned Brendan. 'That thing's made from cast iron, it will smash like a bastard if you drop it. Besides, you eejit, isn't that thing supposed to be inside your engine?'

WEAK WASABI .... ME AND ANDY

I had quit, a month earlier, on the idea of even taking my bike to Phillip Island. I had done the Boxing Day race at the Cemetery Circuit in Whanganui, NZ. I had been bridesmaid in the event twice before and I wanted that winner's trophy. The Cemetery Circuit was also the last round in the Suzuki Series. I was second in points in the series – it had been a rollercoaster. I had either won the races or the bike broke. The Taupo round had been the most amusing. I won the first race by a decent margin. The bike was handling sweet and the engine was about as good as it had ever been; which wasn't very good. It would pull strongly off the corners then run out of guts like weak wasabi. In the second race I kept hitting false neutrals as I downshifted. I had to stop a couple of times, when it jammed in neutral, reach down with my hand and wrench the gear lever into a gear. Fortunately, I had a big lead and could pull away just before the field caught me. The marshals were getting twitchy with their black flags – eagerly awaiting the call from race control to flag the fella on the F1; he was behaving oddly. I made the finish line in first place with the pack close behind. Back in the pits I was convinced the gearbox was rooted. A mate, Patric, took a long look at my gear selector. He discovered a tiny grub screw had come loose by the peg and it was jamming the gear lever from behind. Gremlins.

At Whanganui the bike missed and spluttered in the first race – dying in the corners then coming alive down the straight. I still managed second place but only by riding so erratically that no one dared pass. I tried a new battery for the second race, to no avail. The bike would brake nicely and had great stability, but I would come out of a corner, open the throttle and it would die, splutter, bang, then lurch alive again at 7000 rpm.

Andy had been watching the race from near the overbridge (a walk-through shipping container placed over the track). He was excited and agitated when he caught up with me as I was putting the bike back on its stands. I was less excited, but probably more agitated; I had come second again – which was a good result considering the state of my bike, but second was first loser.

'Flippin eck, your bike was on fire, mate,' spluttered Andy.

'Yeah, right,' I said. 'The dirty bastard would only run between seven and nine thou. Dying off every corner. I would hardly call that, "on fire".'

'No, I mean it was *on fire*,' said Andy. 'Really on fire! There were flames coming out the back of the engine. She's paggered.'

We had both squatted to check it out. The wiring above the carbs was burnt and crispy to the touch.

The bikes were due to be loaded for Phillip Island a week later. The Christmas period was no time to be getting work done, especially engine work.

I got the bike back to my place and pulled the valve cover off. There was no obvious damage but on closer inspection the valve clearances were all to poo. Number one was the worst. The exhaust cam lobe was worn down and there was no clearance. The ignited mixture had been bottling up and finding no exit to the exhaust, it had been blowing back out the carb through the inlet valves which were rushing to try and force more air/fuel mix into the chamber. Hence the fireshow. The exhaust lobes appeared to have rounded off, melted even.

Andy had convinced me to still crate my bike for the island, get the camshaft rebuilt in NZ and take it in my luggage. Fit it on Wednesday in the PI pit garage – the theory sounded good but I knew from years of living with myself that life didn't always flow in a natural direction. It had taken until the age of 60 for me to realise that I must be one of the world's great optimists. My wife called me a pessimist because I complained that everything I tried turned to custard. But I was either the most stupid man to be born or I was one of the world's greatest optimists. I bit down and kept trying new things.

I had half-Scottish and half-Irish genes so life was never going to be easy; but it would always be interesting. One half wanted to go to the pub and the other half didn't want to pay. All the usual Celtic jokes.

My FJ1200 head used shims to obtain valve clearance. A prick of an idea in my view. I had scrounged around for some shims of varying thickness, stuck them in a plastic bag and thrown them in the suitcase.

POPPA SMURF

Poppa Smurf had a long white beard and, being a Smurf, obviously aged slower than humans. He had been around the motorcycle scene for as long as most riders could remember but he didn't appear to be getting older. Poppa Smurf was there to mechanic.

Poppa Smurf had his overalls on early and he was hunting for a job. He and I set to, trying to find a workable range with the shims from the plastic bag. I gave up early and went for a wander to clear my head; mostly to avoid taking a large hammer to my bike. Patience was the main tool required for the job and I had always been short in that department. Poppa Smurf, being supposedly ageless, was calm and in control. You didn't want to be dropping a cam sprocket nut into the depths of the engine. I was clumsy enough to do just that. I had already skinned a knuckle on a cam cap. My older, paper-thin skin liked to come apart at the least opportunity.

MOTORCYCLE MAN

This was not the time nor place for me to demonstrate my repertoire of dolt mechanic moves. I'd had plenty, too many to name. Carefully unwinding the hot oil filter so as not to drop it into the full pan of hot drained oil below, then mistiming on the last thread and dropping it anyway, with a splash of hot oil all over myself and the bike. On the refill of oil, hurrying too much into the funnel and it regurging back all over my leg. Or being clever and trying to wind the tyre valve back into its stem while the just fitted tyre was desperately trying to expel 80 pounds of air which is what it took for me to get it on the bead and the valve blowing past my ear into the never-to-be-found beyond. Then there was putting the rear paddock stand jauntily under the back of my bike only to discover I'd slightly missed one bobbin and the stand slipping and the bike tipping onto its side. Or unscrewing the cap and checking to see how much brake fluid was in the master cylinder reservoir and squeezing the lever at the same time which shot a stream of brake fluid into my right eye. Besides all that, there were the tedious

DC searching for power. Photo: D Begg

mistakes that came with age such as mixing up the main jet sizes for the carbs because 135 could look awfully like 125. An arthritic spasm causing the fingers to unlock and drop the tiny circlip for the carb needle deep into the flatslide.

And so on.

TEAM IRELAND CAPTAIN......................................POG MAHONE

The Ireland team was pitted next door. I went seeking the Ireland team captain.

'Well, if it isn't Mr Pog Mahone,' I declared.

'Well, if it isn't I've got a problem,' said Pog Mahone, straightening from the bike he was working on. He flicked his long fringe back and shook my hand warmly. 'Well, well, to yourself DC. I expect you'll be wanting a dynamo with all this cloud about,' he said, thoughtfully tapping his teeth with a 10mm spanner.

'Typical PI Classic weather, eh,' I smiled. 'Always seems to be rain threatening early in the meeting.'

'It does that. You'll be wanting your cycle clips tight on those joddies and even a backing up of the cheese cutter may be in order,' said Pog, touching his head. He bit on the spanner contemplatively. 'Was it last year or the year before?'

I had learned with Pog, from previous discourse, to not necessarily try and answer a question: especially when I didn't know what the question was. It was good to leave space in the answering; room for multi-choice. Bide time until I had at least a scarce idea of which way the conversation could be going.

'Pretty sure it was either last year,' I ventured. 'Or the year before.'

Pog raised a couple of wrinkles of perplexity to his brow. 'Would have been last year methinks. Murphy was on the team – useless gobshite. The man took to watering his chain while on track – in the quallies.' Pog shook his long brown hair in disbelief. 'Down the front straight, if I'm not mistaken.'

'Ah, yes, the oil in qualifying,' I agreed, as much for my own clarity. 'Simon and I were qualifying at the same time. We came down the front straight, and of course, you don't know there's oil down. We both briefly lost the front but somehow managed to catch it and stay on. We ended up on the grass beside each other all wide-eyed. Turn One is not a place you want to lose the front.'

'Indeed, no,' agreed Pog. 'Yer man is not a toboggan.'

'Never a truer word said.'

'You'll be on the Yamaha velocipede this year?'

'Yes,' I confirmed. 'Thing is still not running right, though. In fact, it's not running at all. I still have to put the exhaust cam back in it. Melted the lobes.'

'That is a curious performance of puzzledom you have there for yourself DC. And I wish you well with it.' Pog scrunched up his face and tapped the spanner further along his teeth; *a form of tuning fork?* 'Would it be a lack of dipping in an Arab well that's caused the conundrum?'

'Yes, we think enough oil isn't getting across to number one,' I agreed. 'It's a pretty agricultural system in the old FJ.'

'You could put the old Enots Drip Feed hand pump on it. 1914 I believe they were the bees knees,' chortled Pog. 'Give yourself something to do while poking down the front straight. Reach down, eh, laddie, and give it a pump.'

I laughed. 'We've gone the easier route and upped the oil flow. Run some external oil lines direct. The top of the head is now bathed in oil.'

'Sounds like you're onto it, my man.' Pog scratched his nose with the 10mm. 'Wife. Is she still in the sexual way?'

This was a toughie for me. I could usually get the gist of it on the subject of motorcycles with Pog. Beyond that was confusing terrain.

'The kids have all left home,' I said, carefully. 'Just the wife and myself now. You still a single man?'

'Yes, the man is not presently a tandem,' agreed Pog. 'It's still two wheels but the frame has the shortening. It can get through corners quicker but it's not so great on the long journey. But back to the business, my man. Tell me, any of your lads running the penny-farthing?'

'We have a couple of the boys on the Manx and one Triumph, I believe. Otherwise, the oldest are the TZ 350s. We have a few of them and the boys are quick.'

'Ah, the 'feather bed'. Now, there's a frame.' Pog brightened. 'Speaking of racing your old bed, I hear the Harris boys are coming to the happening. Great, great, it will be great craic.'

Steve and Lester Harris from Essex were famed not only for their XR69 frames. They had enjoyed success at every level of racing with Barry Sheene and Graeme Crosby being two of their famous customers; to own a Harris frame was a beautiful thing. They would get to see many of their XR69 frames at this meeting and the replica CMR ones run by the likes of me and Simon in the Kiwi camp.

'Okay, good to see you again, Pog. No doubt we will be seeing each other a lot in the next week.'

'To be sure. And good to see you've still got a head on you like a handball alley,' chortled Pog. 'You feck away and we will see another.'

TEAM NZ CAPTAIN.................................... ME, SURPRISINGLY

I had become captain of the New Zealand team more by default than anything else. It was one of those moments in a committee meeting when a new captain was being sought. I happened to be looking the other way when the new captain was nominated. I figured looking the other way indicated I wasn't interested. The others in the room figured that if you were looking the other way you were a fair target; you could brook no argument. It was unanimous and when I turned my head back the deed had been done.

I had endeavoured to prepare; to research the role of a captain. I had begun to read *The Five Dysfunctions of a Team: A Leadership Fable*. It explored a dynamic five-part model of dysfunction – and why teams failed to work cohesively together. The five dysfunctions were: 1 absence of trust, 2 fear of conflict, 3 lack of commitment, 4 avoidance of accountability, 5 inattention to results. The Kiwi team had all those traits. I had all those traits. Those traits were more like a job description for being in the Kiwi team.

KORMA NOT KOALA .... THE BOYS

The teams were asked to be away from the pits by 3 pm. Poppa Smurf had done an admirable job with what we had in the way of shims. But we were short some thinner shims. We needed to shave some meat off the shims we had. After a little debate I decided a belt sander was the best tool for the job; a little brutal but time was not on my side. Thursday was practice day and you needed all the track time you could get to adjust to the big circuit after racing on NZ's tiny tracks. I headed to Mitre 10, leaving the other boys to settle into the rental house for a few quiets. I found a belt sander for $69 plus some belts. Cheap if it did the job.

Andy and Matt were in the kitchen jostling.

'You need to frame yourself out there tomorrow, get on with it,' ordered Andy. 'You look like you're waiting to give someone a croggy to school with all your faffin aboit.'

'Ee ba gum, that's rich coming from you,' countered Matt. 'With your fancy new Dainese leather suit with the bib on the front. What's that for? To stop all the gravy yer chelpin from landing in yer lap.'

The Yorkshiremen nominated themselves to wander up to the local Indian restaurant for takeaways. Poms knew their way around a good vindaloo.

'Make sure that's korma not koala,' called Simon. Being a cop, he had a suspicious nose – and he liked his food.

MOTORCYCLE MAN

I returned to find Simon, Campbell and Brendan slothed out on the couches watching the Aussie Open. Simon was soon asleep - his favourite pastime. The week on Phillip Island represented freedom from the everyday. Freedom was a loaded word and to many it bedded down with words like irresponsibility and independence. Most men found themselves in that 20-year period where they had shed their big toys for the traditions of marriage, mortgage and midgets. It wasn't until their 50s that they once again smelt the whiff of liberation. I wasn't fully emancipated but to many of my friends' wives I had a strong tang of immunity from family ties. I was a little older than my friends in the race world. I had been slow to learn that look from a mate's wife: 'No, Tommy can't come out to play – at least not until he's done the lawns, washed the car, walked the dog and taken the kids to soccer.'

The race week on Phillip Island allowed grown men to become 12-year-olds again; and let's face it, that's the best age to be a bloke. This was a pureblood motorcycle gathering.

Downtime at the rental brought out the sloth in middle-aged men. Talk was usually on bikes and rarely strayed to things such as jobs, wives, children. The best bike was a common topic. Which bike would you have if you could have any? Okay, which bike would you have in the Pre 89 Class if you could have any?

Most riders had a few bikes tucked away in the shed at home. I had eight. I figured that was a good number: one for each day of the week and a spare. My wife thought it was too many until I had shown her an Irish mate's collection of 150 bikes. She was good for a few days after that. Bikes could wear a relationship thin.

I liked to hang with women. In fact, some of my best girlfriends had been women. It was just that man was a basic animal in essence and one of those basic needs was to be able to herd with other basic animals, i.e, men. Motorcycles could become a campfire (especially a Japanese bike at a Harley convention) – a warm hub for guys to congregate around and shoot the breeze. What you did for a job wasn't as important as what you rode. Blue collared guys could hang with white collared guys ... to a point. A white-collar guy probably needed occasionally to wash his white shirt with the coloureds to give it a tinge of blue.

Interludes at the rental house meant deals could come about if you weren't prepared. The year before, I had been at the PI meeting as a spectator only. A couple of months earlier I'd had a massive crash at Manfield while trying to make a move on Eddie Kattenberg into Turn One. The head injury was severe and my race licence had been revoked for several months. It was during this phase, and while we had idle time at the rental house, I found myself buying a bike I could neither afford nor was suitable for a motorcyclist with my character flaws. My defence mechanisms were still smeared on the tyre wall at Manfield and Simon's sales patter left me convinced that I had an almighty need to buy an Italian motorcycle right then and

Photo: D Begg

right there. And what's more, an Italian bike that had been built so tightly around a Japanese engine that you needed to drop the motor just to change the plugs. I was not a patient man, and you needed a much gentler bloodline than mine to own such a bike.

Simon sold me his immaculate Bimota YB8 for $15k. I didn't have the money, as usual, but I had a scheme for how to get it.

I was as excited as an Irish Setter when the Bimota turned up in the transporter. It had only 15k on the clock. I was nearly peeing myself with excitement as I turned the key and pulled the choke lever. The dash lit up and I took a breath, held it, and pushed the starter button. The shiny white and red bike gave a quick cough and nothing else. I wound away but there was no sign of life. I turned the key off and popped the gas cap. I suspiciously nosed the fumes. Skanky and old. Old gas meant fouled spark plugs.

This was when I discovered a little more of the way of Italians and how they built motorcycles. I could remove the outside two plugs with only moderate bad language. The inside two required the engine to be dropped. Of course, to get to the engine one had to remove seat, fairings, exhaust, airbox, etc. I buried every hammer that I owned and went about the job. I fitted new plugs, added new fuel, and the bike started. I then listed and sold it a week later; without ever riding it.

Me, being an unlikely optimist – and with my brain fade –did eventually lapse and buy another Italian bike. A muscular beauty called a Moto Guzzi V11 Sport, Rosso Mondello. It was a Latin reflection of me: didn't do anything particularly well, was basic, but strangely interesting and pretty much up for anything. It was a peculiar animal to ride, with it being driven through a driveshaft. Guzzi forums featured optimistic fatalists describing the V11 handling as being *like it was on rails*. I figured you would need a set of rails to get the bloody thing around a corner. I didn't do forums but if I did, I reckon I would describe riding the Moto Guzzi as like trying to dry-hump a Massey Ferguson 135.

THE GIST .... BRENDAN

I went down the hall to deposit the sander in my room. I had to shuffle sideways to get past Dave and the mirrors. I put the sander and belts in my Fly Racing bag to be taken to the track the next day, then shuffled sideways back to the lounge.

'Brendan, I think I need you when I go to talk to your man, Pog Mahone,' I said.

'Why's that, then?' asked Brendan, perched on the edge of the couch, restless and ready.

I hoped to use Brendan as an interpreter when speaking with the captain of the Irish team, Pog. Pog spoke in bewildering ways that were unlike anything I had ever come across before. I figured Brendan might be able to break it down into plain English for me.

I leaned on the back of the couch. 'I'm not always sure I'm getting the gist of what he's saying. You could interpret for me.'

Brendan sprang to his feet. 'I could that. But yer man talks in ways *I've* never heard so it's not always easy for me either.'

'He's been round bikes a lot. Perhaps a little too much,' I offered. 'I wonder if he talks to his bikes more than people. I wonder how healthy that is.'

I moved to the fridge. Milk, chocolate, chocolate biscuits and beer. The fridge was full. I grabbed a can of VB and took a chair near the telly.

'You're another who spends a lot of time with machines, Campbell. You're either on a digger or in a truck. How healthy is that?'

Campbell smiled secretly and fingers intertwined, stretched his arms slowly out in front and cracked his knuckles. He was just under six-foot tall and loose limbed like a welterweight wrestler. 'I do like my diggers. Just got a new one. A 24T. She's very pretty.' He cracked a couple more knuckles for good measure.

ALL DONE WITH MIRRORS .... SPOTTY DAVE

'Anyways, to more pressing matters,' I said. 'Have you seen what Spotty Dave is up to in the passage? He's putting up mirrors. Hanging them from the ceiling. All the way down the passage.'

'I used to have a ceiling with mirrors on it,' said Brendan dreamily.

'Yeah, and now you've got a Russian wife,' said Simon. 'Spotty Dave's a crazy bastard. But I like him; he's funny as fuck.'

'Anyway,' I continued. 'They're not stuck on the ceiling. They're hanging from it – all at different levels and angles.'

Spotty Dave, on cue, happened into the lounge. As one we turned to look at him. 'What?' he said, looking at us looking at him. 'What?'

'What's going on?' I said. 'Those suitcases you arrived with were full of mirrors. Weren't they? What are you doing?'

'Well.' Spotty Dave smiled indulgently. 'You know how we are getting older, and still racing bikes?'

We nodded.

'As we get older, we don't get faster, we get slower.'

We nodded.

Spotty Dave crossed his arms and smiled warmly.

'Not only are we getting older but there are all these young guns now being brought onboard – to ride classic bikes.'

We nodded.

'You've got Alex Phillis, Jed Metcher, Levi Strauss…'

'That would be Levi Day,' corrected Brendan.

'Levi Day, Paul Byrne.'

'Byrnie's not so young,' said Simon. 'He's nearly my age.'

'Back to the point,' cajoled Campbell.

'When we are young, we race faster,' said Spotty Dave. 'That's just nature. We lose testosterone as we age.'

'Noooo!' gasped Brendan, hovering on one foot. 'I can't do that. I have a Russian wife.'

'Ha, yes you do,' agreed Spotty Dave. 'But I don't want to get slower. I've been looking into a remedy.' He paused for effect: 'Time travel.'

We still nodded. Then slowly we turned to one another with grins: *the man is nuts*.

Spotty Dave acknowledged the man is a nutter grins with a chuckle. 'I know, I know. But when you look into a mirror, you're only seeing a reflection. But – and here's the thing,' said Spotty Dave, raising a finger. 'You are seeing an historic reflection. By the time you look at the mirror and the image is reflected back to you, a millisecond has passed.'

We nodded yet again, but not quite so emphatically this time; we were simple men.

'You are seeing what you looked like in the past, even if it was only a fraction of a second ago. So, what I've been testing is the duplication of this algorithm. I have hung 27 mirrors, that should be the perfect number as it's a positive integer that is equal to the sum of its positive divisors, excluding the number itself, of course.'

There was a pause. A moment of dull silence – a unified holding of breath. The man with the mirrors ploughed on.

'If you extrapolate the theory then you can historically alter your image and hence, your age,' continued Spotty Dave. 'By bouncing the image off mirror after mirror, you can extend the application back in time until you become younger and younger. Gradually at first and then exponentially. Time acceleration is the change in velocity, over the change in time, represented by the equation $A = \Delta V / \Delta T$.'

Collective pausing still.

'Yes,' I said, taking a breath. *Crikey, Spotty Dave*. 'But it's all very well to see yourself as younger, through your mirrors – if you can do that – but how can you capture that image, that age you want?'

'Simple.' Spotty Dave smiled down at us, like God. 'Meditation. It's already inside you, from your past. You've just got to bring it back. Welcome it back and let your inner child come out to play.' He smiled encouragingly. 'The psyche is the core of us. So, why can't we move our psyche around? It's a spirit, it's our soul, it's not limited or anchored to the physical age of our body. We just think it is. So, if I can see myself as 20, then capture that psyche, I'm a young man again. Although, admittedly, the sleeve I'm using is a bit old.' He circled his arms and lifted his legs one at a time. 'But it's still in working order. Ha, the warranty has probably run out. But put a 20-year-old spirit in it and let's see what it can do.'

Fortunately, Matt and Andy chose that moment to burst through the front door with korma, vindaloo, garlic naan and rice. The odours of Mumbai pushed aside the hovering clouds of zany doubt and ignorance.

CAW, PRACTICE DAY .... THE BOYS

We awoke early again; NZ time was still well etched. I had already walked several kilometres through the outskirts of Cowes; I was a terrible sleeper. Sunrise was an incredibly noisy time in the town with all the cackling, cawing and cat-calling. The musical tweets of the red-eye figbird. The familiar 'whoop whoop whoop' of the pheasant coucal. If one was lucky, the 'chu-it chu-eet chu-wee' of the hooded plover.

There were several other walkers out at that time of day and I also spied Jeremy McWilliams decked in Lycra and putting in an early spin on a bicycle. McWilliams, a northern Irishman, riding for the UK team, was always at the pointy end of the International Challenge (IC) and the rumour was that he had a special engine in his Harris frame; he definitely had a special human engine. The boss of the UK team, Arthur, had a particular

Jeremy McWilliams. Photo: D Fitzgerald

liking of the feisty Irishman and had slipped a few more ponies into the mix when building his engine.

It was practice day and a chance to test bikes and riders to see if they were ready. Most of the riders at the Island Classic were aged somewhere north of 50 …or was that south? Easy to get confused: spectacles, testicles, wallet and watch. Naturally one slowed down as one got older. The biological clock, the body chemistry, fought against the daredevil gene; a man of age didn't bounce so well anymore; broke more easily and healed less quickly.

My body was deserting me. I was in denial but only in a half-hearted manner; I was many things, and one of them was that I was a realist. I was clinging onto my organs and joints like a desperate man clinging to the face of the Eiger.

I had only started road racing at 50. Sure, I had done a bit of motocross when I was younger and had owned many bikes. I was also something of an expert at falling off them so departing a bike and going down the road on my arse held no great fears. Still, at 50, to decide it was a good idea to try and hit 300 kph down the back straight at Pukekohe, well, that wasn't going to be everyone's cup of tea.

It was increasingly difficult for me, when I was out socially at a dinner or party, to engage or indeed to be engaged in mundane conversation. Note would be taken of my distracted air, my lack of interest in the inflation rate or the country's GDP, the housing market. *The Dow-Jones didn't arouse a stiffy*. Little did my fellow diners know that behind this average looking man's stupor was a dude who resided in a world where mild panic was de rigueur – let alone to get a hint of the shocking reality of how violent the attack on the senses it was to race a motorcycle. In an attempt to see if there was life in the old dog I would be asked what I did for kicks. I tried not to, but sometimes I admitted that I raced motorcycles for kicks.

Now, if you're looking for a conversation killer, that's the one.

Some men aged with bitterness and regret, others with dignity and integrity. No longer being the focus of the erotic gaze could bring a decent looking man to his knees.

The fortunate man was the one who had discovered the bliss, indeed the solace, of a motorcycle and the understanding that this vehicle, this agency, allowed him to keep body and soul together through much of the fragile aging bullshit. A motorcyclist didn't need to be smothered by psychosocial theories of aging (activity theory, disengagement theory, continuity theory) or even that there was a whole field dedicated to being old: geropsychology. Sanity could be restored just by plonking oneself down in a chair, with a beer, amongst a bike or two. Fire up a bike and listen to it tick over. Or, better still, get a leg over *somehow* and go for a spin. The clan of the rider.

HOGWARTS FOR MOTORCYCLE RACERS .... THE BOYS

Matt slotted behind the van steering wheel. The boys took, what had already become, our accustomed seats; Campbell in the back seat – like he was on the school bus, of course. It was a 10-minute run to the track and this time there was no queue. The road into the infield went under the track by means of a large culvert. It wasn't wide enough for two vehicles and was governed by a traffic light system. Passing through that tunnel, was in a weird way, akin to boarding the invisible train to Hogwarts. The real world where normal people lived was left behind and one emerged into a different reality. The Phillip Island IC was indeed a motorcycle Hogwarts.

The flatmates had six IC bikes between us.

Simon and I had the CMR copies of the XR69: Simon's with the GSX1100 engine, mine the FJ1200. Brendan had the Harris XR69. Matt was on an original GSX1100. Spotty Dave had a GSX1100 slotted into a Harris frame. However, it wasn't an XR69 frame, it was a Magnum; a shorter frame, more of a hybrid that Spotty Dave had tinkered with. Campbell was on an original GS1000R, red like the one Wes Cooley raced back in the day. It had a two-valve engine that wouldn't cut the mustard on such a vast track as PI. He pedalled it furiously on the smaller NZ tracks when it's lack of power didn't always matter; but *there's no substitute for cubes baby.*

Andy was on a Suzuki GSXR 1100. It didn't fit the IC category and he had to slot into the New Era Formula 1300 class.

Photo: D Begg

HAIRY PELT .... POPPA SMURF

Poppa Smurf was a little put out as he had forgotten that morning to put on his towelling hat; his signature towelling hat. He gave a wry shrug, tucked the end of his beard into his overalls and got straight to work belt-sanding the shims. He wasn't a vain Smurf but he had to admit to enjoying the cut of himself in a full-length mirror when he chanced upon one. His beard shone white like a Turkish Angora and he was aware that the belt sander could tear the magnificent hairy pelt from his face. So he tucked it away in his overalls for safe keeping.

He wasn't deterred by the crude engineering that I had asked him to perform. To him it was just another job card: Smurfs being communists were used to doing with no questions asked. There were mutterings from some about the hardening being taken off the shims and the wonkiness of such a practice, or that Poppa Smurf risked being left with smaller fingers from the grinding.

I had no interest in those murmurings. *Just get the bastard together so I can get some track time.*

Track notes: racer rituals

Riders and mechanics went to work sorting last-minute jobs before the first practice run: Making sure there was good brake pressure at the brake lever. Some riders liked a hard lever all the

DUNCAN COUTTS

way out, some liked it hard halfway to the bar, pressure would fade during a race so one had to be mindful; no radial brake parts were allowed on classics. Checking the chain tension and air pressures again *and again*. I noticed Matt was muttering to himself as he messed about preparing his bike. He was deep into the ritual of his pre-ride despair. 'I'm so fuckin slow, no talent,' he thrummed.

All racers had a certain routine they went through when getting ready to go on track. I liked to put just my lower legs into my leathers then slip on my left boot followed by the right boot. Zip the boots and the leathers snug around them. Back protector on then pull the suit up and slip the arms in, left then right. Chest protector in and zip up. Helmet on.

Ha, there was no problem sliding the helmet over my noggin since my Chinese barber had taken to my hair with the same glee he displayed in cooking over his wok. My Chinese barber owned a takeaway bar-*cum*-barbershop. When he wasn't taking the spatula to some sweet and sour pork, he could be found vigorously shaving the sides off a man's head; the dude having been desperate for a haircut and wontonly wandered into my barber's. My barber transitioned easily between jobs and used much the same action with the electric razor as he did with the spatula. A haphazard brisk back and forth motion designed to cut through the stiffest hair or equally to break apart some sticky rice.

I fitted left glove first and got it just so before slipping on the right glove. Do a little up and down squat and get the nads comfy. I *always* mounted a bike from the left; never the right; like a horse.

Some racers wore a certain colour of sock. Some wore the same socks, unwashed, for a whole race weekend. Many riders wore something green when they raced in Ireland. Using the same undies on race days was common. Barry Sheene had the ultimate pre-race ritual. He had a hole drilled in the chin of his helmet just large enough to admit a ciggy. He would get that last nail down before taking to the track.

Many of these routines were just habit but equally many were superstition, although the riders could be completely unaware or in denial about this. Then there was a rider's preferred race number but let's leave that for now.

Track notes: phones get the gig

I gazed around the pits. No one was staring at their phone. Odd in the modern world. But this was a meeting of classic bikes and there was always fettling that had to be done – not much phone time available.

Still, it was a joy for me to see the phone put away. I had been shocked, on a recent trip to explore Thailand, tourists were walking the streets with their phones held out in front like beacons. *Perhaps they were beacons*. They were following the track laid out by GPS on Google Maps. But it seemed to me, that they were missing the sights, the nuances, the interactions with locals. Then when they came to the feature, the site they had sought, they wouldn't wander around it taking it in, enjoying the moment. They would video it on their phone. Once again holding the phone out, a little higher this time, for the device to get a good view. And if there was something live happening, some show, they would hold the device up high, their arm extended to get good footage, totally focussed on the image presenting on the tiny screen.

I was staggered. *The phones were having all the fun.* The phone was getting the tour. The tourist was just the device to hold it.

And don't get me started on selfies. *Don't look that star in the eye and shake their hand and say 'well done you'.* Oh, no, YOU are more important than that star: they must be in YOUR photo. Don't get me started on selfies.

TEAM USA CAPTAIN .... BO

I had time to seek out the American captain, in the pits next door, to see how the Yanks were shaping.

'Gidday Bo,' I said, stepping into the American team pits. 'Long time no see.'

Bo had a large cigar lazily housed in the side of his mouth like an acetylene cylinder. His Stetson was pushed back on his head to reveal a shiny forehead. Brown curls escaped out the sides of the hat. Bo was leaning nonchalantly against a toolchest surveying the US pits like they were yards of fine steers.

He considered me and blew a long plume of blue smoke, 'Well, lookee at what the cat dragged in,' he said, stepping forward to squeeze the air out of me with a very American pound hug. 'It's hell of a good to see ya, pardner.'

'So, what state are you fellas in?' I asked, refilling my lungs and indicating with my head the American pits and the plethora of bikes.

Bo went slightly wide-eyed and glanced quickly around. 'Why, the Lone Star State, boy, of course.' He frowned, 'No wait, wrong! I'm as confused as a goat on Astro Turf. We're in …' He grabbed a race programme off the toolchest and rifled through the first few pages. 'Here, here,' he cried, jubilantly poking his finger at a page. 'The State of Victoria.'

Bo paused, holding the programme limply. Then he threw it like a rag back on the toolbox. 'I don't recall any State of Victoria. Where's Springfield? Son-of-a-bitch! There's a Springfield in every state. That I do know.' Bo lunged for a woman passing by. She had coiffed platinum-blonde hair that sprung lightly aloft as he grabbed her. 'Springfield, Victoria, how far from here?'

She gathered herself a moment, her hair settled and she patted his hand lightly. 'Bo, we are in Australia. I can explain it for you but I can't understand it for you. There are no Springfields in this country.'

Bo's brow shot up with incredulity. 'Well, I never. What kind of godforsaken country is this?' He gradually released his grip on the woman. She was smiling and appeared calm despite the team captain's turbulent condition; she was not surprised by his looseness. She moved away.

'That's right. Yes, indeed we are.' He turned to me and winked. 'We call her Radio Station. Because anyone can pick her up, especially at night.'

'I heard that,' called the calm woman, back over her shoulder. 'And you Bo, weren't so much as born, just squeezed out of a bartender's rag.'

Texas Tornado. Photo: D Begg

'Ouch,' said Bo, admiringly. 'She is hot as a summer revival.'

He gave a quick puff on the cigar. 'God daing. I blame the British. They will dump on anything they can get their greedy hands on. This country was perfectly fine until those Limey bastards landed here.' Bo grimaced: 'Then they gave it only six states. Horsefeathers. The US of A has 50 goddam states. And every one of them has a Springfield.' He glanced furtively about, reached into the cabinet of the toolchest and withdrew a can of Budweiser. He took a long pull and surveyed his pits. 'Bit early to be stirring up the steers. The branding iron will go into the fire soon enough.' He took another drink and crumpled the can in his hand. 'Look, pardner, you carry on,' he said, placing a large hand on my shoulder and looking me square in the eyes. 'I have a dead soldier to see to.'

PRACTICE WHOOPS .... THE BOYS

The stroke of 9 am meant that motorcycles could be started – a time for earplugs to go in; for those still trying in vain to save some hearing. The blipping two-stroke racket was the most damaging. The big four-strokes just needed a steady idle to warm up, then a flourish of big revs to finish; showing who the big dog was.

Poppa Smurf was still sanding the last of the shims for my F1 as the IC riders began kitting up for their first run.

CLASSIC MOTORCYCLE MADNESS

The IC was the premier event and hence its riders got more practice than the other classes; it was the bling event. I was frustrated, no rider liked missing practice.

Brendan led the way out of our pits on his immaculate XR69. It was outfitted in classic Suzuki colours: light blue panel on the top, white on the tank, to light blue again and then dark blue through the middle. The lower fairing went to light blue again and the belly pan featured a splash of bright red. It could be mistaken for no other marque. Brendan turned out beautiful bits of kit.

Matt on his blue and white GSX 1100 was next out of the pits. Its hind end was slightly jacked up giving the appearance of a beast about to leap. Perhaps like a cheetah. Perhaps like a warthog. The bike sounded mean with a beautiful JayGui exhaust system. The shorty muffler was sexy indeed. The exhaust note bounced around in your innards for a few seconds as it went by. People turned at its sound; it had that effect.

Spotty Dave was last to leave the pits. He was parked by the door of the pits and had been warming up his bike for longer than most. It was a unique blend: the spawn of a Harris Magnum frame combined with Spotty Dave's own tweakings. It was shorter in the frame than an XR69 – it had more the cut of a street-café-cum-resto-mod – very nimble on NZ's short tracks. Twitchy was how many fellow competitors described the bike. However, that could have been the ergonomics of the bike or Spotty Dave's riding style. He had the habit while racing of looking back over his shoulder at any given opportunity. If you were lucky he would give you the finger. His riding style wouldn't be quite described as erratic, more like enthusiastic.

The bike was painted white with red spots festered all over it. Spotty Dave described the scheme as 'Scarlet Fever'. Measles was probably more accurate. His leathers were also white and covered with red leather spots. His gloves, white with red spots. His helmet, white with red spots. His boots, white with red spots. Hence, Spotty Dave. For all I knew, Spotty Dave's body could have been covered in spots. I had never seen the man naked and had no intention to.

One of the mechanics eased Spotty Dave off the race stand. He gave it some revs, engaged first gear and let the clutch out quickly. The bike lurched forward, the front wheel lofted into the air and it wheelied across pit lane directly into the pit wall with an almighty crash. The bike and Spotty Dave fell onto their sides. People looked up with shock at the sound of the collision. A couple of onlookers rushed across to help the fallen rider. Fortunately, neither the rider nor bike were injured as it had only happened at moderate speed.

The bike was steadied and inspected briefly, then wheeled back into the pits and put back on its stands. Spotty Dave stood, pale and perspiring, hands on hips. He turned to walk away.

'What the hell, mate,' I called, catching him up and putting a hand on his shoulder.

'I screwed up,' said Spotty Dave. He pushed the hair off his pasted brow.

'I was watching,' I nodded. 'You just dropped the clutch and went straight ahead into the wall.' I lowered my voice, eyeing Spotty Dave carefully. 'It was like you'd blacked out. Like you didn't know how to *ride* the thing.'

Spotty Dave grabbed me by the arm, glanced quickly around and drew me judiciously away from the curious group that had gathered like hyenas round his bike. 'That's the thing,' he hissed. 'I *don't* know how to ride it.'

'What do you mean?' I exclaimed. 'You've ridden it heaps.'

'Yeah. But not like this.' Spotty Dave pulled me closer. 'I used the mirrors this morning. In the hallway – to make myself younger.' He scrunched his eyebrows down and gave me a meaningful look.

'Oh,' I said, doubtfully.

Spotty Dave glanced covertly about. 'I think I managed to make myself 12.'

'What do you mean, 12? Twelve years of age?!'

'Yes.'

'Oh.' *Bloody hell.* I bit on my lower lip. 'I can see that could be a problem.'

Spotty Dave let out a snort. 'At 12 I only had a pushbike. I was stealing lollies, fags, and smoking them round the back of the bike shed.' He giggled and hunched his shoulders up. 'Geez, Wayne, I think the mirror trick might work. I didn't learn to ride a motorbike until I was 15.'

CRAZY EYES .... CHUCKY AND SIMON

Chucky doll was perched proudly on Simon's fuel tank, his mop of red hair as thick as thatch, his crazy blue eyes glaring. The day hadn't started well for Simon. A bolt on his engine, on the oil feed banjo, had snapped. A mechanic had managed to drill it out and fitted a new one. But now the bike had no power, the ignition light refused to glow. A broken wire was found. That was sorted and the beast was wheeled to the starting rollers to fire it up. It was stubborn. The starting rollers wouldn't spin it quite fast enough and the carbs flooded.

Most people wouldn't credit human attributes to a machine but that's just the disposition Simon's bike was displaying. It dropped its lip and clearly didn't want to go out on track. Like a spoilt teenager it was working its way steadily through a box of tricks designed to frustrate any track action. One could argue that Simon's attributes had somehow morphed into his bike's. This bike clearly preferred to be snugged up in its tyre warmers, on its paddock stands, in a pleasant garage – its version of couch time – to the hectic business that was occurring down Gardner Straight.

Simon zipped his white and black leathers and picked up his helmet. The XR69 finally gave up its reticence and reluctantly fired up. Simon took a large gulp of racer air and headed out for his first run.

HAVE FUN FASTER .... THE BOYS

Laptimes came up on the monitor: 1:50 for many of the Kiwi team. They would need to get their heads down: 1:40 was needed. I was frustrated at not being able to get out. I moved to the pit fence, clinging to the mesh with my head poking out through a viewing port watching the bikes speed down Gardner Straight (named after Wayne Gardner: the first Australian to win the premier GP class. Once upon a time it had been called BP Straight). The bikes roared past blasting dust and noise all around; the sound hit you in the chest. The speed was immense and terrifying, as it always was when experienced up close.

It was a fine thing, one of the finest sights you would ever see – a bike hurtling at speed down the main straight at Phillip Island, the roar of the engine reverberating off the Armco and walls as the bike approached, then the strangely mournful wailing as the exhaust note twisted in the air and sung its departing song. Onboard the bike it's a bizarre scene ahead as the heat shimmers feet above the track seemingly all the way up to the famous Melbourne sign hovering over the start/finish line. Beyond that was nothing but blue – the Bass Strait. You were riding your bike at more than 250 kph into the deep blue yonder.

MOTORCYCLE MAN

I hunched my head down into my shoulders like a tortoise as they tore past. I considered the oddity of speed. Speed is a peculiar thing. Next time you're on your bicycle – oh, you don't ride one? okay, your car – as you are driving look just past the front of the bonnet at the road. See how fast the road is disappearing under your car. Then shift your gaze up the road 10-metres. Now see how much slower it's moving. Now shift your gaze 50-metres up the road. Speed seems to slow down as the road is coming much slower towards you than it is right in front of your bonnet.

This is the same with racing. The first thing non-racers always ask is how fast do you go? One problem to specifically answering this is that a race bike doesn't have a speedo as it's not a necessary piece of equipment and you only have what is necessary on a race bike; and as little of that as possible. Most racers do have an astoundingly good feel for just how fast they are going in which gear and at what point of the track. That comes from experience and knowing from GPS data what top speed your bike makes and the speeds at different sections of a track.

200 kph can feel very fast on the road as road builders do not design roads to accept motorists doing that speed. Track builders work at the other end of the spectrum. Grand prix motorcycles were now doing more than 350 kph. Pause on that for a moment and consider the fastest you've been in a car on the road (and reduce that by 10 kph as the speedo will be reading too fast, as they're manufactured to, in a road car or bike.)

I had an Aprilia RSVR 1000 which I rode on the road and then turned into a race bike. I raced it a few times then did a few modifications. I then wanted to test it but I lived several hours from a track so I decided to do what many racers do, test it on a road but a quiet one in the countryside. My choice of test track was from my house at Whangarei Heads to Ocean Beach. The road had a few tight but flowy corners and a decent-size straight. There were some up and down rises in it to add a little spice. The run took three minutes by car. I had no idea how long it took me on the Aprilia but I did know that I only got into third gear and due to the rises and falls in the road I had a lot of trouble keeping the front wheel on the bitumen and I swore both wheels departed terra firma at least once.

I arrived back at my house a quivering mess. Any testing of the modifications had quickly gone out the window as riding the beast at maximum level had become only a matter of survival. I was nearly exceeding the control limits in third gear on that piece of road: I still had another three gears in the box.

The thing about racing a motorcycle is that you ride the machine at the maximum rpm that is possible without blowing it up. Then you change gear and do that again. Then you change gear and do it again. And so on.

Next time you're driving your car – oh, you drive an automatic? Bugger. If you can drive a manual, and hopefully it's got a tacho, look to where the numbers on the tacho go from green to red. Right on that green/red change is where you want the revs to be **every time** you change gear. You will be surprised how the vehicle turns into a different animal when you do that, even a Toyota Corolla.

The racetrack is designed for vehicles to be run at their maximum. Blowing an engine is an everyday occurrence there – not so much on the road.

And here's the beautiful irony. I took my Aprilia to the racetrack, after the mods were done, and the bloody thing was slow. I was screaming for more power. And yet this was the same monster that had terrified me on the run to Ocean Beach – and only in third gear. In sixth gear, yawn, at the track, yawn, I was hitting 250 kph down the straight, yawn, but it felt like I was going backwards. Remember that key to racing: speed is insignificant, it's not how fast you are going but how fast you are going in relation to those in front of you and behind you.

Who in their right mind would strap themselves to the back of a missile and flick the switch. I would have been far better to be on track. Watching was unnerving. It was hard to comprehend that usually I also was one of those idiots hurtling by on the tarmac. Mice began running up and down my spine. I pulled myself away from the fence and headed back into the garage; watching up close was giving me the heebie-jeebies.

Hampton Downs, near Auckland, had become something of a home track for me and yet, every time a coconut, I would go through Meremere on SH1 and round the corner to that first glimpse of the Hampton Downs track, and I would instantly feel sick with fear.

Track notes: Sweats, butter expectation

The riders filed back into the pits after their shakedown runs. Stands went under the bikes and tyre warmers went back on. Helmets off, the riders were wide-eyed with surprise after their first laps of the PI circuit. There were shakes of the head and nervous laughter. This track, the speed you ran on it, took some getting used to – even for those who had been there before. For the newbies, expectation could be a callow beast and letting it run loose in your dreams and nightmares in the weeks leading up to the grand event could give a man sweats wet enough to drown the bedsheets.

First laps on a new track were always hard. Missed apexes, braking too early, too late on the gas, off line. The trick was not to think about it too much; definitely don't analyse. It would come, it always did. By the end of the day they would have it sorted. Hell, even a new job took a week or two to get match fit for. Just dig in and don't think. That's why the word fortitude was invented. That's also why motor racing was probably better suited to the simple man.

There was a vast range of experience in the riders at this meeting but there were no rookies: a rookie could well be overwhelmed by racing at PI. The speeds attained on this track meant that while there were sections where you could relax the body, give the arms a rest, you needed to realise that if things went wrong the consequences were likely to be big. If the dude ahead of you lost the front, you acknowledged it – thought, *one less fecker to pass* – and stayed focussed on the job at hand; eyes on where you wanted to go. It was tempting to follow the action with your eyes as here was a real-life movie playing out in front of you: sparks, scraping, smoke, sliding, chaos. *Who wouldn't want to watch that?*

A rookie may find himself transfixed by the sliding rider and then he too becomes a part of the movie: *where you look is where you go*. A seasoned vet has built an arsenal of reactions that become as natural as breathing. That's not to say a vet doesn't have memory problems.

Short-term memory loss or concussion effects can dull a racing brain.

Perhaps not to the extent where one suffered goldfish syndrome. Probably closer to dog butthole syndrome: a dog will lick its butthole and every time expect butter.

UNSPOKEN CHEATY STUFF .... ME

Poppa Smurf got the last of the shims sanded and smiled thinly. We checked the clearance. Seven thou was what we were ideally after but anything close, preferably over, was okay. I had cable tied the cam sprockets to the cam chain to save time on having to go through the whole timing process again. It wasn't ideal but I was in one of my *let's get on with it* moods. I shared Spotty Dave's penchant for making one's bike look distinguishable. I had gone for a Hundertwasser-inspired paint job on my F1. I was the only one in the Kiwi camp to have a bike with the designation F1. Using the Yamaha engine meant I couldn't run it in the Pre 82 Class in NZ: it didn't come out until 1984. Also, the forks, brakes, wheels and a couple of other things didn't comply.

The Motorcycle New Zealand rulebook was a marvellous feast if you were a carnivorous anorak into the tedium of pulling strips of theoretical meat off bones. Most racers were fairly laid back about it. However, as was the way in all forms of motorsport, if you were winning, your machine went under the microscope. Fellow competitors at the pointy end were loath to believe the other fella could just be faster – it had to be their bike. There was some unspoken cheaty stuff that went on because the fast guys knew, or suspected, the other fast guys were doing it too. Such as the beautiful slipper clutch being fitted. It was illegal but it saved a lot of stress on an old engine when it was violently downshifted a bunch of gears. It should be legal for the good of the bike was the appeasement. Then there were wheel rim sizes. The types of brake calipers used and available back in the day? And so on.

I was of the opinion, apart from glaring abuses such as using radial brake parts, if you can't beat them, join them; but don't make a hullabaloo about it.

My bike had a black and white checkered paint job on the upper fairing and tail unit – although the checks were not clean squares but more of a distorted, fuzzy, stoned shape, as was the Hundertwasser way: no straight lines. The bottom half of the fairings were done in multi-colours. I had heard it described as a 'dog's breakfast'; I had heard worse.

The next practice session, what would be my first, was a way aways so I had time to duck along to the UK team pits and catch up with its captain, Arthur. It was good to touch base with the other foreign captains: we would be together in meetings that weekend to bash out the rules for the IC.

TEAM UK CAPTAIN .... ARTHUR

I strode into the English pits. I couldn't bring myself to call it the UK pits – I didn't understand what the United Kingdom was. It was some sort of allegiance between England and Wales and Scotland. And, that's right, Northern Ireland was tacked on. Allegiance was a very tenuous word. Seemed to me, from my reading, that the allegiance was formed through conquest – not quite slavery but definitely bend one's knee to the Cross of Saint George. From what I could work out, you were British, but if you happened to win something (and you're from England) then you became English. If you lost, then you were British. If you were from Scotland (e.g. tennis pro Andy Murray) and you won something then you were British. If Murray lost he was Scottish. The captain of the England cricket team was Ben Stokes. He was a born and bred Kiwi. However, if England won he was English. If they lost he was Kiwi.

Then there was the Commonwealth Games. The Conquest Games might have been more apt, I reckoned.

Racer Jeremy McWilliams was born in Belfast which was part of the UK. Connor Cummins was a racer and a Manxman: the Isle of Man. Shades of grey.

I spied the team captain in the middle of the UK pits. Arthur was in blue overalls head down over the tappets of a Birmingham Small Arms Rocket 3.

'Top of the morning to you, Art' I said, in my best Irish accent – which was poor by any standard. And doubly poor because you wouldn't meet an Irish person who would say 'top of the morning to you'. That was an American myth.

Arthur straightened slowly, mostly due to being interrupted by an Irishman while he was doing God's work, but also due to his old back. When he saw it was me, he brightened and let out a small chuckle. 'I say, you nearly had me there, old chap. And it's Arthur, not Art.' Arthur pulled a blue rag from his overalls and wiped his hands. His tie was neatly tucked inside the overalls. 'DC, it's awfully good to see you again,' he said, holding out a hand. 'Haven't seen you for yonks.

Photo: D Begg

Frightful accent you were trying there. Beastly. An Irish one I do believe. We try to keep our distance from them, if you know what I mean.'

'Yes, I know exactly what you mean,' I chuckled. 'I've got to say, most of the time I have no idea what Pog is talking about. I think it's mostly agreeable – and usually it has something to do with bikes.'

Arthur grinned, removed a comb from his top pocket and eased some recalcitrant hair back into place. 'There was a reason we set up the colonies and they provided useful avenues for some of the, how can I put this delicately, less desirable people to live. Of course, I would never put New Zealanders in that camp. Oh, golly gosh, no. You, what do you call yourselves, Kiwis? Splendid. You are fine English stock.' Arthur frowned lightly. 'Well, you were; times change I suppose.' He gave his hands another vigorous wiping with the rag. 'Now, how are your chaps looking? What motorbikes are you running? I don't suppose you will be running any Vincents,' he chortled.

I smiled. 'Should I mention here that it was an Australian, one Phil Irving, who designed the Vincent engine?'

'Oh, hush now. Such nonsense.'

'But we are pretty much running all Japanese,' I admitted. 'We have a bunch of TZ 350s. Some Pre-82 Suzukis. We do have a Triumph Trident in the mix though. Our Challenge bikes are Jappas with a GS1000, a GSX1100, a TZ750 and a bunch of XR69 replicas. Seems to be the way. Of course, you are running Yamahas in the IC?'

'Yes, what-o,' agreed Arthur. 'They do have oriental engines, yes Yamaha. But English frames. The Harris. British-built engineering.'

'Of course, you wouldn't be calling them XR69's, would you Arty. Bit of a slight on the old school fellas like Mick Grant and Rob McElnea who rode the XR.'

'Utterly confusing I fear, old bean,' accepted Arthur. 'And it's Arthur, not Arty. We call this new bike, the F1. Couldn't really call it an XR69 without a Suzuki engine, could we?'

I took a considered look at Arthur. He was the archetypal figure of a pensioner; probably some child's grandad. His pomposity and easily offended manner disguised the guile of a very clever manipulator. The serpent has many disguises. Arthur was a man with a plan.

TIME TRAVEL? .... SPOTTY DAVE

The IC riders set out for their second practice session. Spotty Dave decided to skip this one; he feigned that he had some adjustments to make. Most thought he was talking about the bike. Obviously there had been some sort of malfunction: perhaps the clutch cable snagged, throttle return cable broke. I knew the truth; at least I believed I did. I wasn't sure what to believe – *time travel?* However, I had more important matters at that moment, namely getting some track time and fettling my bike to get it performing to some sort of acceptable standard.

Track notes: Noddy blowing engines

It was less-nervous smiles all around as the boys rolled back into the pits after session two. Now they knew which way the track went and were beginning to marry up their speed to it. The bikes were lightly steaming at the abuse handed to them – especially the engines. A good GSX 1100, back in the day, produced somewhere around 70 to 80 horsepower at the rear wheel. I always wondered why they said, 'at the rear wheel'. *It wouldn't be the front, noddy.* Now the poor dears were being asked to front with 100 per-cent more. An old Gixxer 1100 may have dreamed of being put out to pasture. They were now considered gold and if you could find one hiding in the weeds, you could tear it apart, bore it, do indecent welding and knifing to the crankshaft, fill it with race goodies and torture the beejesus out of it. Double or nothing power. Steve Martin had been given a Katana to ride, the year before, with a GSX 1100 engine reported to give 190hp at the wheel. 'Horses Arse' was the common technical response from the rest of the field. No one would get to find out as he blew it up in the first session. His bike was then fitted with one with 180hp. Rumours were like racers running helium in their race tyres, hard to prove fact from fiction. Mr Martin had blown up three engines that weekend.

Katana built by Trevor Birrell and Dale Gilbert. Rider Steve Martin. Photo: D. Begg

JU JU .... ME

I got my bike back on the stands, tyre warmers on, battery charger hooked up and stood back to look at it. Everything seemed to be in order in terms of bits falling off – or, more correctly, in terms of bits *not* falling off. I had safety-wired the oil filter, sump plug, oil filler cap, and brake calipers as per the regulations. I'd also wired the oil line fittings and some other nuts and bolts for extra insurance.

The performance of the engine was at best average, but it was what it was. Unconsciously my racer brain was scrolling down a list of possible ways to squeeze some more Ju Ju out of the beast. *Ha, beast? It was a cheetah by looks but one that had had its teeth pulled.* It needed some Ben Johnson or Lance Armstrong juice.

MACCA ON THE TRACK .... MATT

I noted a gap amongst the bikes in the pits. Simon hadn't rolled back in with the rest of the IC team.

'What's happened to Simon?' I asked, of Matt, as I helped him get his bike back on its stands.

'Don't know, pal,' panted Matt, sweat running like the Niagara Falls off his forehead. 'Didn't see him. I'm so slow. Didn't see anyone. I'm so far back. I'm like a macca on that track. It's embarrassing.'

I asked Brendan. Brendan said he saw Simon pushing his bike off the track at MG corner. He said it didn't look crashed, it appeared to have broken down: it was likely being trailered back by a pickup crew.

Chucky was nowhere to be seen.

HEKKA HEKKA HEKKA .... SIMON

Simon finally arrived back at the pits but on the back of the pickup trailer with his big Suzuki XR69. A huddle of viewers formed quickly at the back of the trailer – they say scavengers can smell blood from more than five miles away.

There was oil spread across the back end of the bike and over the tyre. The bike had clearly been on the floor. He was a lucky boy not to have been hurt; slicks and oil were not a good combination. The bolts on the camshaft tensioner had come loose allowing the cam chain to jump some teeth.

Simon's XR69 had done internal damage. He tried to explain the noise to Poppa Smurf. 'Kind of Hiiiccckkk, hiiiccckkk.'

Poppa Smurf tilted his head and cocked his ears, like a spaniel trying to pick up an odd whistle. He looked away to the sky. 'Like, tat-tat-tat-tat-tat.' His teeth clacked together like castanets. 'Ta-tat ta-tat ta-tat ta-tat ta-tat.'

'No that was last time,' said Simon. 'This one was more, hicka-hicka-hicka-hicka-hicka.'

'Not, rittrrr, rittrrr, rittrrr, rittrrr, rittrrr?'

Job done. Photo: D Begg

'No, that was the one at Ruapuna. This was definitely a more H sound. Hicka, hicka. Or maybe, a hackka-hackka-hackka-hackka-hackka. Yeah, that's probably closer.'

'And you're sure, not an R sound? Not a rroookkk–rroookkk-rroookk-rroookk-rroookk? Not the death rattle?' winced Poppa Smurf.

'No, I know the rroookkk,' recollected Simon, shaking his head and grimacing at the memories. 'That was Teretaunga, two years ago. And Manfield, the year before. I'm nearly positive, brother, this was a hekka-hekka-hekka-hekka-hekka.'

Poppa Smurf tilted his chin to the side and squinted – finely seeking definition. 'So, it's now more of a hekka-hekka. Originally you said it was a, hicka-hicka. In the middle it was hackka-hackka.'

Poppa Smurf assisted Simon with the unloading from the trailer.

'And it was nothing like the first year over here,' continued Poppa Smurf, he wanted to get this clear. 'The first year on your FZR thou when it let go just after the Hayshed.'

'No, no, no,' muttered Simon. 'That was just bang – then silence. Piston punched a hole through the front of the crankcase. I got lucky it happened there.' Simon crinkled his brow. 'Imagine if that had happened going through Turn 12.' He gave a light shiver; so many ways to hurt yourself.

THE FEAR .... SIMON

Simon didn't need encouragement to slow down on the track. His first timed run of the weekend was always his fastest. Most riders had a bit of a shocker on their first run: missed apexes, running wide, running on and not looking to where they wanted to go. But most riders got faster the more laps they did, as the meeting went along. Simon was what could be called, in education circles, an early developer. He was fast straight out of the box. He was busy immediately learning the apexes of a track and because of his great technique, he could read a circuit quicker than the average Joe Blogs.

Simon always nailed his apexes. He had great method and knew his way around a track; any track. He understood the drill innately; this was basically what he did for a job. He taught coppers how to drive patrol cars fast. He also taught them how to drive safely while being quick. However, making decisions on a track were very different to operating in the high-stress real world.

Come the third or fourth session on a bike, Simon began looking at each corner, not in terms of later apexes or earlier application of the throttle, but instead in ways one could be hurt in that particular corner

He had a peculiar tendency which was threatening to dominate his performances. The first session would be a belter but he would never better it for the weekend, despite the multiple sessions that followed.

Simon's burgeoning hiccup was that he was letting sensibility interfere with his racing. He reckoned that the fear factor grew as the weekend progressed; his brain began interjecting 'oh shit, that would hurt if you fell off there', moments. His reading of the track went from a carefully prepared plan of attack to one of full defence mode. Simon was a big fella with bulk muscle. His theory was that it was better to carry some beef in the situation of a crash. The body would absorb the impact with its mass – a skinny chap had no chance as he would just shatter.

Cookie time for Simon.
Photo: D Begg

MOTORCYCLE MAN

I know – actually every racer knows – there is no way of explaining to a *normal* person that racing a motorcycle is a good idea. A motorcycle racer could appear to be a decent man, intelligent even. The business model called classic motorcycle racing falls down badly. Vintage bikes are worth far too much to have the bejesus thrashed out of them on a racetrack. And yet, that's what hundreds, no thousands, of racers do to them every year. They consumed tyres, fuel and parts at a fearsome rate. Then there is the cost of race entries and transporting bikes to godforsaken places where tracks are built.

And it could be a deadly pastime, stressful, hard on relationships, tough on the body, terrible on the sleep and only the most devoted racers stuck with it.

Racing a motorcycle is experiencing a shorthand version of life itself.

Hope, fear, despair, disbelief, betrayal, love, confusion, passion, anger. All the emotions a bloke is unlikely to talk about – but put a race motorcycle under him and he is living them.

Motorcycle riding is exceedingly scary to the normal human being and motorcycle racers are the hardcore of the motorcycle world. Forget about your gangster on his pimped-up, bog-slow Harley, he is just a blowhard who likes a lot of noise. By comparison, a stock Yam R1 off

CLASSIC MOTORCYCLE MADNESS

the showroom floor is deathly quiet yet can do 100 miles per hour in first gear; and it has five more in the magazine! Conversely, the weekend warrior on his R1 thinks he is 'the man' as he tears around the Coromandel Loop. But put him on the track and he would be mute with shock at just how slow he is compared to an average racer. He has no idea you can brake that late, or lean that far, let alone what happens when you ride a powerful bike on the stops in every gear; that takes a particular verve.

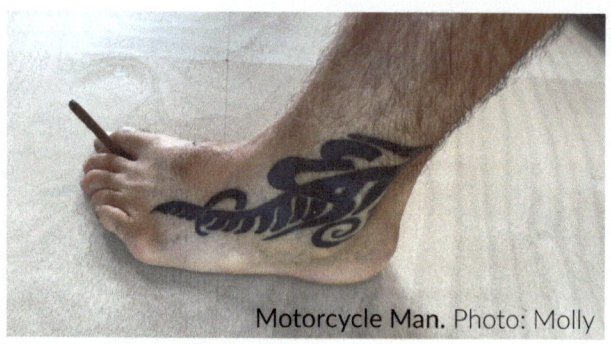

Motorcycle Man. Photo: Molly

Once you've done a bit of racing it soon becomes clear that riding on the road is a fool's errand. On the track the twistgrip is always wound to the stop, hell breaking loose in the high rev range and a rear sticky slick tyre gnashing its rubber teeth into the blacktop.

What if you took even a smidgen of that race lunatic mode to the street amidst all the road furniture and the restrictiveness of riding within the road code.

You could if you were that particular badger who religiously believed in nonsense slogans, such as: 'Live each day like it's your last.'

Last day on earth: 200kph through town; even better, on the back wheel.

'Hey officer, I'm living each day like it's my last.'

'Yeah, well sunshine, it is your last day with that licence.'

We also love to race - not to die. Sure, there are risks and inherent danger while racing on track but mostly the control is in our hands, not in the sweaty palms of some dickweed behind the wheel distracted by the next txt.

The feast is indeed finest at the track.

BEAUTIFUL BUT OILY .... SIMON

Simon and Poppa Smurf wheeled the beautiful, but oily, XR69 to the back door of the pits to clean it before taking it inside.

Simon took his helmet and gloves inside and plopped them on his tool chest. He lowered himself onto a plastic chair, took a deep breath of resignation and began unzipping his boots. He paused mid-zip, glanced up and about. *Where was the wee man?*

'Has anyone seen Chucky?' he asked, looking about.

The nearest riders glanced up from their tasks. One by one they shook their heads. Simon didn't pick up on it, but they were shaking their heads that, no, they hadn't seen Chucky, and no, sorry about your bike, you poor prick: but what were you thinking bringing that son of the devil to a racetrack? *No wonder your bike is buggered.*

BLARNEY BLARNEY .... POG

I dragged Brendan with me to see Pog. I had a couple of things to discuss with the Irish leader. I could understand Brendan. Brendan could understand Pog. It made sense.

'You'd be bringing the lucky Limerick peddler with you,' greeted Pog, shaking our hands.

'I'm not sure on your pronunciation but I'm thinking pedaller,' I said.

'Can sound the same but, you know, different meanings.'

'Aye. If you want two things that are the same but different, you've come to the right meeting. Take the XR69, Pops Yoshimura would be rolling in his grave. Pops would drill the barrels, pepper the plug seats – he was yer man.'

'That's what I wanted to ask,' I said. 'Why are the Irish running the GS1000 engine in the Harris frame? Why not join the party. Why not join the English and the Americans and throw a GSX11 or XJR 1300 at the job? Even your TZ750 is running the original skinny forks. You could be running an R6 front end in that.'

Pog let out a small squeak. He put a hand to his mouth.

I continued, 'And, you're running that Nico Bakker Kawasaki, with the original Z1 engine.'

Pog moved his hands to his face and gazed at me between splayed fingers like a man looking out through prison bars.

'It's even got a 16-inch front wheel and an 18 on the back. You could be running 17-inch wheels.'

Pog gave a startled look. 'Oh, the puzzledom, the puzzledom,' he groaned incredulously, and began gnawing on a knuckle.

Photo: D Begg

Pog took a minute, slid his hands down and clasped them reverently, monk-like, before him. He considered me. He made a couple of shapes with his mouth before settling on the one he wanted. 'Do you see a little one from Fairy Bridge standing afore yee. Do I have wings? Am I a wee person – a leprechaun? Aye, no, you see the real thing.' He shook his woolly mane emphatically.

'We don't do fakes or imaginations of great things. Our bikes may not be technically replicas, but they are tributes and as such very close to the original. You'll be needing all your ears and spares around our wheelers. You want beefy? You want muscle? All the talk of riding the beast, taming the dragon, yer man's bike, etc, etc, blarney blarney blarney. I have consummated the bringing over of a pikey pack of CBXes. Now that's yer man's bike. Race that if you still have some monster in yer marrow.'

Pog paused, and let out a low chuckle. He placed a hand on my shoulder and his eyes went deep blue. 'Ah, you can ride the beauty that is the XR69 but she's still a motorcycle at the end of it; she will break your heart. As Yeatsie would say, "We have an abiding sense of tragedy that will sustain us through temporary periods of joy".

I was reminded of the tale of the two teddy bears in the bath tub. One asked for the soap. The other teddy bear said: 'What do you think I am, a typewriter?' Surely this was in the same bewildering category. I was often a step behind the game but in this conversation …

I turned to Brendan, turned my palms upwards and raised my eyebrows in a please explain gesture.

Brendan chuckled, and shuffled his feet lightly. 'Yer man said you're a fairly fine-looking good sir with your eyebrows making Frida Kahlo all ablush. And your come-by-them-honestly knocky-knees. You may not have the abundance of locks of your good man the Pog afore yee but a man who's lived long enough to lose his hair will no doubt know a thing or two about life – experience is the comb that life gives a bald man. The character of teeth ye filled your maw with would play an untuned din on the ivories and your ears are going to spin you a whirly round come a goodly breeze. The nose you've mounted could sit high on the manor wall with the finest elk and goat – many a time a man's mouth broke his nose. Are you worried – no sir. You'll not be having the plastic surgeon put his sticky silicone gel spoon all over you – no Botox in that face the birthing doctor mistakenly slapped in thinking it was your arse end. You've got your very own swagger-jagger. You are as God made you.'

Brendan gave me a nudge with his elbow. 'And God loves a trier.'

I stood, mouth agape, shocked. What had I just been assailed with?

Was it possible Brendan spoke an even deeper malarkey than Pog? What was this foreign unintelligible profundity they spoke?

I looked from Brendan to Pog. From Pog to Brendan. They both appeared to be as happy as clams. On the contrary, I felt like my brain had just gone through a blender.

'Obviously I have no idea what you buggers are talking about,' I said. 'Now I feel like I need an interpreter for the interpreter; especially as I asked what I thought was a simple question.' I shook my head again, endeavouring to find clear air. 'I was just trying to say that your bikes are not quite as competitive as they could be. The Irish bikes are beautiful. No doubting that. They are certainly great replicas. But…'

Pog folded his arms, a warm smile settling on his face. Then he stepped forwards and put his hands consolingly on my shoulders. 'The man is not a plastic paddy,' he said. 'But perhaps we have a wee trick or two still left up our sleeves.' Pog winked at me.

A HUMID EYE .... THE BOYS

The flatmates finished tidying up their bits-n-bobs and piled into the van. Matt was driving. We'd had a great day riding our bikes on what many thought was the best track in the world. However, Simon's day had been a disaster so one had to tread carefully.

Andy saw himself as a problem solver, something of a counsellor. He enjoyed finding a solution. Or, at least having a meeting to form a committee to write an agenda and get some minutes down so that a process could be put in place that could be voted on and discussed and a postponement made while an appeal to an item in the minutes was heard and another meeting could be planned.

'Do you think you can fix it, Si?' asked Andy.

'Don't need to, brother,' said Simon turning a humid eye on Andy. 'It's sweet just as it is.'

We kept our eyes out the windows, carefully avoiding looking at Simon. This wasn't good. Simon must have gone into a 'fuck the world' funk. *Fuck racing. Fuck all of it. Fucking fuck fuck.*

Simon snorted, like a bull on first paw. He snorted again. Then he let out a low chuckle. He hooted: giving a ludicrous cackle. This was definitely not good. He had gone over some kind of edge. He had been let down by his bikes so many times and this was the last straw.

Classic racers lived with the knowledge their bikes could blow at any time – especially two-strokers. It went with the game. You were asking unholy questions of your internal combustion engine. It was an old engine. Not steam engine old, but still, closing in on at least 40 years old. It wasn't only men that crinkled, warped, bent, and went off their toddy; race engines were people too.

A few top motorsport people just upped and walked away. Mike Thackwell up and left Formula One in 1987 after being top of the game.

Jody Scheckter was the only South African driver to win the F1 Championship and he just upped, and off. Eddy Merckx arguably left at the top of his game – but that was cycling. There were the highs but there were plenty of lows in sport and motorcycle racing was definitely a school of hard knocks.

Some racers in Simon's position just walked away from the sport, never to be seen again. There's only so many shattered pistons, holed crankcases, topless valves and snapped crankshafts one man can take.

My favourite blowup of the dozen or so I'd had, had been at Eastern Creek (now known as Sydney Motorsport Park, but doesn't have the same ring to it). My GSXR1100 had let go just as I came onto the front straight. It had started with a mild vibration that grew rapidly. I could feel it through my throttle hand. I kept it pinned and pondered on it. One didn't want to get out of the throttle without good reason. There was a bevy of racers up my butt that I had worked hard getting by. I wasn't going to give all that hard work up without careful consideration.

This was all happening at high speed but that was normal for a racer. Everything was happening at high speed on the track and racers had the innate ability to be able to compartmentalize a situation; to slow it down into bite-sized chunks. When a racer got in trouble, out of control, he didn't go 'oh shit' and cover his eyes to wait for the crash. He fought to regain control. To diagnose, fix and recover; all the time knowing he was losing precious time to his rivals. A racer did not have victim mentality. He raged against the situation until the bike either recovered stability or threw him off. Hence the invention of the elbow slider developed by Marc Marcus as a way of saving a situation.

Could it be a wheel vibration, I pondered, throttle still wide open. Perhaps a front tyre slightly deflated. Little lies you told yourself to avoid the awful truth. The vibrations got worse; they never got better. I decided I better get off the track and out of the way. I was already running the outside edge of the track. I shut the throttle however the bike didn't get the message. It tore onwards on full throttle. *Interesting; analyse.* I wanted to get on the grass, just in case there was any oil or liquid coming out the back of my bike. Little did I know that I was leaving a wall of blue smoke behind that would have made a July 4th party happy. Vince Sharpe, a fellow Kiwi, was behind and had to ride through the blitzkrieg. I couldn't veer onto the grass at full throttle, that was obvious. Well I could, but I didn't want to. The chances of controlling a bike with slicks on the grass at full throttle were minimal; I was no Ricky Carmichael. I hit the kill switch: no change, the bike kept rocketing forwards with a wild, death-defying urgency. *Still analysing at close to 200 kph.* I had killed the ignition but the GSXR 1100 was now providing its own spark: self-detonating. This baby was on its own launch mission. I didn't know it then but the number four piston had destroyed itself and blown out through the inlet valves in the head, out the intake ports and into the carburettor, jamming the carb slides on full open. The other three pistons were still intact and intent on giving it full berries.

RASH DECISIONS .... SIMON

I scrambled back to the present and snapped my attention back to Simon.

'I've sold the bugger,' stated Simon, laughing.

'You've what?' asked Andy, spinning in his seat.

Even Matt, who was supposed to be steering the van, spun in his seat with shock. The van took a minor detour to run over an orange cone.

'Sold it,' repeated Simon gleefully. 'It's gone.' He laughed again.

I also pivoted in my seat to consider Simon. He looked good. Happy even. Happier than he had been for some time.

'Sold it within 30 minutes of blowing it up,' continued Simon. 'Rastus has bought it. He said he always wanted one. Now he's got one.'

'You sure?' I blurted – *like I could comment on rash decisions.* 'Not being a little hasty.'

'Nope,' declared Simon, and gazed out the window. 'There's two good days when you own a race bike.'

'The day you buy it and the day you sell it,' we all chanted – and laughed; we all had our Post Classic race bike war stories.

'Besides, I've still got the Katana,' said Simon. 'I will spend some of the money from selling the XR and put a new frame in the Kat. Already spoken to Dale Gilbert and he's going to send me one of their frames.

Same as the ones Giles and Martin are running.'

PART TWO
DINNER WITH MEN

BEER BELLY AND SKINNY FORKS

Thursday dinner was RSL night. The Returned and Services League had a club in Cowes and it was popular. It allowed the general public in so long as they signed in and weren't drunk on entering. The food was great pub food and the prices were good. There was a sprinkling of other racers in the club. Kiwis were welcome as they had fought alongside the Aussies in many conflicts: brothers in arms. So long as you weren't rough (not too rough), or intoxicated (not too pissed), decently dressed (your jandals were clean), you were allowed in.

The place was full of your *standard ocker*. 50-years-old, faded Stubbies, thongs (jandals/flip-flops), singlet traded in for a T-shirt, pencil-thin legs, brittle-looking moustache and a beer belly slumped over the top of the shorts.

For the Kiwis it had become something of a custom to get at least one meal at the RSL. Roast of the day was popular and you got your plate filled.

'So, what do you reckon about PI, Campbell?' I asked, plopping my plate down at the table. This was Campbell's first PI event.

'I reckon it's good,' he replied, waving his fork enthusiastically. 'It's fast. I've never been on a track that fast, that big.' He waggled his fork even more expansively. 'I need a bigger engine, my little two-valve is struggling.' He dug his fork determinedly into a spud. 'I feel like the sheriff on the boat in Jaws. "You're gonna need a bigger boat."'

'Yes, you do,' I laughed. 'That track has no respect for the weak. It requires only one speed, flat out.'

Campbell's cheery red Suzuki GS1000, even under the genius of Wes Cooley, wouldn't have been on the pace at PI. Talk about a knife to a gunfight. His bike was one of only a few two-valves in the IC. It was a beauty, but beauty was up against the beast: the four-valve GSX1100. The difference was probably about 15 horsepower stock but the 1100 had more potential. Talking about horsepower numbers was like talking about which spell was strongest in the magic department of Hogwarts. People not well versed in the dark arts of engine building and performance would often claim exorbitant figures for how much their bike was putting out. The reality of the early Superbike engines was more conservative than most realised. Horsepower at the wheel was usually in the 70s. Engines were built to industrial strength like everything in those days. The sheer weight of the engine, plus the frame, plus the running gear was staggering. *Try lifting a cast alloy Katana front wheel?*

'And my forks are too skinny,' said Campbell, lowering his knife and fork to the plate. 'They start doing this by the end of the straight.' Campbell put his arms out and violently twitched them back and forth like the agitator in an old washing machine.

'How does that go?' laughed Brendan.

'Like this,' grinned Campbell, repeating the gesture. 'Then I've got to try and stop the bugger for the corner.'

There were plenty of bikes with only two-pot brake calipers – although the PI rules said you could have four-pot. The new two-pot calipers were actually pretty good and combined with modern brake pads of the carbon or sintered compounds, they did a remarkable job.

Brendan had been quickest that day amongst us. He came from a family of boys that all pedalled race bikes and there was plenty of fierce sibling rivalry. I figured I could get up to Brendan's speed but the planets would need to align. My bike was going fine, just gutless. It certainly handled beautifully. Denis Curtis had done a fine job in designing the replica frames. Unfortunately, Denis had passed away recently from cancer. The frames were now part of his legacy and it was special to own one. They came with your initials stamped into the serial number.

'So, what the hell happened to you, yer Spotty Dave?' asked Brendan, as he chased some peas around his plate. 'You, yer man, did yer get a bit of the whisky throttle.'

I had been the only one of us to see the incident when Spotty Dave had put his bike into the pit wall. The others had already headed out on track, the mechanics were on the pit wall, their heads poking out between the mesh to catch the first riders tearing past down the main straight.

'I will be on it tomorrow,' promised Spotty Dave, manfully trying to muster some courage. 'Was a little off my game today.' He gave me a faintly haunted glance.

I figured Spotty Dave was on a bender of his own making and it was best to let him run. I was certainly not his minder or his mum, *imagine that*! But where was the line between letting him go wild with his novel mirror time travel invention, if it became a reality, and a responsibility for his wellbeing? Was Spotty Dave becoming an alien? Was he already an alien? How well did I know the man? Did I, as captain of the Kiwi team, have a responsibility to pull the man if he became a threat? Geez, he might become a threat to not only himself but to other riders on track. I selected another frown line from the worry basket and pasted it above my brow. I was rapidly becoming the reluctant confidant to too many crazy notions and activities.

Sleep was a distant planet to me and the classic motorcycle madness filling my head wasn't going to bring that planet closer to me; or me to it. I had the job at hand of racing to occupy the mind, let alone having the intrude of another layer of conjecture and wonder.

I shook my head a couple of times. 'Okay, quiz time,' I declared, going for a diversion as much for myself as for the crew. I mopped up the last gravy on my plate. 'I give a name, you give the bike they ride. Okay. Jock?'

'TZ 350,' said Campbell.

'Rastus?'

'GSX 1100, like mine,' said Matt.

'Used to be, now an XR69, thanks to me,' said Simon, ruefully. 'The fucker.'

This brought some chuckles. Simon seemed to have moved on quickly from his misfortune. Few men had this ability.

'Foxy?'

'CB 1100R.'

'Beaker?'

'GS thou,' said Simon. 'Although I think he has an 1100 donk in there now.'

'Butch?'

'Norton,' said Campbell.

'Vince?'

'Guzzi,' said Campbell.

'The Wilton brothers.'

'What and who the feck are the Wilton mothers?' bleated Brendan.

'TZ 750 and TZ 700,' proclaimed Andy. 'Trevor Taylor has both those bikes too.'

'Wiggles?'

'That would be an FZR 1000 at the last sighting,' said Spotty Dave.

'I don't know any of those feckers,' complained Brendan.

'No, all Kiwis,' I admitted. 'Croz?'

'Ah, now I'm on yer,' smiled Brendan. 'A bunch of bikes yer man rode but let's go Moriwaki Kawasaki Z1.'

Unified nodding agreed with that answer.

'Smiley?'

Silence.

'That would be a fella I know in Whangarei,' I said. 'CBX 1000 – like new. Keeps it in the lounge.'

The boys were still adjusting to Australian Eastern Standard Time. We hit the sack early.

GOO GOO

Chucky had turned up. Simon found him at the foot of his bed when he awoke.

I arrived back at the house after an early morning wander. I did enjoy the peace of Cowes, aside from the bird cacophony, as the sun took a peek, saw all was clear and eased itself above the horizon. I had a bit of a walking circuit I liked to do. The wharf down from the main street was first port of call and usually had a few hopeful fishermen on its railings. Being an insomniac, I was 'on the drugs' for the PI meeting. My current tipple of choice was Amitriptyline. It came with a warning to not get too much sunlight and that it may cause sleepiness. *Duh – the whole point.* Amitriptyline did work in that it turned my brain off: its busyness at 1am was the essence of my non-sleep. However – and there's always a however when drugs are concerned – restarting my brain was no easy matter. After taking Amitriptyline it was like having to coal-feed a steam engine to get the thing firing again.

I arrived back to find Spotty Dave sitting on a stool in the hallway gazing distantly into his mirrors. I assumed he was making some adjustments to the ranks of mirrors; *he better have*. I didn't disturb Spotty Dave's trance-like state but just slid sideways past the mirrors to my room, taking care not to bump one. I hated to think what would happen if that occurred – *some rippled time continuum bouncing back to the future*. We might find Spotty Dave wrapped in a nappy with his thumb in his mouth all a-goo-goo.

ZEITGEIST AND TEENAGERS

The IC boys had one more practice session before qualifying began. It was now getting a little more serious. This was the run where you needed to have your gearing nearly sorted and a fair idea which way the track went. Graeme Crosby time: 'Which way does the track go, and what's the lap record.'

If you could hit all your apexes then your lap times were probably going to be okay. That was a truism for most tracks. Racers always wanted to go faster. Speed was a thrill on the road but it was meaningless on the racetrack. What counted was whether you were gapping the rider behind, or more importantly, closing on the geezer ahead; speed was irrelevant at that point. Velocity was relative. You might be doing 250 kph compared to the ground but compared to a fellow competitor the difference may only be 3 kph. And *that's* the speed that counts in racing.

I had my bike as ready as it was going to be. It had new slicks fitted, the battery was fully charged, the mix of avgas and premium was set at 50/50. I knew it would be good on the downhill charge from the

Southern Loop to Miller. It was the pull up from Siberia to the top of Lukey Heights where it would be found out: that it couldn't pull the skin off a rice pudding and would be as weak on that climb as a mountaineer who's shed his hobnails. *What a pain.* All that time and money put into it and it was coming up short.

I wandered to the front door of the pits to Spotty Dave's spot. 'You got this?' I asked.

'Yeah, mate,' nodded Spotty Dave enthusiastically, locking the fuel cap down.

He looked to have regained his ken. I thought he had the grin of a young man – but hopefully not too young. 'What age do you reckon today?'

Spotty Dave pursed his lips. 'Pretty sure I've brought it forward to the late teens, maybe 20.'

Spotty Dave ran the tip of his tongue across his top lip. 'Looking back through the mirrors this morning I think I spotted me in my first pair of Levi's.' He grinned. 'At least, this time, I'm old enough to know how to ride a bike. I feel good – really good,'

I smiled. Spotty Dave was about to mount his Harris GSX1100 as a late teen and oh how I wished I could again feel what that was like; *if it was really happening!* Spotty Dave was riding his own personal zeitgeist and it might only be the god of deus ex machina that could save him.

'Go well, mate,' I said, simply.

'You too, mate.'

TEAM AUSTRALIA CAPTAIN .... WALLY

I decided to catch up with the Aussie captain first thing, before things got too busy. There was a captains' meeting scheduled for that afternoon, so it was good to touch base with all the skippers before that. I ticked them off mentally: Arthur, the UK captain: Bo, USA: and Pog, Ireland. And Wally, the Aussie.

'Gidday, mate,' I said, walking into the Aussie pits.

'Gidday, cobber,' replied Wally.

Photo: D Begg

Wally's voice sounded like a fibreglass surfboard being ridden down a gravel wave. There was nothing but sand and grist in his vocal cords. He was perched lightly against a lovely Honda CB1100R, his arms loosely folded. Wally didn't quite cut the figure he used to but you could still tell the man had been an athlete. He had the rangy build and strong shoulders of a footie player. He was wearing the Duckhams cap he always wore. It was oil weary and worn to the stage where the peak was shedding cotton strands.

I looked around the pits and the settled scene. Unlike the minor bedlam in the other pits, the Aussie ones were calm with everything seemingly ready. There was a plethora of exotic bikes. The Irving Vincent 1600cc four-valve took pride of place. It was in the exceptional exotica category of race bikes – and there were more about than you would think. It was up there with the Britten V1000, the Brough Superior, the Norton RCW588. It was an unbelievably tight package. The saying was that the Vincent engine must have been put into the frame with a chair and a whip.

'Looks like you fellas are ready,' I observed, neatly.

'Yep, seems that way,' agreed Wally, taking a sweeping glance. 'We set up a couple of days ago.' He nodded his head. 'Yeah, no dramas. Saves all the messing about last minute.'

'Home advantage, eh?'

'Something like that,' agreed Wally.

'So, you got the measure of the Poms this year?'

Wally raised a hand to his day-old growth and gave it a rueful scratch. 'Fair dinkum, but it's not a level playing field, is it I? They manage to be the flea in the ear of the Phillip Island management

CLASSIC MOTORCYCLE MADNESS   61

and bend the rules a bit more each year.' He paused. 'Now, I know you blokes are in the same situation that we are. You run the Pre-82 Class under the same rules as we do. The Poms have managed to get this pushed out to Pre-84 which is no help to me, or you. They've got these Yammy 1300 engines and put them in Harris frames. Those Yams weren't around before 1984 – so what do they do? Change the rules to suit the Poms.'

Wally's neck began reddening up. 'And it was an FJ 1200 that was the bike in 1984. They've got an XJR 1300 and stuck an FJ 1200 head on it – so it looks like an FJ. Nikasil bores come standard and you can run the 1300 stock, with just some high-comp pistons. Don't even have to split the cases. It's straightforward cheating; there's no other way to describe it.' Wally hunched his shoulders and inclined his head. 'Now I'm not one to complain, as you know. But how far can you let them go with this? You are in the same boat as us. What are your thoughts, cobber?'

'We are just small fish in this pond,' I sighed. 'We basically just come for the beer and skittles. We don't have the bikes or the riders to compete against you fellas.' I reconsidered, 'Well, we do have the riders: there's some bloody fast boys in NZ. We just don't have the bikes.' I grinned, 'I guess your home advantage will be put to the test.'

LUCKY LUNCH

Simon was all smiles and ridiculously happy considering his lovely XR69 had been lunched the day before. He looked like a man who had been shipwrecked and washed up on an island to find a bottle on the sand beside him with a winning lottery ticket inside. He perched Chucky on Brendan's toolbox while the Irish/Kiwi rider was out on his practice laps.

KING KONG

The IC boys rolled back into the pits after the morning session. This time it was Brendan who was missing in action.

He soon turned up with his bike on the back of the pickup trailer. He had gone down at Miller. It was just a light low-side so the bike was barely scratched. The bolt on the steering damper had bizarrely sheared off jamming the damper rod into the engine and locking up the steering. Brendan walked into the pits with his helmet in hand while some ready helpers unloaded the XR69. He spied Chucky on his toolbox a moment before Simon whipped the doll away.

'I told you to keep that fecker away,' snapped Brendan, unzipping his leathers.

'Come on brother, he's just a doll,' cajoled Simon.

'He's no *feckin'* doll! *And you, yer man, know it*!' Brendan was bright red in the face. It was hot. He banged his chest protector down on a chair. 'If I see him around my kit agin, I'll have at him.'

'Chucky, don't listen, he doesn't mean it,' cooed Simon, stroking Chucky's hair. 'He's a big meanie. Let's go somewhere else.'

It was disturbing for those around, however, no one said anything; it was better not to draw attention to oneself. Simon was a big fella with a shaven head and a slightly intimidating look. If he wanted to walk around with a doll in his hand, well… *but it wasn't quite right*. It wasn't quite The Hulk kidnapping Barbie or King Kong swooping in to take Ann Darrow, but it was disturbing. But no one wanted a scene; besides, riders had their own demons to wrestle with.

ALL TALK NO DORK

Qualifying for the IC was held in two groups: the slow and the fast. It was up to the rider to decide which category he fitted into. So help you if you thought you were a gun and put yourself in the fast group then got in the way of the top guns as they were trying to set a time. 'All talk, no dork' would be considered a kind comment. There's not a lot of room in racing for blowhards and it takes very little time to be found out. You could well sprout about how fast you were while perched in a pub or café but come track time there was nowhere to hide. Laptimes were truth. Tell a racer how shit hot you were at a certain track and they would inevitably ask you what laptimes you did. You could say your bike wasn't running great – and it may not have been – or it was underpowered – and it may have been – but a slow laptime was a slow laptime. The thin air at this meeting was to be found in the higher 1:30s. Laptimes were an automatic form of cattle drafting.

Brendan was the only one of the flatmates prepared to put his name with the quicks. He did a more than respectable 1:43.448. The others went in the slow half: Campbell 1:55.229, Matt 1:51.501, Me 1:47.585 and Spotty Dave 1:49.666.

INTERNATIONAL CHALLENGE ORIGIN

The IC originally began as an Aussie versus Rest of the World competition 30 years ago. The ROW team was made up of mainly Kiwis and a few Aussies who couldn't make the Aussie team. We had four adopted Aussies in our Kiwi IC team: Damien, Glen, Roger and Alex (son of the legendary Robbie Phillis). Alex qualifying time was 1:39.441. He wasn't happy with it; I would have torn your arm off for it. Anything sub-1:40 was legend status. 1:40 - 1:45 was respectable. More than 1:50 meant you needed to pull your finger out – or you were riding a two-valve; and your bike couldn't keep up with the speed of the track.

RASTUS

There was one other Kiwi in the IC team: Rastus. Rastus was from Stewart Island. Stewart Island was NZ's third largest island. Next stop south of Stewart Island was Antarctica. You wouldn't last long on Stewart Island if you weren't hardy. Stewart Island was separated from the South Island by a

30 km stretch of water named Foveaux Strait. The strait was a rough and treacherous body of water, which claimed many lives: from 1998 to 2012 there were 23 fatalities. Bodies were often not found as great white sharks patrolled the strait. Rastus worked as a paua diver and cray fisherman. His job, while working the ocean floor, required him to keep an eye out for the great shadow above. He was probably the only man racing at PI that had motorcycle racing as a safer recreation than his occupation.

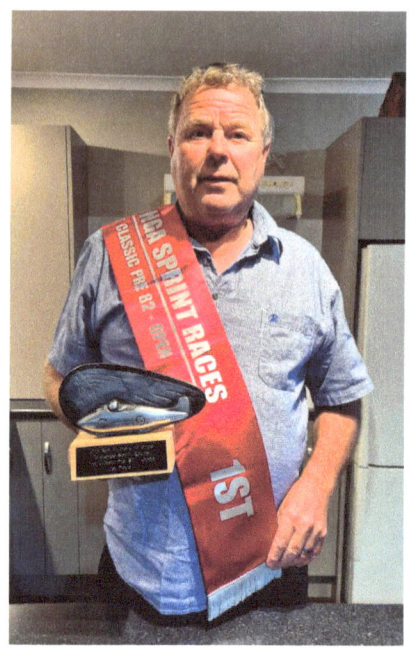

Rastus's GSX1100 was parked amongst the two-strokes. It was beside Kev's TZ350. Kev owned the Invercargill Yamaha dealership and was a best mate of Rastus. Kev, Rastus and I had come up with a plan to try and hide Rastus bike amongst the two-strokes. Try and make it inconspicuous; Lord knows Rastus was anything but. He was larger than life. He had a cheerful, ruddy, boisterous complexion. Rastus was a kind of larger version of Campbell – the welterweight. Rastus was all heavyweight and had the easy nature of one who knew he could have you in a full nelson before you could take your next mouthful of tea.

His GSX was running on methanol which was highly illegal at PI. You couldn't run avgas anymore let alone the dangerous methanol. The alcohol-based fuel had a high octane rating. It burnt clean and cool. It could light up a motor, even a tired one. However, the lighting up was one of the significant downsides. A methanol fire was all but invisible and produced no smoke. A mechanic in pitlane could be jumping up and down, waving his arms and screaming because his race steed or rider wasn't performing, or he could be engulfed in a methanol fire. In NZ you had to run large M stickers on your bike to signify that methanol was being used. At PI, Rastus and I surreptitiously peeled the M stickers off his bike.

We figured putting his GSX with the strokers meant the sweet pungent aroma of methanol could be hidden amongst the skank of the two-stroke emissions.

Speaking of which, the two-strokes fired up filling the pits with hard noise; talk about a conversation killer. People couldn't hear themselves let alone others. Smoke wafted out of the pits as the support classes wound out for their final practice.

CHUCKY GOES AWOL

Simon squatted beside me, 'Have you seen Chucky?' He sounded slightly panicky, like a parent who's just noticed his three-year-old has wandered off. I was busy inspecting the rear tyre on my F1. I reckoned I could get the two races on Saturday out of it, by flipping it, then bung a new one on for Sunday. The beauty of slicks was that you could run them in either direction. Sure, they had an arrow showing the direction of rotation but anyone who knew anything knew you could flip

Kev and a TZ's familiar perch.

them. Some said the belts inside the tyre would tear apart if the direction was incorrect. I had never heard of that happening. I doubted there were even belts in them.

Simon, of course, didn't have tyre issues. He also no longer had to work out how to smuggle avgas into the pits and into his tank. Or how early he could get on the gas at the Southern Loop. He wasn't fretting on how late he could brake into Miller. His self-defence mechanisms were now on vacation and Simon, secretly, thought this was a beautiful thing. His immediate life had been simplified a lot. He was just worried about his little buddy; or evil mascot depending on your take.

'No, I haven't seen Chucky,' I said, indifferently. 'How long's he been missing?'

'I'm not sure. A couple of hours, I think. I've been up on top watching the qualifying. He wasn't here when I came down.' Simon rubbed his bald dome. 'Geez, Chucky. The little bugger can't be far. *The Chuckster*. Where are you, son?'

'Let's ask Rastus,' I said, straightening up and wiping my hands on a rag. *Hopefully Chucky has fallen down a deep well*, I secretly thought. 'Also, you need to be involved with Rastus and his …' I was a little lost for words. 'Let's call it, his fuel issue.'

We walked across the bay dodging sprockets, circles of tyres, stepping over spanners to get to the other pit garage.

'How's it going?' I asked Rastus. Rastus was holding a suspicious 20-litre white can. It had no markings on it.

'Box of birds, mate,' said Rastus, happily.

'You wouldn't have seen the Chucky doll would you?'

CLASSIC MOTORCYCLE MADNESS

Rastus thumbed over his shoulder. 'Someone said he was down in one of the Aussie pits.'

'What!' barked Simon. 'The Chuckster has gone to the other side?'

'I doubt it,' laughed Rastus. 'He's having too much fun up here. I'm just glad I'm over this side of the pits, away from the little bugger.' He addressed me: 'I'm nearly out of methanol. Down to one can left.'

'Ssshh, not so loud,' I cautioned, looking quickly about. 'You know we can't be using that stuff. Don't even *say* the word.' I paused briefly to think. 'Let's call it M. Abbreviate it.'

'Or meth,' suggested Rastus, brightly.

'Hell no, man. Are you crazy?' I looked with bewilderment at Rastus. 'Imagine someone overhearing us talking about getting some meth. *Geez,* I've got enough trouble trying to keep you mongrels on a leash without your drug habits coming out.'

'Okay, let's go for M and M's,' chuckled Rastus. 'We will call the meth, M and M's.' He was from Stewart Island, the last El Dorado, and wasn't used to playing covert games. Pretty much anything went as far as he was concerned, except stealing a fella's bike – unless he deserved it. He had just recovered one of his own in Invercargill after it went missing. A gang contact had pointed him in the right direction to find the missing bike. He found it in a wardrobe standing upright in wheelie position on its back wheel. How it had gotten in there was a mystery. Rastus had to pull the wardrobe door frame apart to get it out – which was easily done by the big man. He could leg trip and take down a 14-stone wrestler, he wasn't going to be bothered by a pine framed wardrobe.

'The bloke supplying me is nearly out of M and M's,' resumed Rastus. 'He's getting low. Don't know if someone else is on the M and M's at this meeting, wouldn't be surprised. But there's not going to be enough to go round.'

I chewed on this for a moment. 'I think I know someone who will know where to get the M and M's,' I said. 'You and Simon can go and get it. The pair of you can look after yourselves as I imagine the process could be slightly dodgy; if you know what I mean.'

Simon grunted. He didn't appear all that enthusiastic about the mission. It had complication written all over it just when he thought his life for the next few days was looking sweet and simple. Couch time was being threatened; it was now turning into hammer time.

He was growing tense. Good. That's how I wanted him.

'Take the Chucky doll with you,' I advised. 'He finally may be of some use to us.'

CAPTAINS' MEETING

I had a captains' meeting at 1pm to further work on the rules governing the IC races. It was the first of several meetings over the weekend. Setting rules was an important part of any sport but a rulebook in motor racing could quickly grow to be the size of a brick.

I was one of the last to arrive in the conference room of the Phillip Island Racetrack. I was also a little behind the game in regards to the rules of the IC as basically I'd been given a bit of a hospital pass when I was anointed Kiwi captain. The Phillip Island International Classic was run under Motorcycle Australia rules for its vintage classes.

However, the IC class had been hijacked and was being violated by basically one person: Arthur; the UK captain, who possessed a mouth in which butter wouldn't melt.

Arthur outwardly was a genteel man of kindly appearance – kind of like Ken Barlow of Coronation Street, seemingly patient and all-caring – but he was no mug; he was there to win. The British had their arses handed to them by the Aussies in the first couple of years of the IC and they were hurting.

The Brits had obeyed the Pre-1982 Rules in place in Australia (and NZ) and mainly used the Suzuki GSX1100 engine as the powerplant, with unreliable results. The UK team (Arthur) had then campaigned subtly for changes with the rules and this was proving successful. Of course, this changed the nature of the IC races. There was no Pre1982 race class in England – there was in NZ and Australia. Arthur reasoned that Pre-1984 was a more suitable race age limit for the bikes, allowed, more choice of machinery. There were no Pre-82 rules in Britain and there was no Post Classic class at all in the USA – at least for big bikes.

Arthur had beavered away in his workshop in dreary Shropshire and designed a bike to have an engine that, while not bombproof, was much sturdier than a volatile GSX 1100 powerplant. He began by using heavily-modified 1984 Yamaha FJ 1200 engines. He then discovered that the XJR 1300 engine was identical except for the head. The beauty was that the XJR was manufactured from 1999 to 2016 so there was no shortage of them. Plus, they used Nikasil bores. He could run the XJR 1300 block standard and just add high-compression pistons. The FJ 1200 head bolted straight on and hey presto it all looked FJ1200: the veritable wolf in sheep's clothing.

Arthur put them in XR69 frames, designed by the renowned Harris brothers, Lester and Steve, and called the model, F1. He then went out and employed a bevy of pro-riders to pilot them. Arthur had wheedled a fair chunk of money out of the Phillip Island office to bring these stars downunder, and for the motorcycle jockeys it sure beat hanging about in a gloomy British winter. Isle of Man riders were the mainstay of the team: Ryan Farquhar, Conor Cummins, Gary Johnson, James Hillier, John McGuinness and Peter Hickman were amongst them.

Arthur was dotting his I'-s and crossing his T'-s in an effort to win the IC.

ISLAND CLASSIC – CAPTAINS' MEETING 1

Captains: USA-Bo, Ireland-Pog, NZ-DC, UK-Arthur, Australia-Wally

Agenda: Item
1. Size of brakes 2. Size of wheels

The Phillip Island GM was chairing the meeting. I took a seat beside Bo. There was a chair free beside Wally but I didn't want it to appear as if there was some sort of Australasian front.

'Welcome all,' began the chair. 'Good to see you fellas back here and let's hope for some great racing. This meeting is a continuation of the previous years' meetings regarding the rules for the

International Challenge, the IC for short. We have made gradual changes to the rules and we seem to be reaching some sort of consensus …'

'Well, mate, I wouldn't go as far as that,' interrupted Wally. 'I think we all know what has been said, or purported to have been said, at previous meetings and there is room for dispute there. Now I'm not one to rock the boat, but …'

'Wally, we will all get our say,' blocked the chair, raising a hand in the universal stop sign. The chairman was an uncomplicated man. Sure, he had difficulties now and then, *who didn't?* But he always endeavoured to row his boat to calmer waters.

'I say old chap,' said Arthur, rising from his chair and picking up a biscuit from a plate on the table. 'These biscuits look tasty. Perhaps, if I may, I suggest we could look at the motorbicycle and the rules that pertain to it in parts. If I may.' Arthur broke the biscuit into several pieces. 'Can get frightfully messy, eh what. Now, if we take this biscuit to represent the motorbicycle …'

'It's a god-damn motorbike,' snarled Bo, sliding his chair back and crossing his cowboy boots on top of the conference room table.

'Pardon?'

Bo leaned back in his chair and looked toward the ceiling. He figured the English had been the cause of all the git uppity back in the day in the US of A. Bo had enough trouble in dealing with Yankees: they were the spawn of people like Arthur. *Ah, maybe he was being a little harsh.* 'The thing is called a motorbike, pardner. Not a motorbicycle.'

'Quite,' mused Arthur. He smiled benevolently at Bo. If only the Yankees had wiped out all those southerners when they had the chance. *Hush now Arthur, that was a little harsh.* 'We, shall use the Queen's English. I understand you're *new* to the language in your part of the world, but one must maintain one's decorum. Don't you think?'

'Are you saying what *I think* you're saying?' Bo levered his boots off the table and leaned forward. 'You limey bastards and your cheap tricks. What do *I think* you're saying?' He paused, momentarily confused. *Anyone worth his salt knew Americans spoke the best English. Sure, they had taken the liberty of jazzing up the Oxford dictionary a bit but the Merriam-Webster (America's dictionary) was a whole site better bible, in Bo's humble view. Still, he had to admit, the Brits could certainly fuck with English words in a dazzling kind of way.*

He removed the unlit cigar from his mouth and pointed it at Arthur. 'If I think you're saying that I think …' his voice trailed away. A small smile crept onto his face relieving his features. '*I think I know what you're saying* … and it's not what I think.' He put the cigar back in his mouth and smiled broadly.

Arthur was slightly unnerved by Bo's odd behaviour but he batted on: 'Old chap, I'm just saying that perhaps we should regard each component of the motorbicycle one piece at a time with regard to the rules and what is incumbent on us.'

'Yes,' gulped the chairman. He mentally tried again to row that boat towards calmer water – his boat was named *Little Leeky*. 'That's the way to move this forward, I think,' agreed the chair. 'And Arthur, you don't need to stand each time you speak.'

'Tut, tut, of course I do,' beamed Arthur. 'Decorum, my good fellow, decorum.'

'Right,' said the chair, struggling to keep a straight face. 'Let's begin with the wheels. No, let's start with the brakes. Are we all in agreement that four-pot calipers should be legal? DC.'

'In New Zealand Post Classic Rules, in the Pre-82 Class, they're not allowed. They are allowed in Pre-89. That would mean changing back and forth for us Kiwis.' I puckered my lips. 'We would need a set of calipers for NZ and a set for here. Plus making the adaptors.'

'You could use a lathe. Strewth, you blokes got electricity over there yet,' chortled Wally, reaching around Bo to give me a friendly slap on the shoulder. 'Haha, no offense. I am really in agreement with my Kiwi cousin. We too have to come up with a four-pot system for this one meeting. Otherwise, the Poms and the Yanks have a huge advantage.' Wally smiled cordially. 'Now I'm not one for having a whinge, but we seem to be favouring one team in this setup. The rules all seem to be going in one direction. Now I realise we are going faster each year at this meeting …'

'Yeah, because you boys keep turning up with souped up engines,' I chimed. 'Then blowing them up. What about a limit on the number of engines you can run. Our fellas turn up with just one.'

'My good old mother kept four pots by the foot of the bed,' interjected Pog. He held up four fingers. 'One for each and a spare for the sheep herder. They surely stopped enough for us but it's best to use the rear first before applying the front – in my experience. My granddaddy wasn't with us by then, he'd gone to pasture. The back paddock was the best place for him and he could give it a right lick as he went past – he was still quick. If you know what I mean.' Pog abruptly quit speaking. He silently opened his mouth wide and threw his head back quickly a couple of times like he was taking tequila shots.

The group stared, transfixed. *An odd tic or some kind of expression?* Pog settled himself, smiled benignly and gazed around the table. *We waited for more but that was it.*

Wally reluctantly dragged his eyes from Pog. 'I had a bit of a wander yesterday, no dramas,' he said.

'Couldn't help noticing a lot of fancy machinery in the Yanks boxes. Now I'm not one for spitting the dummy but there were some bikes in there running six-pots.' Wally folded his arms meaningfully and looked hard at Bo.

'Is this true?' asked the chair. He could feel orderliness departing – *Little Leeky* was taking on water. A sinking feeling came over him.

Bo removed the cigar from his mouth and considered it. It was getting a little chewed on the end. He rolled it slowly round in his fingers.

'And wavy discs,' I added, with a smile at Wally. 'Although I'm not one to complain.'

'Well, son, the best things come in six-packs,' grinned Bo. 'And, Bud, I reckon we invented those.' He looked meaningfully at Arthur.

'*Well I never*,' spluttered Arthur. 'What a *beastly* idea.'

'My boys are travelling hard,' continued Bo, unperturbed. 'They're not hanging about. They've got more guts than you could hang on a fence. You can't expect them to haul ass and not be able to haul up. We didn't become the greatest country in the world by being no pussies.' Bo took a small plastic capsule from his pocket. He popped the lid and shook a couple of pills into his hand. A small silver hip flask appeared in his other hand. He downed the pills with a slug from the flask, and smiled, 'Gotta keep the nerves steady in these hi-roller boardroom meetings.'

'Okay, gentlemen,' intervened the chair. *He could figuratively feel the water in his sinking boat; it was part-way up his legs. So much for rowing to quiet waters.* He scrolled clutchingly down the sheet of paper in front of him. *He would soon need a lifebuoy.*

'Perhaps, we could meet halfway,' he suggested. 'Four-pot calipers that would be. Umm, let's move on to wheels. Now, we agreed a couple of years ago that 17-inches was the only way to go, what with modern race tyre sizes and all of that. But what composition of the wheels we never fully discussed – didn't think we needed to. Bo, what are the Americans running?'

'Carbon, baby, carbon.'

The scraping of a chair: Arthur rose to his feet. 'That is preposterous. Totally out of order. God forbid we would go down that path, old chum. It is total poppycock. We run magnesium, as they did back in the days of the empire.'

'The only mag I know,' drawled Bo. 'Is the 44 Magnum. Now that little mother will blow a big hole right through you.'

'Wally, DC?' expostulated the chair. *The water was now streaming into Little Leeky.*

'We can't afford either,' I said. 'We run street rims. Whatever we can find, obviously some are lighter than others. But nothing fancy in our team.'

'We too run a lot of street rims,' agreed Wally. 'We do have a couple of bikes on the mags. Now I'm not one to complain, as you know, but come on, carbon fibre. What's next? We've got rid of methanol, and now avgas, soon we will be down to racing lawnmowers. Geez, you bloody mongrels are moaning like sheilas. It must be time for a coldie.'

Little Leeky was going under. The water was metaphorically at mid-thigh. The chairman grimaced: *this was way too early in the race weekend to be getting his nuts wet.*

Pog raised a placating hand. 'You can get away quickly with a load of damp sod on your handlebars – even with the wooden leg – and there'll be nary a splinter in you. You pop one spoke and it's not complaining. You pop a family of them and she'll wobble you like jelly at Easter. There is impedimentum to the momentum whether you be a boxer, flat-twin or a Wankel. It's no difference to the man out after rabbits – or the man working the thrashing mill – or the man who bashes the tin for the tinker – or the man who carts the soil from the night box – or the man who irons his horse's feet. It's about spinning the hoop around the bends.'

AIN'T MY FIRST RODEO

I caught up to Bo as we were leaving the meeting. Bo was pulled up outside the offices.

'Can I have a word, Bo?'

'Sure cowboy,' agreed Bo. 'And that word is, horse.'

'*Horse?*' I questioned.

'Yessir, where's my horse to get back to the pits. Someone should be picking me up. And by the way, your barn door's open and the mule's trying to run.'

'Huh.'

'Pardner, your fly's open,' smiled Bo.

'Oh. Thanks for noticing … I think. Maybe I'm saving energy – it will need unzipping again in the not-too-distant future. Come on, we can walk this,' I encouraged. 'I need a favour.'

'God dang, I love a favour.' Bo fell in beside me as we began the walk back to the pit garages.

'Yes, well, this is definitely a favour. I need some methanol.'

Bo grinned, lifted the Stetson from his head and laid it back on with an expression of delight. '*Well,* I am cooking on the front burners today. By the end of this meeting, dude, you and I may be brothers.'

Photo: D Begg

I laughed. 'Brothers from a different mother. What do you reckon, can you help?'

'You know I can help. This ain't my first rodeo, pardner,' he chuckled.

'That's why you came to me.'

I was a little wary of Bo, who wouldn't be, but he did appear to have a pretty good pipeline to a lot of things. There was something about him that I liked. He had a certain cracked charm. Perhaps it was Bo's struggle with himself that fascinated me. The hardnose man from Texas – perhaps he wasn't really from Texas; perhaps the whole pardner/cowboy persona was a charade. Maybe he was in fact from Queens, New York, and his Texas act was a way to blot out the boy from the Big Apple. Any man who could pull that off with the punch he showed was a man worth listening to, unless you had something a hell of a lot better to do with your time.

Bo led me to the American pits and tore a back page out of a notebook. He wrote a name and directions on the piece of paper and said he would call ahead to tee it up. He smiled and held it out. 'These boys will do the business but don't dig up more snakes than you can kill.'

SEAL DE-GLOVING

The final qualifying session got underway mid-afternoon. The temperature had reached 40 degrees. The track temp was well into the 50s. It was a case of getting one quick flying lap on the board ASAP:

the slicks didn't like the conditions and were turning to liquorice with too much running. For most of the Kiwi team the qualifying times were about the same as in the morning session, if not a little slower. The conditions weren't ideal for bike or rider.

Racing leathers were the only outfit on the track but a rider quickly became overheated off the bike. Campbell was so sweated up after the session it was like watching a seal being de-gloved. Two helpers endeavoured to peal the leather suit from his soaking body. People often questioned how it could be so physical just sitting on your butt riding around a beautifully smooth piece of tarmac. But ride a heavy bike on the stops, brake late and wrestle it from side to side through the corners and most people would sweat. Leathers were designed to be a tight fit: the track was no place for flapping clothing. Campbell's training regime (lack of it) meant the leathers were a little tighter this year. The modern leather suit was totally unlike the leathers of motorcycle jockeys in the 60s and 70s. Those leather suits were wafer thin and mainly about low wind resistance. If you fell off they would give some very limited skid protection which was testament to the quality of steer that was used in their construction. However, they contained no plastic shock-absorbing pads, titanium skid plates or nylon elbow guards. You could even walk normally in the old suits –in an upright position.

The modern leather suit was designed for the rider to always be in the riding position. When the rider was off the bike he was still constricted in the riding position. So, when you saw a rider walking in his leathers, he had not reverted back to neanderthal; he was not dragging his knuckles because that was his comfortable pose – he was forced into that situation because of the restrictions of the leather suit. If he dared try to straighten up his nuts would be cut in half. The modern leathers were made of a combination of kangaroo and cow leather. This made them malleable while retaining strength. Leathers were still the best material for soaking up speed while not disintegrating. You could slide at 200 kph on asphalt for quite a way so long as you didn't stay on one spot on the suit: it paid to roll around. This would stuff the suit but if you didn't move you were going to second degree the hell out of a part of your body. Your leathers would be pretty knackered afterwards but your skin would be fine – well, maybe a little speed rash.

Street riders had some delusional idea their lovely fitting Gore-Tex apparel would protect them. In a slide a Gore-Tex suit peeled apart like a banana shedding its skin. God help you if you were wearing a jacket and pants. The jacket would ride up and you would be given a jolly good skinning around the midriff and hips. That would also happen if you were wearing a leather jacket but at least your upper half should be fine.

Armour in motorcycle street suits basically did nothing and in many cases caused injury by directing the impact to one particular area rather than dissipating it. Air suits were the new kid on the block. However, a Post Classic rider would rather spend the money on knifing the crank, or Carillo rods, or a set of Keihin 36mm round-slides, not an expensive airbag suit.

MISFIRING .... ALEX / BRENDAN

Alex Phillis wandered down the Kiwi pits and found me talking with Brendan.

Alex was the only chance the Kiwis had of a winning rider in the IC. No one else came close.

John McGuinness. Photo: D Fitzgerald

He had competed at the highest level in World Superbike. He was one of the youngsters competing at the Island Classic but he did have pedigree with his father, Robbie, being a WSBK legend.

'How's the bike this year?' I asked Alex.

'It's a beast. Bit of fine tuning to do but I reckon it's good.' Alex paused and frowned. 'But have you guys been having any misfire problems?'

'Nope,' I said. 'Well, at least, not anything new. My bike is always off-song at the moment – but not missing.'

'I have,' advised Brendan, nodding. 'Had it a couple of times in that last session. I've checked the coil wiring and battery earth. Haven't found anything.'

'Intermittents are the worst,' said Alex. He screwed up his face with recall perplexion. 'It was weird. It only happened a couple of times and it was only when I passed a bike. Well, tried to pass a bike. Can't make the move when your bike starts missing.'

Brendan fidgeted lightly up and down and nodded again. 'Yeah, I had the same. Strange thing. Just about got alongside a bike and mine started missing – like it was running on two. Like a coil had cut out. That's why I checked the coil wires.'

'Same as me,' said Alex, looking perturbed. 'I got alongside this bike and it dropped down on the cylinders, so I couldn't make the pass. Backed off and it ran fine. Then when I tried again, the same thing. Too weird.'

'That is a weird coincidence,' I agreed. 'The same thing happening to both of you – and in the same situation.' I folded my arms.

The three of us paused in consideration. I noticed there were hairline cracks running through the concrete of the pit floor. Oil and smudge inked into the cracks and crevices – Phillip Island history

– who's grease was deep in that floor? Gobert, McCoy, Melandri, Doohan.

'What bike were you passing?' asked Brendan, momentarily pausing his restless energy.

Alex reflected. 'McGuinness. What bike were you passing?'

'Not sure yer man that was on it. But it was a red, blue and white one.'

'That's McGuinness,' said Alex.

'Yeah, they've got it painted in Honda colours,' I confirmed. 'It's a Yam FJ in a Harris frame but they've painted the fairings red, blue and white. John McGuinness is sponsored by Honda so they're trying to do a little hush hush. Pretending it's a Honda.'

'*Too much*, those cheeky feckers,' chuckled Brendan.

'But isn't that weird?' asked Alex.

'Not really,' I said. 'He's contracted to Honda so can't ride anything else or he will be in breach. I would say they're turning a blind eye to this one. It's just classic racing.'

'No, no, I don't mean all of that. I get that,' said Alex. 'I mean, it's weird that it was his bike that Brendan and I pulled alongside and then our bikes started missing.'

The three of us chewed our cuds on this. Could only be a coincidence. *What else could it be?*

'I'll look into it, see what the Gods of Speed are up to,' I said, somewhat arcanely.

MAGNETIC FIELDS

Arthur, as usual, was in his grey overalls and buried deep in the thick of some ancient British steel. He left the fettling of the 'oriental' bikes to the mechanics who worked on modern stuff; he was all about old English bikes.

'I say there, old chap,' I mimicked.

'Oh,' said Arthur, straightening from his task. 'I say old sport, we will make an Englishman out of you yet.'

Not a chance in hell, I thought. *A lot of nicey-nicey on the front porch what-oh but beware of the British bulldog out back.*

'How was qualifying, Arthur?'

Arthur smiled warmly. 'Well, it was somewhat splendid. Jerry did well, as he always does. A couple of the other chaps struggled a bit. It's a fast track, eh what. A little different to Brands Hatch.'

'That extra gear in Jeremy's gearbox must help,' I smiled.

'Oh…' Arthur looked closely at me, to see if trouble was afoot. 'That. Common old box, that. What a bore – only six speeds.' He put an arm around my shoulder. 'Do you remember those early Japas. The Honda RC166, the 250-6. A glorious four-stroke that revved to 20,000 rpm and ran through a seven-speed box. And it could do more than 150 mph. Ah, Hailwood, he won the 1966 world title on that. And what's more, he won each and every race that year.' Arthur became even more stimulated and gripped me tighter. 'Your good man, Hugh Anderson, had already won the 50cc world title in 62 and 63 on a Suzuki two-stroke. Frightfully smelly and noisy, but golly-gosh, it could go. Then the Orientals went to the square-four, two-stroke. It was a 125, the RS67. It only revved to 16,000 but it had a 12-speed gearbox. Those were the days, eh what? The RK, its little brother, had 14 gears. Imagine how tiny those cogs were? It would have been like working on a timepiece.'

I shook my head. 'That is crazy, hard to even imagine it. You'd need bloody good eyesight.'

'Yes, old fellow. That's why they canned it all. In 1969 the FIM said enough and gearboxes could have no more than six gears. So here we are.'

'Anyway Arthur, you can rest easy, I'm not here about that six-speed box in Jeremy's bike. I'm guessing it's a Nova box.' I paused long enough to let Arthur know that even if I was a Kiwi (that flightless bird from the bottom of the world), and a simple man, I was aware of some goings on. 'No, a couple of the guys in my team had a curious thing happen on track.'

'Oh, *curious*. I do love a good mystery,' enthused Arthur.

'They were going to pass McGuinness and their bikes started misfiring.'

'Misfiring, you say.' Arthur squinched his brows.

'Yes, misfiring.' I concentrated my gaze on Arthur. 'And they weren't riding together. They were riding separately, different parts of the track, and it happened a couple of times. Very mysterious.'

'Mmmn, somewhat.' Arthur scratched his chin; a study of consternation.

'What sort of misfire – did they say?'

'They both described it as the bike felt like it had suddenly dropped a couple of cylinders.'

'Oh, *excellent*,' tittered Arthur: then quickly sobered. 'I mean, *awful*. A jolly bad show, old chum,' he huffed.

I smiled intently. 'What did you mean, "excellent"? What's up doc?'

Arthur looked about guiltily. No one was within earshot. 'Whoops-a-daisy,' he gulped. 'Sorry old chap. I've been playing about a bit with some magnetic fields and the current they produce. I think I can tell you, as you are a man of honour. But mum's the word.' Arthur touched the side of his nose.

'Yes, mum's the word,' I pledged. *Here I go again*, I thought. More *crazy shit,* as Simon would say. I was being bombarded with schemes, themes and dreams from all quarters. A nice relaxing weekend pottering around a track with classic bikes, they said. Bit of R and R, they said. Rubbing shoulders with the famous, they said. Some beautiful bikes, they said. You'd make a great team captain, they said. You're so reasonable, they said.

What could possibly go wrong? they said.

'Back in the 19th century, Michael Faraday, an Englishman of course, was playing with electric currents and producing magnetic fields with them. Faraday, along with a professor of experimental physics, James Maxwell, proved that an electrical disturbance could produce an effect at some distance.' Arthur paused and frowned. 'Are you following, DC?'

'Yes, just hanging on,' I confessed. Spotty Dave had lost me down *his* rabbit hole. I felt like I was about to disappear down another; wallabies and little blue penguins digging furiously and burrows everywhere. This Phillip Island Classic was beginning to feel more like playing a part in Alice in Wonderland, rather than attending a motorcycle festival.

'I've got a little …' Arthur paused to find a word. 'Shall we call it, a little *unit*. This little unit is in the tale piece of John's bike and with the push of a button.' Arthur dug into his overall pocket and produced a small black device that had an extendable aerial. It looked like an old-style walkie-talkie, on a small scale.

'I can turn it on and off with this,' said Arthur, showing me the face of the object. It had a small on/off switch, and that was all … very simple.

'What does it do?'

'This little contraption just turns the unit on John's bike on and off. The unit sends an electrical pulse out. If something, such as a motorbicycle, happened to be in the vicinity, why, my dear old thing, it will connect with its electrical pulse, which will bounce back to the little unit and there-in create a circuit.' Arthur smiled lopsidedly. 'It could cause an ignition system to go missing in places.'

I looked aghast. 'How far can this electrical pulse shoot out?'

'Oh, several feet. You have to be close.'

'*Close*! Like you are when you're overtaking?' I spluttered. 'That kind of close.'

'Precisely, old bean.' Arthur was practically hopping from foot to foot with rapture. 'Brilliant, don't you think.'

I shook my head in bewilderment. 'Highly dubious, is what I think.' Perhaps lawn bowls wasn't such a bad idea as a hobby – far less complicated than this racing gig. *Did I really need this kind of stimulation?* No doubt there were dodgy tricks going on in the world of bowls too. Arthur would probably put some sort of homing device in *his* bowls were he to go down that recreational pathway.

'I wouldn't think this little device of yours is quite in the spirit of things,' I said, with some understatement.

'No. Quite. You *do* have a point,' conceded Arthur. 'I find it distasteful.' He pursed his lips fervently. 'But in a time of war one must do what one must do. The bloody Hun has no morals, he will do anything. Those V2 rockets will be the death of us.'

I snapped my fingers in front of Arthur's face. 'Hello. Earth to Arthur.'

'What. Yes. Oh, good job old chap.' Arthur grinned foolishly. 'Reliving another time for a minute there. What a bore, forgive me.'

Lukey Heights. Photo: D Begg

'No worries,' I laughed. 'We were talking about this little device in McGuinness arse-end.

'Well, I wouldn't quite go that far as to describe it like that,' cackled Arthur. 'I'm not sure John would approve … perhaps he would. He has a somewhat ribald sense of humour. No, it's really just a backup in case those awful Americans try something preposterous.'

'Or, the Australians?'

'Well, yes, them too,' agreed Arthur.

'Or the Irish?'

'Well, that goes without saying.'

'And the Kiwis?'

'Oh no. No. That would be most out of order. God forbid. That would be most boorish.'

'Yes,' I smiled evenly. 'But you've *already* used it on us.'

Arthur looked affronted. *What was he being accused of?* 'Oh yes, that,' he conceded. 'Quite the little hiccup with your boys trying to overtake John. I'm so pleased it works. Let's just call that a little test. Of course, I would never use it on the New Zealanders in a race.'

'Of course,' I said.

'Anyway, my good chap. Let's keep this under our hats. I'm sure it won't be necessary this weekend. But it is nice to hear that it works on the main stage,' Arthur said slyly, 'and that I can count on you to keep this strictly in confidence.'

ROOT CANAL

I got back to the Kiwi pits to hear news had filtered up that two of the Aussie/Kiwi bikes had issues after the very hot qualifying second round. It sounded like Glen's had dropped a valve and Damien's had oil seeping out of the head gasket. A dropped valve was like a root canal to a postie rider; you were going to suffer a couple in your lifetime. It was game over for that engine. They were going to try and crank the head a little tighter on Damien's leaker and see if that did the job – could have just been the high heat sweating the oil out.

CHUCKY KEEP YER HEAD DOWN

Chucky was found in the Aussie/Kiwi pits. He was being filmed by a Channel 10 news crew scouting for a different angle. He would get more TV coverage that week than any other participant in the NZ team. Simon scooped him up protectively.

The flatmates headed for the rental van. Matt took the wheel.

'*Wait for yer man,*' whispered Brendan, from the back seat.

'*Fock,* I was so slow,' groaned Matt, doing up his seatbelt.

'Hee hee hee,' sang Brendan, sounding more Chucky-like than human.

'Knew it was coming. Yer man never fails.'

There was laughter about in the van.

'What about you, Andy?' I asked. 'How was your qualifying?'

'Near as makes-n-matter,' replied Andy. 'The usual. Somint up wi me brakes the first few laps.'

'Nothing new about that,' I proclaimed. 'You always have no brakes because of all the Pledge you spray all over your bike.'

Andy smiled loftily. 'Eyup cock, the lekkin can go both ways but she comes up with the sun does my Gixxer. Still, I'm not really here to race. It's more about the participation.'

'Yeah, right,' said a chorus of voices. *Participation, Bullshitashin.*

'You, yer man, need to tuck your lard under that screen,' offered

Brendan. 'I watched you going down the front straight.'

'Ee, ba gum, *I was* tucking me ead down,' said Andy.

'*Bollocks*. Your head was going down, sometimes. Not your body.' Brendan guffawed. 'It looked like you, yer man, were reading a book.

You'd look down, then look up, then look down, then look up.'

'I was tucking in.' Andy was affronted, being spoken to like this – *and by an Irishman.*

'It might pay for yer man to lower your whole body then, not just your head,' repeated Brendan. 'What are you doing, with that up and down with your head?'

'I'm checking ahead.'

'Checking what? That you're on the right page?' laughed Brendan. 'Is yer man reading a book?'

The boys couldn't help laughing. You couldn't buy this entertainment.

Andy maintained his sobriety. 'No. For your information, I'm avin a gander to check I'm not catching anyone. There's a lot of dust and shite down the front straight. Haven't you *noticed?*'

'Isn't that the whole idea of racing?' I asked. 'To catch the person in front and overtake them.'

'To some, it may be,' conceded Andy.

'Brother, are you worried about sucking dirt in through your intake?' asked Simon. 'Aren't you running a filter?'

'Yes, I am. Of course,' said Andy, huffily. 'But that dust and muck gets all over the bike. And my leathers. Bugs and dirt everywhere. It's a bugger to clean off.'

TIGER SNAKES AND BOURBON

We had time to grab a shower and a beer. Then it was off to the barbecue: the annual Kiwi and American get together. It had become something of a tradition thanks to Kiwi team stalwart Ann McDonald. She was the organiser and usually last on the tee towel at the end of the night. The Kiwis hosted the Yanks; and paid for it. Good American bugger Paul Schaffer came up with a bottle of bottom of the barrel bourbon. It was nectar and had enough strength to power a sprint car.

Robbie and Alex Phillis were at the barbie. Robbie was into a story from a few years before, when he was racing a Katana Post Classic bike in a support race for the Aussie round of World Superbike.

'Anyways, I came out of Siberia and she was a bit loose. I was maybe a bit wide for the Hayshed but I hung in there. Then the bastard came round on me and at the same time the front folded. You know that kerbing there …'

The listeners nodded.

'I went across that kerbing face down. When I came to a stop I thought, *Shit, I've wiped the old fella off.*' Robbie looked gravely around at those assembled.

'What, one of the marshalls?' said someone.

'No, you muppet. *The old fella.* Jolly Roger. I honestly did. I'd hurt my hands – one of my gloves had come right off – and I couldn't get my zip open. I didn't really want to look anyway … if you know what I mean?' He grimaced at the recollection. 'Anyways, the meat wagon arrived and this nurse came running over.'

'Nurse?' questioned someone.

'Nurse. Medic. Ambo. Whatever they call them,' said Robbie, not needing the interruption. 'I can tell you, she wasn't no nun.'

Everyone had a chuckle at that.

'I said to her: "Can you have a look down there and see if it's still there, please?" Ha, she didn't know what I meant. So I said again: "Can you check down there and see if I've still got the old fella. I think I might have wiped it off on the kerb".'

Robbie paused and took a moment and a sip of his drink – he allowed the gravitas of the situation to settle on the listeners. 'She had a quick look – she didn't want to. She said it's still there. Hee-hee. She really said: "There's something there. I don't know what it looked like before".'

The listeners erupted in laughter.

Robbie held up his hand. 'Fair call. Anyways, it was still there. Sliding across that ripple strip, geez. Well, a week later the bruising came out. All yellow and purple. It looked like a tiger snake.'

I was enjoying the American bourbon so much so that Paul eventually gave me the bottle. Knob Creek, Barrel #5999, 120 proof. Paul enjoyed a man that liked his bourbon and I was that man, that night. Under the effects of the bourbon, I felt incredibly in-tune with the racing

Chappie, Danny, ?xy and Muzza. The Brains Trust.

vibe. Phillip Island may be a fast track but right there, right then, I felt like the Master of the Universe: the PI Universe. I was the equivalent of the Head Gamekeeper of the Hunger Games. That sweet elixir was a brief portal into domination of the track. When Alex told me you could go through Stoner Corner flat out in top gear, no worries, mate, I nodded my head, eyes bulging enthusiastically. *'Course you can.*

PART THREE

RACE DAYS

THE ZONE

I awoke a little fuzzy. It could have been the bourbon or the sleeping pill. *Now, what day is it? Friday? … Pretty sure it's Saturday.*

I pulled on some shorts, managed to also get a t-shirt right way round, plunged my feet into sneakers and headed for the shore. Rising light struck through the gum trees and splintered the water like startled sprats.

During my morning sabbatical walk I thought my way around the track; many riders would be doing the same thing. Alex had clearly said, flat out and in top gear through Stoner.

Alex was a quicker rider on a quicker bike: if he could do it then so could I. Alex was 30 years younger than me, that was a factor. It just required bravery, confidence – and an empty bowel. I *needed* to make up time. I wasn't overly slow, my bike performed a bit like a shitbox – was a sack of spuds on the straight – but there was time to be made through Stoner. I needed to get a wriggle on.

If only I could get 'in the zone' as some pro's described it. To try and find a zone where strange two-wheeled music played. Riders like Rainey and Gardner spoke, in later years, of how they would sometimes have out-of-body experiences where they found themselves floating above, in the air – kind of like a drone – and looking down on themselves racing. They felt time slow down and everything became so in tune that braking, turning and accelerating became symbiotic. Aryton Senna described *the zone* as falling into a kind of trance.

Of course, those racers kept mum at the time about these happenings. You start talking like that and no sane race steward is letting you loose on a racetrack.

I wasn't seeking an out-of-body experience, although that could be cool. I was more just looking to put some corners together; to get a bit of flow on. If I could downshift and brake in harmony, using the full power of the brakes and the compression from the engine to pull the bike up as late as possible, then drop it into the corner at the perfect moment for it to quickly hunt the apex, off-throttle, stabilise it there with a little throttle then pick it up, use some rear brake, and drive the bugger hard onto the fat of the tyre. If I could put enough of those corners together I could make a lap time. You could win races like that. A near-perfect lap was infrequent for me – for most racers – and if achieved it would stay with you for a long time. In the following weeks you could be up to your armpits shovelling sheep shit, or draining sump oil, or digging a trench, but that sweet lap would still be as real to you as what was on the end of your rake.

THE ORIENTAL LATRINE FLY

I made it back to the house as the sun began putting some warmth into the day; it promised to be a good one. Getting out early, aside from the health benefits, meant you missed being attacked by the Aussie fly. Or, more correctly, the Aussie flies. They were late risers but woke with a nasty appetite for flesh.

Many of the Aussie flies were just plain annoying. Such as the long-legged Fly, the house fly and the grey-striped fly. One of the most annoying was the bush fly as it could hover startlingly close beside your face even if you were running or cycling. It was after your saliva and would grip the corner of your eye or mouth and suck like a greedy infant.

There were flies, you just knew by their sounds, that they were *carriers*.

The laden drone of a blowfly, or worse still, a sheep blowfly. There were blue and black mottled blowies, and grey ones with prominent bristles on the thorax and abdomen. Go forth and multiply has never been more fully endorsed than it has by the Aussie blowfly. If you're sluggish watch out for the snail parasite Blowfly. And the ultimate bad boy was the oriental latrine fly. It was a shiny greenish-blue with a yellow face and large red eyes. Unmistakeable – kind of dressed like a clown: *you didn't want to suck the venom out of that bite.* But the one to be avoided at all costs was the horse fly (March fly). It was the one with the mandibles from hell. This was no metaphor but it was only the females that bit, as they needed blood to produce the next generation.

There were other buzzy flies such as the hover fly, the common hover fly, the wasp-mimicking hover fly, the fruit fly, the Mediterranean fruit fly and the native drone fly but they were small fry.

BEACH BOYS

Spotty Dave was sitting motionless on a stool at the far end of the hallway, looking into his mirrors and humming softly to himself. His morning ritual. I bent an ear expecting to hear what I thought would be a steady 'Oom.' An Eastern chant or meditative rhythm; one that wouldn't be out of place in the far reaches of India or Tibet. A yogi, on a rock, in saffron, 'Oom.'

I listened intently for a couple of minutes. I *knew* that sound – it was a tune. No Eastern chant: no 'Oom.' More like pop. It sounded like the Beach Boys. 'Get Around Round Round I Get Around.'

'Mmmn Mmmn Mmmn Mmmn I Get Around.'

BRAAAP AND THE MUMBO

Campbell had his scrambled eggs down to a tee, fluffy and light and the bacon crispy but not too crispy.

I complimented: 'Most important meal of the day, eh Campbell?

He smiled. 'A doctor friend told me that protein will set you up for the day. He also told me to eat 10 raw eggs a day.' Campbell chuckled. 'He told me incontinence.'

'What do you mean, incontinence? You mean, in confidence.'

'Well, nudge-nudge, wink-wink, you should never trust a fart. And I don't trust my doctor friend.'

'Hei-ho, I was avin a gander at McWilliams and Beau Beaton yesterday,' intruded Matt, bent over his muesli. 'How do those guys go so fast?'

'They hold the throttle on,' answered Brendan. 'Waaap.' He raised his hand and gave the universal full throttle twist of the wrist sign.

'Yes, but they're giving it a right wick out of the corners.'

'Braap,' said Brendan, again giving the sign. 'Yer man is just slow. Face it. Yer slow as fook.'

'Thanks. Wanker.' Matt, at 6' 4" and 95 kilos, did have a built-in disadvantage. Motorcycle racing was a rare sport in that it favoured the smaller dog. Not necessarily jockey small as you still had to be big enough to muscle a heavy bike. GP racers Pedrosa and Capirossi were borderline too small but they were terriers; hard as nails.

'That McWilliams went past me into Siberia, yesterday,' I said, pulling up a stool at the breakfast bar, beside Matt. 'Then he pulled a big crossed-up wheelie coming out of it. That bike has got some mumbo.'

There was a moment of silent considered admiration. *What was it like there, up in that rarified atmosphere that the great inhabited? To inhale that alluring fume just one time.*

Simon shook his head in wonderment. 'Bugger that. A bike only has two wheels. Put it on one wheel and you half your chances of surviving.' One of Simon's memories was of his Superman crash at Timaru's Levels racetrack on a practice day. He was riding his beautiful R1 (all his bikes were beautiful) and had just gone through the decreasing radius left-hander. The next right was innocuous and required hardly any lean angle but it was the corner that everyone crashed on. People had put thermometers onto that corner: some suspected a stream ran under it making it cooler. One fella, Butch, had even lain naked on that corner to see if he could feel a temperature change. It was after a crate of beer, so it could have been just a lie down. No one really wanted to know why he was naked. The real reason people crashed there was because it was the first of only a couple of right turns on the goat track and there was a long time for the right-hand side of the tyre to cool down. Simon lost the back, then it gripped again and high-sided him. Well, attempted to high-side him. Simon was a big lad and he was not one to be flicked off easily, plus he was holding tight to the bars like a lizard. Your normal sized rider would have been flicked to the moon and eventually come back down to earth to a world of pain and a wish that he had never been born. Simon's body came back onto the bike but in fully prostrate Superman position; he was stretched out flat like a surfboard on top of his R1. Like Rollie Free on the Bonneville Salt Flats, only Simon wasn't wearing budgie smugglers like Rollie had. The weight of the remount jerked his hands back causing the throttle to go to full. The acceleration combined with his bulk over the rear of the bike caused it to rear skywards and wheelie off across the paddock.

Simon hung on grimly as it continued to wheelie over the grass cutting the corners between turns seven and nine. The grass was still damp from early rain and the slicks found no bite and began spinning. This was fortunate because it brought the front back down to earth. Using the strength gained from doing bicep curls at the gym, Simon hauled himself forward on the bike. He just about got his legs back onto the pegs as the bike regained the tarmac on the start/finish straight. He still had a death-grip on the bars, regrettably he was still on full throttle. The rear slick spun nastily on the bitumen and then found bite. The front went skywards again and Simon slid back off the bike, once again prone in full Superman flight mode. He careened over the finish line on one wheel and straight ahead at turn one. A large billboard had recently been erected on the infield, 30 metres in – advertising All Black, Dan Carter, in Jockey underwear. Simon and his R1 tore Dan a new one on their meteoric hell ride. The billboard timber frame swiped Simon cleanly off the back of the R1. The Yammy, being finally free of its weighty burden, careered off serenely on its merry way, as a riderless bike is wont to do, until it ran out of momentum and plopped happily onto its side.

WHY DON'T YOU MARRY FULL THROTTLE?

I looked to Matt. 'What you doing through Stoner?'

'Fourth gear, rolling it on,' said Matt.

'I have it on good authority,' I said, with some conviction, 'Top gear, full throttle.'

Matt paused mid-mouthful, 'Is that what you do?'

'Yes. I mean, no. But, I will.' I realised I had made a commitment. *Whoops, have to follow through now.*

'Yeah, boss,' chimed Brendan. 'Full knackers through there. Sweet as.'

Campbell sat at the dining table with his cooked breakfast captured in front of him. 'I'm full gas everywhere! My poor girl is struggling.' He considered the piece of toast held lightly in his fingers. 'This is no place for a near stock GS1000. What are the P6 boys doing, Andy?'

'Aye up, I'm not sure. I don't get too close to anyone in front of me,' said Andy, smugly. 'Don't want to get dirt or muck flicked up onto my bike. She's a pretty thing my bike.'

'Yeah, pretty like a show pony,' I said. 'But what about through Stoner, what you doing?'

'I have to ho-up before Stoner. I'm catching guys after the Southern Loop so I go back to third; there's a lot of little gravel on the inside. Don't want that lamping up on the paintwork. The belly fairing would take a hammering.' Andy smiled proudly. 'I've got that tinted pearl-white paint, you know.'

'You don't say. Why don't you marry it?'

Matt. Photo: D Begg

THE NEED FOR SPEED

The usual Irishman was on the gate as the flatmates arrived at the circuit and he gave his usual greeting and circumspect look; as if he knew something we didn't know; that look that said he thought we were in way over our heads, we just didn't know it yet.

I had the need for speed – I went seeking some help. I wasn't looking to the sciences like Spotty Dave. I was limited by the performance, lack of, of my stunted F1 engine. However, my riding could do with some points of improvement. The Pommy pits had a bunch of fast riders, all professional or at least semi-pro. Spike Edwards was sitting in front of a laptop. I could see a lap being played out in front of him care of an onboard camera.

'Mind if I take a squiz?' I asked.

'A what, lad?' replied Spike, slightly surprised at the intrusion.

'A look at your onboard.'

'Sure,' encouraged Spike, adjusting the colourful peakless cap he wore constantly. 'Pull up a chair.'

'I was in the same race, you wouldn't know,' I said. 'I was down the back with the other plebs.' I gave a thumb over my shoulder sign to indicate my grid spot. 'But I'm looking for a little more pace. My bike is slow as but I know I can ride the track faster.'

Spike nodded and smiled encouragingly. 'Okay, first things. Where are you braking for Turn One?'

CLASSIC MOTORCYCLE MADNESS   85

'I'm not really braking,' I confessed. 'I more just go down to fourth at the 100 and tip it in.'

'So, if you go to the 50-metre board, stay on full gas to the 50, then do this.' Spike squeezed my upper arm firmly but gently, like a friendly bobby. 'Do that with the brake, just that much, and go down a gear and then tip it in. You've just done another 50 metres on full gas.'

I beamed. 'Brilliant. And easy. Well, easy sitting here. I haven't tried it yet. What was that, that Simon Crafar always said. "It's not he who gets on the gas first, but he who gets on full gas first that counts"'.

'That's it, lad.'

Spike talked me around the track. I looked to be getting most of the track about right, apart from T1. I just needed to up my belief and courage. And tidy up my entry and exit – and apexes. And show a little more commitment. And go a little later on the brakes and a little earlier on the throttle; the two simple principles of racing faster. *So easy, not.* Perhaps I too needed a suitcase of mirrors. Perhaps I should consider another sport. Croquet?

Arthur spied me loitering in the UK pits. 'Ahoy, I say, old chap, you wouldn't be spying on Old Blighty?'

'Kind of,' I confessed, rising from my chair. 'Just stealing some knowledge from your good man, Spike.'

'Oh, righty,' said Arthur, taking a quick glance at Spike, and drawing me away by the upper arm; a different move to Spike's arm squeeze. *It was a squeezy time.*

'He's probably not the man you want to talk to,' said Arthur, conspiratorially, then grimaced. He looked meaningfully at me. 'He's from *north of the border.*'

'What, Scotland?'

'No, my good fellow, *worse.*'

'Sweden. Denmark?'

'No, silly.'

I raised my eyebrows. 'Norway. Iceland?'

'No, no, no. Lovely chaps, those Scandies.' Arthur dropped his voice even lower. 'He's from *North Yorkshire.*'

'Oh,' I said, somewhat perplexed. 'I thought Yorkshire was part of England.'

'So do *they*,' said Arthur, inclining his head in Spike's direction. 'That's just the problem. They think they are part of the empire, but … between you and me.' Arthur dipped his head. 'They are, really, part of the problem.' He straightened and smoothed his overalls with his large hands and checked that the knot of his tie was straight. 'Anyway, my good man, how are the New Zealanders doing?"'

'Well, we've had a bit of bad luck, but not too bad, at this stage – and considering the age of our bikes.' I laughed. 'We aren't really in the hunt though. Just making up the numbers. How are you blokes going? You think you can beat the Aussies?'

'We are in the game, old bean,' said Arthur, touching an educated finger to his nose. 'But by jove, those Yanks have gotten faster. Of course, their machines are totally illegal, highly irregular, ghastly pieces of work. And that Bo, how he could be the captain. Atrocious, utterly absurd. What a crude man. Should be sent to Coventry.'

'He's probably alright,' I laughed. 'Once you get to know him. They do, do things differently where he comes from. He does seem to be, um, enthusiastic. And he likes a drink … and more.'

Arthur pursed his lips. 'Oh, yes. I'm sure he likes all sorts of things that you or I would think of as abhorrent.' He brightened, 'But tell me, how are your oriental bikes going?'

'The what?'

'The bikes that have come out of the orient.'

Arthur bent once again to my ear. 'I've heard them called "rice rockets",' he tittered.

GOOD TO TRY NEW THINGS

Bikes were being warmed up in the pits. Quick revving, a hand placed on the engine fins to feel them warming. Perhaps a hand down by the header pipes checking for combustion heat from each cylinder – make sure it's running on all pots. Tyre pressures checked now that the tyre warmers had brought them up to temperature. Battery tenders working. Fuel levels being topped up with whatever dodgy mixture was being burned.

Matt set his bike to a fast idle and wandered over to my bike. 'What pressure you running?'

'30 front, 26 rear.'

'Ow much?'

'30 front, 26 rear. That's hot. You?'

'32 front, 28 rear.'

'That's up there on the back,' I replied, pushing the choke in. 'I will probably go down to 24 but I'll see how this run goes.'

'I wouldn't go *that* low,' murmured Matt.

'You could try it. Good to try new things,' I said, with a grin.

'Mmmn, I doubt it, lad,' replied Matt, with Yorkshire gravity and wandered back to his GSX. His grandfather's house was 500 years old. His father's was at least 300. You wouldn't go willy-nilly changing your tyre pressures because some mongrel Kiwi thought it was a novel idea. Matt was living in New Zealand by choice but he didn't have to accept the whims of a Kiwi who had little foundation to fall back on and certainly not a Yorkshire pedigree which required that one remain steadfast and belligerent, or at the very least, stubborn.

Happy with my preparations, I shut the F1 down and went to check on Rastus. The big man

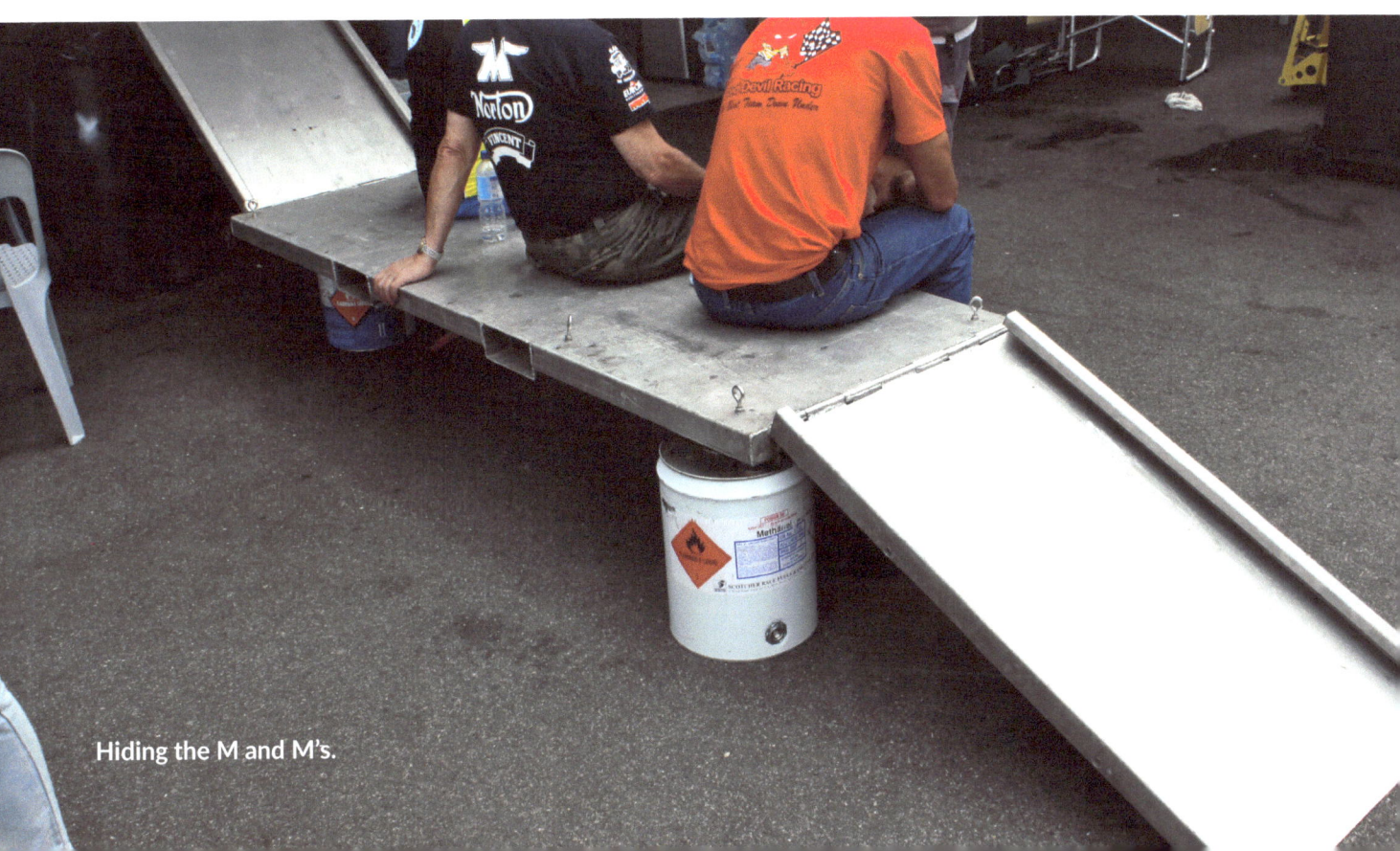

Hiding the M and M's.

was standing, arms folded, contemplating his GSX. Rastus only had one eye. Well, he had two but the right one was not in full working mode - in fact it was made of carbon fibre much to the delight of Rastus. Most people would be downcast and a little sullen at having lost an eye in an industrial accident. Rastus saw it as an opportunity to sport a carbon fibre orb and not only that, one with equally as much sparkle as his good eye.

'Are you ready?' I asked.

'Born ready,' declared Rastus. He was his usual bonhomie, full-of-life, rosy-cheeked self. 'Last meeting with this frame, I reckon. That donkey will be going into the XR I've bought from Si.' He bent his mouth to my ear. 'Little low on the M and M's though.'

My ear had been getting a good whispering to at this meeting. It would have done a Chinese Whispers convention proud.

'Has your man got none left?'

'They've *run out* on the island.' Rastus rocked back on his heels with mirth and guffawed. 'I guess I used it all up.'

I was astonished. 'Geez, mate. How much do you use?!'

'Two litres a lap,' said Rastus, delighted with this fact. It appeared that he was more excited by litres-per-lap than kph-per-lap. 'Think I've got just enough to get through today.'

I considered that Rastus must be doing well with the paua diving and cray fishing business: methanol was expensive.

'Okay,' I said, thoughtfully. 'I'm onto it. You and Si will have to go on a wee mission this evening.'

THE CURSE OF SPEED

Mechanics were swarming over the bikes of those lucky enough to have help; those hired guns who didn't actually own the bikes, just rode them. Those pros might not have had the pressure of getting the bike tuned for the occasion but they had the pressure of performance expectation. They had been, or still were, professional racers and as such, couldn't have an off-day. They set their personal standards very high and pride dictated they give it their all. Peer pressure demanded nothing less.

Professional racers generally didn't know when to give up the sport. Many thought they did and retired, only to be back in the saddle a year later, once again mainlining it. Racing at the top level required an inner rage. When that fury dissipated it was time to hang up the leathers. Pro-racers were paid to be psychopaths on track.

But a retired racer wasn't an easy person to live with: broody, listless, restless. Always trying to quench that fire with other pursuits: walking, cycling, or God help the world, golf. He wrestled with his mortality, injuries, courage, family pressure to be around more – but a racer had spent his life honing and developing himself into a humanoid: part human and part, a fine bundle of neurons carefully programmed to operate at maximum volume. Like the G.O.A.T of pro-cycling, Eddy Merckx: half-man, half-bike.

Some former pros found an outlet in classic racing: McWilliams and Corser loved it. However, many, like Troy Bayliss, wouldn't settle for anything less than an extreme modern bike that was often trying to kill them.

My mates and I didn't have that hardcore pressure but we still knew the amateur pecking order, or thereabouts, and if we didn't finish somewhere close then questions would be asked. The goal was to hit good laptimes; at least once during the meeting. When the lights went out the talking stopped: *when the flag drops, the bullshit stops.* Laptimes showed what you were made of.

RACE TIME / 100-YARD STARE

Steve McQueen said: 'Racing is living. The rest is just waiting.'

Racers got into their leathers early, that faraway look building in their eyes: the thousand-yard stare. Riders went into a blank, unfocused gaze and became emotionally detached from the speed and potential horror of what lay out on the track. Their focus went to braking markers, late apexes and how early they could get on the gas. Tenths of a second that could be made here and there.

My gaze was a little more limited; more a hundred-yard stare. My concentration was broken by Brendan goosing me from behind. I turned to swat the little Irishman but he had already ducked. We both grinned and stood together to ponder the pit garage, alive with sound and energy, a steady hum of industry, like a busy bee hive. Our smiles froze momentarily as Chucky gazed petulantly back from on top of the gas tank on Simon's expired XR69.

Sex. Photo: D Begg

'Why did yer man bring that little fecker along?' asked Brendan.

'Not sure. As some kind of mascot,' I ventured.

'*Not good*. I have a bad feeling about that.' Brendan broke his gaze and turned to me and offered his hand. We shook. 'Have a good race, mate. See you back here.'

'You too.'

'Hey, and remember …'

'What?' I asked.

Brendan hooted. 'Stoner. Flat-out!'

I grimaced. 'Yeah. Right.'

The Tannoy announced the two-minute warning for the first IC race. People swarmed to get the tyre warmers off and bikes lowered from their stands. Many bikes had their starter systems removed to save weight and because they got in the way. The GSX engine's starter gear poked out wide on the left-hand side. If left original it would drag like a bastard on left-hand corners. The common remedy was to ditch the whole starter system, cut the end off the crank and fit a modified cover over the crankcase. This gave the necessary ground-clearance to get the behemoth around most corners. It didn't give modern sportsbike clearance but it was enough. If you were scraping your modified crankcase it was probably because you were crashing.

With no starting system you needed a roller starter. Rollers went from basic design to sophisticated – much like race motorcycles. If you were chasing some cheap entertainment, go and watch classic race bikes being started on rollers. In a similar league to watching weekend warriors launching their boats at the public boat ramp or novice skiers dismounting from a chairlift.

Pitlane boomed with sound, the pit garages became monster echo chambers as big bore, massively carburetted IC bikes began flowing out and down towards the start tower. Interspersed among the muscle of the beefy four-strokes was the very occasional and rare exciting bird called the Yamaha TZ 750. It's nasty two-stroke crackle was at total odds with the big boomers. Fifty kilos lighter, these exotic beauties needed a steady hand and constitution to run.

The bikes started backing up at the pitlane exit, revving and bulling to be loosed onto the track. Overstimulated riders endeavoured to remain calm as they jostled together like trout waiting their turn to rush at the opening in the weir.

The harried marshal waved his green flag and then it was all smoke and noise as the mob erupted on the run out to the track. Every rider had his or her own theory on how to ride a warm-up lap. Some immediately slowed to the side of the track and swivelled on their seat pad to watch the field go by. Troy Corser liked to pull a big mono before hitting the blend line onto the main track. Most got their heads down and pushed on – not race pace but close enough to get the tyres working. Some liked to weave to warm the tyres. Some tried braking hard, on and off a few times – the ones who had been watching too much MotoGP. There were no carbon brakes in an IC race – *well, not legally*. The warm-up lap was a last chance to check out particular corners and ideally where one should be on an apex. The big black numbers on white background boards signifying 150, 100 or 50 metres until the corner. Those were the regimented braking markers but most riders adopted other objects as well. Perhaps a piece of coloured kerbing, a marshal shelter, a bush. The braking markers had been noted during the past couple of days of practice. A car didn't make a good braking marker. Like a dog didn't make a good braking marker. Neither did a grey goose.

The warmup lap was as much about getting the head into the mode of racing as it was getting the bike ready. The racer left pitlane and emptied himself/or herself of thoughts on friends, family, loan sharks, pesky debts. This was a time to feed the race addiction, the selfish all-consuming lust to race; not just because the racer wanted to win but because he/she needed that high.

THE TRACK / THE GRIP / THE GO

The track was in great condition. The grip level was good. The air temp was 24 degrees, the track temp was 49 degrees; all was perfect.

Rounding the last corner, T12, I slowed to allow those allocated spots in front of me on the grid to go past. Jason Pridmore and Barrett Long went past. Both riding for team USA, their dads had competed against each other back in the day. Reginald Charles Pridmore lll (Jason's father) was an English professional racer who emigrated to the USA. He won the inaugural AMA Superbike Championship in 1976. John Long (Barrett's dad) raced all over the world, including many of the big ones: Macau, Isle of Man TT, Suzuka 8 hours.

Aaron Morris and Dave Johnson for Australia glided past. Davo had a Kiwi dad so technically he was eligible for the Kiwi team.

Hang on, the Kiwi team already had Irish, English and Aussie racers in it. Eligible, yeah right, if you had a Pre-84 bike and could get on the seat you were eligible. Mind on the job, DC. You're about to begin a race. On the famous PI track.

The average man, the club racer, was down the back of the field with me, in the last few rows. We were the guys with grease under the fingernails. We fettled our own bikes and were

And they're off. Photo: D Fitzgerald

now mentally running through the condition of our bikes as a last-minute check that all was fit for racing. The pace car was safely tucked in against the wall by the back markers. There was the usual rejigging of a couple of start spots. Racers could be the most intelligent of people and yet still not be able to count. A good racer was a smart racer – *but you don't want to be too smart.*

A nervous lump of fear sweated in the pit of my stomach. Like a small animal it crouched there, sweltering in its defilement. Strangely, I liked it. It was right that it was nesting there. I would soon eject it come the drop of the flag

GO

The grid marshals moved a couple of bikes to achieve an orderly grid that matched the one on their clipboards. The marshal at the back waved his green flag. The marshal at the front then waved his red flag and limped like hell to get off the track. I briefly pondered why the dude with the red flag, no matter which race meeting you were at, always seemed to have a limp. You always wondered if he was going to get to get off the track before the tidal wave engulfed him.

We engaged first gear (or second) and hunkered down low, upper body weight forwards over the tank. Revs rose as the red lights came on. The lights went off and it was go. I got my usual average start and after an initial lurch and wheelie I was underway, revving the bike to red line then shifting gear. My grid position was in the middle of the row but I worked myself to the outside of the field as we approached turn one; *my go-to move.* I had figured out early in my racing career that turn one off the start line was the one place where racers acted like sheep. The first few scrapped for the same piece of tarmac while the rest fell into an orderly line behind them. This meant they were inevitably going slower than the next time they would come through turn one – then they would be in fourth gear and honking at more than 200 kph.

On this opening lap, however, they were only in third gear and shuffling forward like emperor penguins – very fast ones. I stayed hard on the gas and went around the outside of several riders. It always worked although it came with a large hazard factor. If there was a coming together of bikes inside me, or someone lost traction, the front let go, or there was a bashing of bars, I could find myself with another rider in my lap.

Then it was hard into the Southern Loop and third gear: you needed to get this gear change made early as once you tipped the bike over there was no getting your foot back under the bike and onto that gear lever. Try and hold the bike tight to the apex but these big suckers would fight you, endeavouring to run wide, which was OK; this was still a double-apex corner for most of the IC bikes. Superbikes were twixt and tween on single or double-apex. MotoGP bikes were now entering Southern Loop a metre or so wide and making it one continuous corner with one late apex. I think Rossi may have been the one to start using that line; he was the innovator of many GP habits.

I had visited one October when MotoGP was at the island. I had watched the bikes go through the corner called Siberia in the first practice session. There was a slight hollow in the track

Photo: D Fitzgerald

just after the apex and the bikes would become unstable when hitting it. I noted that Rossi only hit the hollow in his first lap. After that he lofted the front wheel just enough to clear it: perhaps six inches. Talk about awareness.

That was why he was called an alien.

DUMMKOPF

I hit full gas asap coming out of Southern Loop as it was downhill and early gas had big rewards, but beware the dreaded high side as the tyres were still coolish. The exit of Southern Loop was blind, in that the corner dropped away; you couldn't see the outside line of the track. Fully wind the bike out and shift to fourth and then the same to fifth. Get the knee down, must hit that next apex, and full throttle through Stoner Corner. I would wait a couple of laps to try that; *yes, yes, I had said I was going to go through there on the stops in top but I didn't say when.* I held the throttle just back from full; *dummkopf,* I scolded myself, *could have made it on full.* To watch Casey Stoner go through this corner was to witness something other-worldly.

STONER

MotoGP racer Danilo Petrucci on Casey Stoner: 'The stages of life should be: you're born, you grow up, you see a Stoner tour at Phillip Island, you breed, and then you die.'

CLASSIC MOTORCYCLE MADNESS

In his own words… Stoner: 'Phillip Island, T3 is fifth gear, it's 265 kph going into the corner, down through the dip and because you're always getting a big push of wind from the inside going out to the ocean, a lot of the time when you're pushing in through there the front end wants to go, and I was saying before I don't like the front end, I don't like the feeling of it compared to other people. I never had confidence. So as soon as you cock that front end dirt track-style, you can't crash with the front.

'So basically I would slide before I even got to the corner. And this is where people don't realise: number one, the difficulty, overcoming the fear. And then why it works. When you get into the corner and you have to get the rear to break before you get to the corner, otherwise when you get to the corner the front end is dictating everything, and you don't start to slide until you come out of the corner. That's not hard, these bikes have a lot of power, it's really not hard to slide these things.

'But sliding them before you get to the corner … I've got to go in, back off just to get the front to load a little bit and then I would crack the throttle on as soon as I could to get the rear to break. So then I could control it, try and almost stand it up and straight line it out of that corner to Miller.'

(I reckon this was some sort of insanity that you even considered getting a bike to start spinning up when you were already doing more than 200 kph?)

Stoner: 'My will to win was greater than the fear, so then I had to … if I let fear control me then I would never have gone as fast as I did.'

MARRY YOUR COUSIN

The braking marker boards appeared on the left. At the 150-metre board I waited a very brief moment then switched off the throttle and in the same instant went to full brake with a smooth but quick motion. I also went down three quick gears and left the slipper clutch to do its dark magic. Technically you weren't allowed slipper clutches in classic racing but the quicker guys all had them; like marrying your cousin, it was something you didn't talk about. There was such beauty in a slipper clutch, especially on a bumpy approach to a corner. The busy little workers in the clutch went at it pushing springs and lifting clutch plates and settling them back down. Fettling the fibre plates from the steels and hush-hushing any misbehaviour.

I had enough on my plate with just trying to stop the hefty bugger. Dunlop Corner was the most crashed corner on the PI circuit. I was sure that the in-road back to the pits was the reason. The in-road went straight ahead at Dunlop and it gave the illusion that the track went straight ahead, or at least was very wide there. Dunlop also appeared, from onboard, to just be a right-hander. The startling truth was that Dunlop was a very tight hairpin: first gear on a Superbike or GP bike.

Most Pre-84 bikes would never taste first gear in a race. That morsel was reserved just for starts or tootling back to the pits. Dunlop Corner was second gear. Depending on your gearing you could shift to third before going back again to second for Siberia – or you could wind it out onto the rev limiter in second. Siberia needed a very late apex to give the run up to Lukey Heights. The best approach on the F1 was a couple of metres wide and then bring it back to that late apex. No nimble loft of the wheel for my bike; it was about as nimble as an aircraft carrier.

The drive out of Siberia was a very compelling section as you short shifted and went knee down, full throttle in fourth through Hayshed. Hayshed was one of the corners that gave the track the distinction of being one of the best. There had been plenty of riders depart the track here and it was always a spectacular crash: the speed was high. If you missed the apex slightly you would find yourself on a dirty part of the track and, because you were a racer and refused to get out of the throttle, bad things could happen.

Then it was the beautiful Lukey Heights. It was my favourite corner. It was named after Len Lukey, a businessman and car racer who owned the circuit in the 60s. There were a bunch of different lines you could take on approach to Lukey – like many of the PI corners. Tracks were a funny thing. Some of the most spectacular tracks in the world could make for some of the most boring races to watch. Cota, Aragon, Sepang, those tracks must have been amazing to ride, I supposed, they sure looked amazing, however, the racing was usually processional and dull with uniform gaps between bikes. I had pondered on this and why. It appeared to me that if there was really only one line through a corner then the racing was bound to be processional. If there was a choice of lines, then you had a contest. PI looked simple to the simple eye but because of its sheer speed and wide flowing corners, it invited choices. It probably provided the closest racing of any track in the world and MotoGP and WSBK riders uniformly rated it their favourite. It was also the most dangerous in terms of crashes. PI was the least crashed track on the GP calendar but it provided the most injuries: *think about that.*

The quickest line into Lukey was probably, depending on your bike, slightly wide and then pull it back to the apex. It was back to third, a smooth squeeze of brake to the crest, then back on full gas. If the geezer in front of you took the tight entry then it was a grand place to drift ever so slightly wide which gave a run down the inside for MG Corner. MG was originally Lane's MG Corner, a Melbourne Nuffield dealer. Some liked to say MG was short for Mother of God. It was possibly the tightest corner at PI.

Photo: D Fitzgerald

Lukey was a blind entry; it was a matter of faith and commitment. After that brief burst of full throttle it was throw everything overboard and try to haul up – snick it down to second. MG and Dunlop were the corners where the most overtakes were made – and featured the most crashes; they were the only two hard-braking corners on the track.

Early gas exiting MG, short shift to third, then gradually and continually roll the throttle on exiting T11. T11 had been called The Copse due to some bushes on the inside of the bend but they were long gone; so was the name.

A FLYING VINCENT

I am not without scars on my brain and my body, but I can live with them. I still feel a shudder in my spine every time I see a Vincent Black Shadow, or when I walk into a public restroom and hear crippled men whispering about the terrifying Kawasaki Triple... I have visions of compound femur-fractures and large black men in white hospital suits holding me down on a gurney while a nurse called "Bess" sews the flaps of my scalp together with a stitching drill.

Hunter S Thompson.

I came out of T11 and it looked like a bomb had gone off. There were bits of bikes all over the track and a couple of bodies lying in the gravel trap on the right. I had only time for a quick glance

Photo: D Begg

– *where you look is where you go* – and then it was into fourth gear and peel into T12; the beautiful launch pad for the front straight.

Red flags began waving furiously and inevitably as I tore down the straight: they weren't going to clear that mess up before the field came around again. The USA rider, Jason Pridmore, had been running in the front few and got on full gas just a smidgen before his rear tyre was ready; no traction control on these big air-cooled monsters. The tyre slipped and spun, only momentarily, but it was enough for Pridmore to shut the throttle – an automatic self-defence reflex. The tyre said, *thanks for giving me back the gift of traction* – and it gripped again. This grip caused the lovely CMR frame to give a quick flick and send Jason over its high side and into the air. It wasn't a high, high-side; those were usually the slower ones – and arguably the ones that did the most rider damage. This was more a bucking bronco slapping, *'get your arse down here, mofo'*. He was rag-dolled down the road. The unfortunate Aussie, Beau Beaton, on the magnificent work of art that was the Irving Vincent, had nowhere to go and ploughed into Pridmore's F1. Both Beaton and the Vincent performed a forward roll over the F1.

Beaton was knocked unconscious as his head led his body into the sand-trap. The Vincent took to the sky, a beautiful black spectral wraith, twisting gracefully in the warm air. Unfortunately it was no stealth fighter; it had no wings. NASA would describe such an incident as a rapid, unscheduled disassembly.

The Vincent came back to earth, landed on its tyres, then spring-boarded several metres again into the air; it was sure having a good crack at flying. The take-off speed for a Cessna 172 is only 112 kph. A motorbike can easily achieve that, it's the staying aloft part where it falls down. That Vincent was glorious in the morning light, twisting, pirouetting, valiantly trying to break the encumbrances of earth's pull. Truth eventually prevailed. The Vincent was heavier than the Haast Eagle and gravity did what gravity does. It slowed the big V-Twin, halted its magnificent climb to the sun and brought it back to earth where it proceeded to destroy itself.

$250k would reportedly get you a new one.

Beau Beaton was already unconscious but the Vincent gave him a side-swipe for good measure as it finally came to rest near his fallen body. Jason Pridmore was conscious but not moving.

RIDER'S BLOCK

Jed Metcher had been leading the race for the Aussies but his bellypan had come loose and was dragging on the track. The red flag was a lucky break for him and his mechanics as it was likely he would have been black flagged out of the race. McWilliams, for the UK, had been running second. Pridmore and Beaton had been next in line.

The riders filed in an orderly fashion off the track at Dunlop and back to their pits to refuel and check over their bikes in readiness for a restart. The meat wagon was already out attending to the fallen riders.

'That was a biggie,' I said to Matt, as we put our bikes on stands and got the warmers back on. 'Those boys got rolled, bowled and rissoled.'

'A war zone, pal,' gasped Matt, eyes wide. 'Never seen anything like it. Oh that poor Vincent. I was down the back, trying to hang on. I was so far

Jed Metcher on it. Photo: D Begg

back I got to come in at the pit entrance before turn 12.'

'Oh,' I considered. 'You *were* far back! Tell you what, next race why don't you ride up with us fellas.'

'Ee, you're a right comedian, you are.'

Riders got busy checking fuel levels, tyre warmers operating correctly, battery chargers plugged in, perhaps re-checking tyre pressures. It was good to be busy because you didn't want to stop and consider too deeply what you had just witnessed between T11 and T12. Racers were very good at blocking that stuff out. You had to be or else you wouldn't be going back on track.

BRACE YOURSELF

The modern motorcycle – and let's face it, these IC bikes were pretty modern – is an incredibly fast animal. The sheer acceleration of a high-powered motorcycle is an awesome phenomenon. You can go to your local Suzuki dealer and plonk a wad of cash down and ride out the door on a new GSX-R 1000. That street bike could accelerate from 0 to 100 kph in 2.3 seconds. A Formula 1 car took 2.6. And the truly crazy part was that you could legally ride it on the road, then take that bike to the track and go to the straight and put it on full throttle, keep it on the stops, and hit the limiter in every gear. It takes a racer to do that – or a fool, or a priest. Not many people liked to admit it, but at the highest level, people love to race because it is dangerous.

An easy and simple test to see what sort of person you are – your makeup in terms of adrenalin and risk – would be to attend the Isle of Man TT and stand at the bottom of Bray Hill as the bikes go past. The vast majority find it to be insanely disturbing madness. The racer finds it to be insanely exhilarating and he/she wants a piece of that.

MOTORCYCLE MAN

Simon and I confessed to a little squirt of nervous pee on the start line. Adrenalin junkie is the term often used for people doing an extreme activity. A squirt of adrenalin is different to a squirt of pee but one could argue they have the same birthplace. An adrenalin squirt is less wet and lovelier. It makes sense then that more adrenalin is even lovelier. To get adrenalin the body needs to be put under stress, under danger. A person would naturally look for a way out of that situation, the heart would race, the palms would sweat. Fear and danger causes a neuro-transmitter to ring the alarm in the brain. This cranks all the five senses – sight, hearing, smell, taste, touch – off the chart.

Blood is directed from the skin and organs to the major muscle groups. Adrenalin is set free in a rush to defend the body. Aches and pains are often not felt under this rush. It's not that they have disappeared, it's just that adrenalin has taken centre stage. Adrenalin heightens your senses, makes you feel stronger, invincible even. The bigger the danger, the more the adrenalin rush.

Ask a Roberts, a Schwantz, a Doohan, a Stoner, what their favourite track or corner was and the answer would inevitably be one that was incredibly dangerous; and probably now off the calendar or modified due to health and safety protocols.

Circuit de Spa-Francorchamps, Nurburgring Nordschleife, Daytona International Speedway, Dakar, Baja 1000 and then there's the Isle of Man TT.

The most sumptuous part of this chemical banquet produced by the adrenal glands is at the end: the dessert, the Cognac, if you will. Once the danger has passed, the body floods itself with natural opiates or endorphins. The mistress dopamine comes out to play and arouses the pleasure centre of the brain; it stimulates the body for hours after. Dopamine is the chemical reward for all that hard charging.

Basically, there is a massive drug-fuelled party going on inside you and it is all legal, and what's more, natural. No wonder the body craves more. No wonder it is so hard for motorcycle racers to give up racing.

The appetite for risk is gastronomical.

Photo: D Begg

STREWTH, MATE. THE DARK SIDE.

Simon bundled into the pits looking flushed. He had been on the roof viewing platform above the pits. He had a grand view of the accident. Simon feverishly grabbed me by the arm, 'Bugger me. Did you see that crash?!'

'What crash?' I deadpanned.

'Strewth, mate! The one out of turn 11!'

'Oh, that crash,' I said, nonchalantly – outwardly, not inwardly. *Of course I saw the crash – well, the after-effects – but I was endeavouring to stay in full block-out mode.* I tried to turn away from my husky mate.

Simon gripped my arm tighter, 'It's madness this sport! So many ways to hurt yourself!'

'I think Campbell is calling you,' I gulped, anxiously freeing my arm from his grip. *Crikey, Harry, I didn't need this right then.*

Two truisms about motorcycles: If you ride one you will eventually fall off - shucks, they only have two wheels. If you race a motorcycle for a decent period of time you will get hurt. Some racers get hurt more than others and it doesn't necessarily correspond to the number of times they fall off. And some racers get more hurt than others.

This is the dark side of racing (getting killed is darker). The big question is, how well do you bounce back from an injury? Probably pretty quick from your first one. Maybe not so quick after your fifth or sixth, or 15th or 16th.

The brain starts asking small questions about your need for continuing to do this mad sport. Or perhaps, to just slow down a bit: but you ain't going to win thinking that. Every rider who's been at it for a while is going to have those internal battles.

A recent study by Dr Joseph Riley, at the University of Florida, involved participants in two age groups: eight healthy older adults, whose average age was 68, and nine healthy younger adults, whose average age was 21. The study sounded like a lot of fun if you were into that kind of thing. Participants had their feet plunged into hot and then cold water to test their pain sensitivity. The researchers were aiming for a pain level of four, no more, because they didn't want to scare their subjects off.

Oh yes, nearly forgot the best bit, the researchers also inserted a catheter into each participant before the pain stimulus and at 15, 30, 45, 60 and 90 minutes after the test. This was to test something, but I'm unsure what. After three identical sessions, Dr Riley's team found that older adults perceived pain significantly faster and more intensely than the younger adults. In short, the older adults were smarter. The novelty of being asked to 'bear down' while a catheter is inserted wears thin pretty quickly. They also found that pain lasted longer the older you got. No shit, Sherlock.

That's why an older racer will just smile knowingly when a young hotshot, who's 10-foot tall and bulletproof, is bouncing around the pits sounding invincible. Let's wait and see how hotshot comes back from the dark side.

PONTIFICATION / THE GREEN FLAG

The five-minute horn went off for the re-start. Riders zipped up their leathers and put their helmets back on; the action was a bit more real now. The warm-up lap gave the riders time to re-adjust and get back into racing mode as they pushed it in a couple of corners to keep the heat in their tyres and warm up the brakes. I was using some SBS carbon pads so initially I kept a little pressure on the brake lever to lay some carbon on the rotors.

Between T11 and T12 the marshals had done a fine job in sweeping up the debris of the crash. However, there was no making the scrape marks on the hard asphalt disappear. The white lines were scoured onto the track as beacons for the rest of the weekend. Most riders took a quick peek, but they were well into race mode, so it was more just an acknowledgement of the crash site. They had moved on. That was then, this was now. If Simon had still been riding, he no doubt would have dwelt on it a little more: filed it into his terrifying portfolio.

Matt just wondered how they could go fast enough to make such a big mess. Most of the Kiwi boys lined up near the back of the grid. Brendan was mid-pack. Alex was on the second row; the Kiwi shining light – even if he was an Aussie. Spotty Dave was next to me. We caught each other's eye. I winked. Spotty Dave gave a cheeky grin.

Looks like he's in the mood, I thought. And he looks to have a decidedly young attitude – *wonder what age the bugger is riding at?*

In the idling stillness just before the start, a helicopter could be heard taking off, bearing Jason Pridmore and Beau Beaton to the hospital.

This was no time for pontification, the green flag was waving. The heat haze made it dance as the steward hurried off to the side of the track. All eyes went to the lights. The block of reds came on briefly and then we were off, again. I got a better start this time and began my swerve to the left-hand side, the outer side of the track. Spotty Dave got his skittish Harris away well and

Alex Phillis. Photo: D Begg

found an opening slightly right; he would take his chances in the mob. Matt had qualified with a 1:51 and Campbell with a 1:55 – that put them in the second to last row. They were both good starters and got themselves up a few places before T1. Campbell's was one of only three two-valves in the race. The others being a Kawasaki KZ1000 and a Moto Guzzi LM1000; they were on the last row.

The re-started first race of the weekend saw no further crashes. It did see a plethora of bikes go out with mechanicals: a wondrous term entombing a myriad of quandaries. I came out of MG on lap four and noticed three large grey geese on the outside of the corner. I kept my focus and peeled into T11. The next time around I noticed Aussie speedster Jed Metcher pushing his highly modified but broken-down Yamaha FJ 1200 and behind him in orderly file were the three geese; odd.

I finished 26th with a best lap of 1:46.2. I had one of the slowest speeds of the day down the straight at 236 kph. Matt did a quickest lap of 1:52.9 – he had done 1:50 in qualifying. I was a little dejected with the speed of my F1. It did finish the race but on the uphill half of the track the engine was about as much use as a golf club made of water. Matt was just dejected – but he wasn't last.

Brendan did an outstanding job and grabbed 18th spot with a 1:43.2. His speed down the chute was 254 kph. Spotty Dave did a 1:48.1.

Aussie Shawn Giles was the fastest rider down the straight at 271 kph, with a fastest lap of 1:38.1 – he finished third.

Campbell was 223 kph down the chute and 1:53.6. The Guzzi did 223 kph and 2:03. The KZ hit 209 kph and 2:09 – definitely lapped.

I had been lapped once the year before on a stock GSX 1100 I had brought back from the USA. In a misguided moment of madness, I had entered it in the IC. 220 kph and 1:54, my best on the GSX.

That bike was a handful and would corner alarmingly like it had a hinge in the middle. Strangely, this appealed to my ken and I thoroughly enjoyed riding the weaving brute once I knew its faults; it added a new dimension to the sport. I had already straightened a bent fork on it in a press – I found later that was just a symptom of the problem. The frame was bent, it had obviously been in some kind of high-impact crash.

ISLAND CLASSIC – CAPTAINS' MEETING 2

Captains: USA–Bo, Ireland–Pog, NZ–DC, UK–Arthur, Australia–Wally

Agenda: Item
3. Engine size 4. Fuel – only pump gas 5. Allowance of FJ1200 engine

'Welcome back, all,' said the chair, smiling grimly. 'Unfortunate fun and games out there this morning.'

'Yeah, no place for the faint-hearted,' endorsed Wally, with an equally grim face.

'Lost one of my best men,' grimaced Bo. 'War is hell.'

'I came out of 11,' I said, shaking my head. 'And it looked like there had been one hell of a rough party. Junk all over the place.'

Pog whistled empathetically. 'Behold ye mighty Vincent. Nae a bike to tarry and be tethered to this good earth.'

The chairman considered the gnarly assortment of classic men before him in the room. Stitches, scars, burn marks, grazes, bumps where there should have been collarbones

This could as easily have been a War Room. These weren't men to be trifled with; they had been in a scrap or two. This game of high-speed chess was nothing new to them. The chairman felt a little out of his depth. He felt like a very small fish. Like a sprat with the constant fear of the shadow above; about to be gulped up. A spooky numbness crept up his body engulfing him. Shakily he looked to the agenda before him. Suddenly he was struggling to breathe, water was flooding his gills. *His gills?* A weirdness slowly immersed him. He looked up and round the table at the assembled captains. *He was in a large aquarium, hovering mid-water, his fins and tail impotently paddling – and he was surrounded by large fish but fish with the faces of the team captains'.*

A part of the chairman's mind warned him that he could be having a turn, some form of mini-stroke, a transient ischemic attack (TIA).

DC was a mahi-mahi. He was moving head-on steadily towards him, his humped green back quivering and his eyes bright red.

Wally was a great white and glided powerfully past, his black eye of death unblinking, unfeeling – sheer malevolence as he circled to come round again.

A rapidly moving wahoo with Bo's face sawed through the water only inches away.

Freakin' hell, thought the chair. *This is terrifying – where am I?*

Ah, but there was Pog. He was a dolphin. Oh, the relief: one of man's best friends. He was no man-eater.

Or was he? Did Flipper have a sinister side? The chairman tried to recall. Weren't there increasing reports of 'Dolphin Attacks Man'?

Pog displayed his teeth-lined smile and nodded his head up and down in a Flipper-like manner.

But what kind of fish *am I?* wondered the chair, endeavouring to see down to his body, not an easy feat when you didn't have a neck.

However, he did have protruding eyes that he could circle downwards.

He had droopy fins and a motley-grey body. Some sort of bottom-feeder.

A guppy or mud dweller that lived off crabs and seaweed. Yet he couldn't help noticing, all of the captains were predators and not only that, they were apex predators.

He sensed a sleek form.

Arthur was very close. He was a barracuda. He was hanging motionless in the aquarium, thin-lipped with a large voracious eye placed squarely on the chairman. Arthur opened his mouth and needle-sharp teeth lined up in a sharp greeting.

'Let the games indeed begin,' Arthur cackled, and loudly clapped his hands together. 'Mighty beasts and Christians beware.'

Then there was silence. It went on for quite some time. The chairman snapped to attention, suddenly realising all eyes were on him. He had been having some sort of hallucination. His eyes jagged up to check the captains' were indeed human. His mouth hung open. He was dumbfounded. But he was no longer in an aquarium.

But was this the real world? 'Ummmn,' he ventured, closing his gaping mouth; trying to sort himself. 'I think ….'

The eyes on him were intense: but they *were* human. *Pull yourself together, man. They're just ordinary blokes with an unordinary habit called motorcycle racing. He looked to the sheet of paper before him.*

'Okay.' He took a deep breath and forged ahead. *Stick to the agenda, mate.* 'Well put ... I think.' He looked again to the sheet of paper before him. 'Okay, second item we have to consider. No, correction, third item: the engine. We've agreed, up to 1300cc. And no methanol or avgas allowed. *Right?*' He looked up and surveyed the table.

We captains, to a man, had our heads down studiously studying the one-page agenda in front of us; avoiding the directive/accusation being levelled.

'Only pump gas. Correct?' he repeated.

There was a chorus of muffled snuffles which sounded faintly affirmative.

Avgas and even methanol was allowed in NZ, USA, Ireland and the UK. The bikes were tuned for it and here, in Australia, it was all illegal.

'Now,' said the chairman, feeling the return of a measure of authority. 'We allowed the FJ 1200 engine in as a trial, last year. What are your thoughts on that?'

It was a gunslingers' standoff: who would make a move? Vested interests were a pack of cards and these hands were being held close to the chest.

The chair realised he had dealt a good hand. He took the initiative – *this was more like it.* 'Arthur, you were the one who introduced it. What are your thoughts?'

Arthur stood and slid the chair back behind him. He was formerly attired as usual, in a plaid sports jacket and a dark tie. 'Ghastly business, this morning with that prang. My sincere condolences go out to the riders and their families. A shocking business.' He gave an ironic chuckle. 'A shocking gladiatorial game we are in gentlemen. It is a battle of sorts but no charge of the light brigade: "Cannon to right of them, Cannon to left of them, Cannon in front of them, Volleyed and thundered; Stormed at with shot and shell, Boldly they rode and well, Into the jaws of Death, Into the mouth of hell, Rode the six hundred."'

The room was silent. *What was the response to that?*

Bo gave a slow hand-clapping. 'That was mighty impressive, pardner. You can't beat that with a stick. I have no idea what you are talking about but I like it. I also don't know what you are on, but I like that too.' Bo formed a pleasant O-shape with his mouth. 'Shrooms? Yes sir, must get me some of them.'

Arthur frowned. 'To continue, my good fellows. The FJ engine has been a bit of a godsend. It appears to be a competitive engine and gives one, another choice.'

'Gives you another choice,' I corrected. 'You sometimes conveniently forget that Downunder we still run a Pre-82 Class, not a Pre-84 Class. The FJ is not legal for us.'

Arthur smiled warmly at me, 'Precisely my point, old chap.'

'Yeah, cobber, but it's not a level playing field,' injected Wally, crossing his arms in frustration. 'It's not fair and it's a bit underhand.'

'That would be underarm,' I corrected. 'And you Aussies know all about that.'

That brought a laugh to all assembled, except Bo: cricket wasn't his strong point.

'I see it as a marvellous opportunity, old chum,' enthused Arthur. 'What are your choices of engine in the Pre-82 Class? The Suzuki engine seems to be pretty much the only one that's available to the average man – the only competitive one, that is.'

Wally scratched his nose and considered: 'Well, we have all the manufacturers. Kawasaki, but that's a two-valve. Ducati, two-valve.

BMW, but that's ...a BMW.' This brought some communal mirth.

'Harley-Davidson.'

'Now, you're really taking the piss,' I laughed.

Wally grinned. 'True that. Umm, Honda, four-valve – but only a 750 or 900.'

'Or a CB1100R, of course,' I reminded. 'That's if you know a dealer or collector of extinct wonders like rocking horse shit.'

More laughter. This was turning into a merry old time.

'Hooray the unobtanium,' chortled Pog. 'Because we are a confidential crew, and you sir,' he said, addressing Wally, 'are indeed a sempiternal man. We have been at the limit of the ocean's galleons. Bashing Viking oars and sweating in the very gunnels when lo and behold a splashing and uniformity of paddles behoves to and we perceive a new vessel with great steam clouds belching from its stacks. We are gobsmacked and as a man, drop our neanderthaI scratchings for here is a new space odyssey – but not 2001. That year, my sirs, would be the XJR 1300,' said Pog, with an enormous wink.

Wally chortled. 'My very point. I think.'

'Would you sit down, dude.' Bo addressed Arthur, who was still standing as if on ceremony. 'You're like a spare bride at a wedding.'

Arthur, with reluctant dignity, lowered himself into his chair.

'Bo,' said the chair. 'You fellas are also running the FJ. How does that fit with your situation in America.'

'We don't have a situation, as you put it. What we do have is some confusion. Hell, I ate so many armadillos when I was young, I still roll up into a ball when I hear a dog bark.' He paused and considered. 'We don't even run any classes for the big bikes. The Nancies out East in the hippy states like Vermont and New Hampshire wrote the rules for 'Merican classic racing. Japanese classic racing. And those good-fir-nothin' layabouts are all riding kids' bikes: 250s or 300s, or even 150s. Goddam hippies.' Bo smiled. '*Although,* they do say the Vermont green is the *finest* weed you'll ever try. But those hippies can all eat shit and die, as far as I'm concerned. We race men's bikes. You've gotta be brave as the first man that ate an oyster. Faster than double-struck lightning. Nothing under 1000ccs.' He chuckled, 'We love the FJ. It's a purty hunk of love muscle.'

'My point,' remembered Wally, 'is that the FJ1200 looks exactly the same as an XJR 1300, except for the head. You put an FJ head on an XJR motor and you wouldn't know.'

'The proverbial wolf in the sheep's breeches,' intoned Pog. 'You could harry the man about the presence of the three-speed and its usefulness when the road takes to its climbing hobnails – and you keeping the rules on your single-speed, but if he keeps ringing the Spurcycle bell you will never have the converse, or even the chance of a civil telegram, or a redressing of the ignoble situation.'

'Pog,' said the chair. 'Before next year I will take some sort of course on gibberish, then I might be able to understand you.' He rubbed his face with both hands. 'But Pog, what are you Irish running? Have you got the Yamaha FJ motor … or XJR … or whatever the bloody thing is?'

The chair kneaded his eyeballs until they went pink. He was gradually losing the plot. The thread of the meeting had once again unravelled. He was not a motorcycle racer; he was not even a motorcyclist. *Bugger me, those things are freakin dangerous.* He was a promoter; just a promoter. Motor racing was mostly car-based but he did love the motorcycle race meetings that PI hosted. They had the MotoGP, World Superbikes, the Island Classic, Australian Superbikes. However, as far as he was concerned, all those involved in bike racing shared the same nugget of DNA: they were all mad.

Pog had sparkling blue eyes. When he turned them full on you it felt like you were but a pebble caught in a fast flowing but friendly thermal alpine stream. A clear crystal blue warmly enveloped you and it was lovely to be part of such an effervescent tide; to bumble along in the drift. It was tough to dig in and get a hold, find some purchase against the flow.

Pog now turned his hypnotic gaze to the chair. 'We have a couple of the lovely velocipede frames hand-built by the good sirs, Lester and Steve. Two XR69's and we are running the original GS1000, two-valves, in them. Also the TZ750. Nico Bakker Kawasaki. Katana. We are running three charming CBX's.'

'Bttt anngrrr,' coughed someone.

'Pardon? What was that?' said the chair.

'Bottt aangerrr.'

'Sounds like boat anchor,' said the chair, then quickly realised it was a joke.

His surprised look brought a bout of unanimous laughter.

'Truly true, my good sirs,' rebuked Pog. 'The CBX is of the same behemoth family that birthed the Titanic. Not to be messed with by a breeze. Not pushed around by a Siberian wind.' He chuckled wryly. 'Not so good with an iceberg.'

'Getting back to my point,' pleaded Wally, gruffly. 'The XJR is still being made in the 2000's. It runs a Nikasil bore. You don't even need to split the bastard. Just bung some hi-comp pistons in and do the work on the FJ head. You can get plenty out of it, can't you Arthur? You're even gone one more step ahead, Arthur. We took a video recording of McWilliams bike. He's got *six gears*, hasn't he? You running one of those Nova boxes?'

Arthur, for the first time, looked a little flustered. He took out his comb and smoothed the side-parting in his hair. 'Surely that's not illegal.'

'Don't think they were running six, back in the day,' said Wally, waggling a finger.

Arthur huffed, 'For goodness sake, old bean. Next, you'll be wanting them to wear leather helmets.'

BABY / CHEESE ROLLING

Andy rolled into the pits, in neutral, engine off. He stayed aboard and removed his helmet, shook his head at me. 'Madness out there. You'd think we was racing for Whitby Abbey.'

'What do you mean, did it get a bit keen?' I asked.

'Keen? Keen? It's not the *huffing* MotoGP.' Andy, red-faced, dismounted. 'People carving each other up all over the place. Bashing fairings. I felt like I was in the Coopers Hill Cheese Rolling Competition.'

I put the rear stand under Andy's GSXR. 'Oh, so once you got through them and pushed on, what was that like?'

Andy regarded me as he would a madman. '*What do you think*?! No, I acted rationally and backed off. Left them to it. It's just not roight.'

He scuffled urgently with the top of his toolbox before getting the lid open and freeing a bright yellow spray can of Pledge. Andy took a deep breath to steady himself and grabbed a cloth – *baby's alright now, here comes a little Pledge.*

#56 Justin Mellerick. #93 Drew Sells. Photo: D Begg

'If you just got on with it, you'd be holding a trophy, not a can of polish,' I said, lamely. I knew there was little point in trying to reason with Andy when he was in such a flustered state. Still, 'Your bike's fast and you are fast enough to run up the front.'

'I'm happy to be up front.' Andy paused with his rubbing. 'But a little room is all I ask for. *Is that too much?* Just a little common respect. Fer feck's sake! It's not rugger!'

Andy sprayed a uniform row of Pledge onto the fairing. He unfolded the lint cloth and began rubbing in slow circles. The circles got smaller and the rubbing more intense. Andy squatted beside his bike, his face very close to the side of the fairing. He rubbed slowly and rhythmically – mesmerising. I moved away, *a little sicky in the back of my throat*. Private time with your bike was the right of every racer, but there was a limit. Even Valentino had been known to sneak into the pit garage late at night to spend time alone with his M1. The similarities of affection between owning a horse and a motorcycle could not be overstated.

A SPUD IN THE SUN

The sun was near the top of its arc. It was still coolish but the heat was coming. A beautiful day.

Pog was wheeling a Honda CBX past the Kiwi pits. The CBX was a conversation stopper with the sheer width of its carriage: six cylinders side by side. It's six beautiful titanium exhaust header pipes were all myriad blue; blue enough to leave grown men unashamedly drooling and weak kneed.

'Ahoy, flightless birds,' called Pog, on spying me standing by Simon's bike.

I wandered over to Pog who had pulled the CBX to a stop.

Pog beamed. 'Behold the Kiwi pits. Ah, but the velocipede became the saving grace for a country of birds that can't fly. The passenger of the foot was looking extinct methinks and he was looking out for being tootled vigorously off the track.'

I sniffed curiously. *What was that?* There was a smell about the magnificent CBX that Pog was wheeling. *Mmmn, McDonalds French Fries!* Lovely, although it was a warming day, hardly the day for Maca's.

'What's that smell, Pog? You been cooking your spuds on the mufflers of that CBX?'

'Lovely jubbly,' allowed Pog. 'The ending of the resulted epistle methinks. A chemist's parade ground. Take a grand Irish potato and liquefy with amylase at 80 degrees. Don't be worrying about your good self's outfalls; a little amylase in the blood and urine is normal.'

'Fair to say, I haven't noticed blood in my pee for a long time,' I said. 'Last time would have been 2015 at Manfield when I took the big one into the tyre wall. Peed blood for two days after that.'

We both took a moment of silence out of respect for blood pee inducing crashes.

'What do you mean, liquifying potatoes?' I said, breaking the minute of silence. 'What you got going on, Pog?'

'You're a tinker – you know very well, DC, how the rules and laws of this game have been a changing.'

I nodded pensively: *by the year.*

'We're not being allowed yer man's good stuff anymore. The methanol, she's gone. The avgas, too. We've tried the natural gas, the hydrogen, even the acetylene – that's a bomb of a fuel. *Baboom.* Well, us folk on the island called Ireland like to do some queer experimenting in the wee small hours. *Now, what do we have here in good ole Ireland that could run an engine?* What's the saying in fishing? "Fish your feet first". It's staring you in the face, you bloody great Daft Punk. The Irish potato.

What's more, the Irish Lumper. A potato, a little gnarly in its oblong form – a knobby codger of a spud. The Irish Lumper.'

Pog indicated for me to come closer. He unscrewed the gas tank cap.

'Have yerself a nosing of that.'

I sniffed cautiously inside the tank. I was a foolish man, not a fool; *fine distinction.* Very earthy smell – furrowed fields. Peat? No, not peat. Definitely a smell of soil.

Pog then thumbed me to the rear of the bike. 'Now have a nosing to the outfall spigot.'

I duly put my nose near the exhaust. Ah, the French fries. The source of the Maca's. 'You're burning some sort of ethanol mix,' I offered.

'Aye. Ethanol. It's in your everyman's pump gas of course. We're all sheep-head's and duly using it whether we have a mind too or not.'

'I was going to say ethanol is illegal as a race fuel.' I contemplated – reconsidered: 'It's not illegal. It's impractical! It doesn't even put out any grunt. Not nearly enough for a race engine. Car fuel only has 10 per-cent ethanol in it, right?'

'Aha,' said Pog, conspiratorially. 'But it is used in nearly all of the racing hereabouts and thereabouts. It's even being used by NASCAR petrol-in-their-heads.'

'Yeah, mate. But only a tiny amount; to keep the greenies happy. You use too much of it and it won't burn quickly enough.' I was no rocket scientist but I did understand a motorcycle engine. 'You would have to run very high compression. And somehow you've got to make the sucker burn hot.'

'Yes, it's incredible. Stupendous magnificence. We've got the CBX up to 18 to 1 compression.'

'No way!'

'Way.'

I was talking/thinking my way through this: 'Ethanol – terrible for starting if it's cold. Cold like in Ireland.'

'Aye, but not cold like in Australia. This lucky country runs hot. Unfortunately, my good DC, today, not hot enough. But the forecast for the next few days is heaven's runway for spudders.'

'And ethanol sucks up water,' I added. 'Any moisture in the air and that fuel is like a sponge. That's why you can't leave a bike sitting for a few months. Roots it.'

'And that's why, my sunshine from down under, I happen to be pushing this CBX wonder-bus through the paddock. She's sucked up too much of the H2O with this humidity from the overnight showers. By the bye, if you could just keep this under your cheese maker, my good son, it would be much appreciated.'

'That would be cheese cutter,' I corrected.

'Would it now?'

'Think so. And ethanol isn't illegal as far as I know. I would have thought it would be promoted.'

'Yes, well there's some weird ideas amongst the assembly of captains at this here doh-reh-me. They don't need to know *all* of our undoings, do they sir? Plus, there's a small technical innovation we use to insert the ethanol – which could cause some pause of dissent.'

'Insert?' I asked, with wonder. 'I've never heard that term used before in relation to an engine.'

'A little shuffling of the alphabet and insert can become inject.'

'You're fuel injecting!' I yelped, unable to restrain myself.

'Good God man, a lid needs to be firmly held down.' Pog looked anxiously about.

'Sorry,' I breathed. '*You're using fuel injection.*'

'Yes. Direct injection to be more precise. It suppresses the engine knocking at high pressure. It allows the high compression. It's also more economic, although God knows, we aren't saving the planet with this sport … unless you consider burning up fossil fuels as quickly as possible will bring a quicker sunrise to new technologies.'

I gave the CBX tank an affectionate pat. 'Where are you making your ethanol – how did you get it here. I mean, is it fresh?'

'Fresh is best, my friend. It's absolutingly fresh. There's no shrinking and sheering away from it. We are making it in one of the rental houses here. Murphy is making it: God bless his plaguy soul. We brought sacks of the potatoes in the shipping container with the velocipedes. Never such a pretty sight: spuds amingling with motorised bicycles. And of course it would be no great quest, we would be Hittite's, without the gear to turn the formula into fuel. Murphy is running the lab. Well, it's not really a lab,' Pog guffawed. 'It's just the kitchen.'

I laughed, 'Like Breaking Bad.'

Pog examined me closely. 'No … I don't think so.' *Was I not keeping up?* 'I'm not sure it has anything to do with braking badly. It's more the going of things rather than the stopping we are interested in.'

'No, no,' I corrected. 'Breaking Bad, the tv series.'

'Ah, the brainless box. The televisionary.' Pog shook his head. 'I'll not be having one of those in my humble cave.'

'So you've got your fellas making ethanol in the kitchen.' I tried to picture this. 'It must be awful messy.'

'Oh yes,' giggled Pog. 'Very messy. Murphy has to mash the potatoes to release the starch. Then add enzymes to convert the starch to sugar. The fermenting and distilling the mixture. *It gets very messy.*'

'Yes?'

'Most afternoons we are getting home to find Murphy on the floor, a complete mess.'

I was concerned. 'How so. The fumes?'

'Well, you know. Come mid-afternoon, after you've been bashing potatoes about all day; a man is not a camel. He heads for water. You've seen the state of your average Igor in the Slavic land. The Russkie and his wants to keep a warm toddy about. The Irish Lumper is no mere potato. It makes a delicious and very smooth vodka. The line between ethanol and vodka is a fine one.' Pog chuckled. 'Murphy has been known occasionally for pushing the boundaries.'

I also chuckled. 'Is this the same Murphy who dropped oil all over the track in qualifying a year or two back?'

'Oh no. The Murphy making the ethanol is a different Murphy. That Murphy is still riding one of our velocipedes. The ethanol making Murphy has his cousin, Murphy, helping him in the kitchen. And yes, his brother, also of course a Murphy, helping him too.'

I couldn't withhold a broad smile. 'So, there's three Murphys making ethanol in the kitchen of your holiday rental, as we stand here?'

'Possibly.' Pog rubbed his chin, and considered. 'There's a couple of other Murphy's kicking around somewhere but sometimes I get confused.'

'No kidding.'

RING RING A DING

An announcement came over the pit speakers that due to the many holdups there would be a rejigging of the schedule. The New Era Formula 1300cc class was bumped up the programme: Andy's class. But first it was the two-strokes turn.

The ring-dings fired up early as was their wont. RRRipp, RRRipp, RRRipp. Over and over. Yam Ring a ding, a ding, a ding; Yam Ring ring a ding, a ding, Yam a ring a ripp, a ring a ripp, ripp, ripp, Yam aring aring a ripp a ripp……

The four-stroke boys looked across the garage to the bay containing the fleet of stink-wheels. To a man they were thinking: *Why the hell do you wankers have to keep blipping the throttles?*

To a man, the two-stroke jockeys were looking back and thinking: *You wouldn't understand, you ignorant diesel riding slobs.*

A two-stroke racer abided in a strange cosmos where needle settings and jet choices allowed God to exhibit his love through blue smoke horizons. Sweet crisp blips were the trumpets heralding the main event. On track the sound was manifested in an alluring symphony which played in a very fine gossamer layer called the power band. Getting the bike *on the pipe* and in the middle of this melodious tune was key and the rider shifted gears like an orchestra conductor, using the gearbox to delicately maintain the melody while increasing the majesty of the performance in a display of increasing velocity. There was no doubt that a 500cc GP bike was the pure essence of motorcycle racing. The NSR 500 reportedly weighed 130 kg

Craig Ditchburn. Photo: D Begg

and made 180 hp. Riders of 500 GP bikes would soar amongst clouds of strange music. Vibrations moved deep within their vestibular systems in a sensory dance of balance, spatial orientation and movement. It took a special rider plus big nuts to make all of that work.

TOO GOOD TO MISS

TZ 350's peeled out of the pits like fresh spuds and sprinted for the track entry. Line astern down Gardner Straight they were a thing of beauty – seemingly attached by an invisible thread, they slipstreamed close, weaving and screaming in a cacophonous falsetto as they fought for advantage. The haze rose off them to mix with the heat blear, smearing the sea of Bass Strait to a gauzy blue. It was a fight to the death into T1: Doohan Corner.

This corner was originally named KLG Corner after Kenelm Lee Guinness. He designed a spark plug that could be disassembled for cleaning. Perfect for a two-stroke racer; they spent many hours inspecting plugs arranged in front of their spectacles.

KLG plugs, 'Too Good To Miss'.

The plug chop was the gospel back in the day for the two-stroke rider. Hold the bike on the pipe and go through the gears to top gear at full throttle, then hit the kill switch. Push the bike in, remove the spark plug/s and diagnose. Too rich/too lean/just right.

The Devil was an ever-present hovering force manifested in the words: 'It's seized'. There were terms that paraphrased this terribleness.

'Nipped up. Picked up. Locked up'. But the most common word became in itself a terrible one-word sentence: 'Seized'.

'What happened?'

'She seized.'

'It was going so well.'

'Seized.'

MOTORCYCLE MAN

I had chatted with legend John Woodley when he was back in NZ to race at the Shorai Batteries International Motorcycle Classic held at Hampton Downs. John had breezily mentioned that he'd had to 'clutch it' when the bike seized as he was tipping into T1. T1 was the fastest corner on the track at Hampton Downs. I had been flabbergasted at the casualness of the comment. I was double-flabbergasted when John said it was the second time it had happened that weekend.

John had so much experience on two-strokes that he could instantly detect the pitch change of the engine and pull the clutch lever before the seizing engine could lock the rear wheel and throw him down the road like a badly spanked child.

Two-stroke riders were uniformly deaf; ear plugs could stop you hearing that vital change of note that heralded imminent destruction.

A seized two-stroke could be revived if the seizure was caught early. Diagnosis was the key. This was where riders and mechanics morphed into scientists – masters of the chemistry of the air/fuel ratio.

A seizure on track by a bike was one thing. A seizure of a rider was another but not unheard of especially as many riders of the classic two-strokes were indeed classics themselves. There was a medical form to be filled out to ride at the Island Classic; to get the insurance. The most daunting part of it was passing the electrocardiogram (ECG) test. This test was supposed to be done while the client was on a treadmill.

Have a peek inside a pit garage at a classic motorcycle meeting and ask yourself how many of those old gits could even step up onto a treadmill let alone survive it when it was set into motion. Imagine the treadmill being thrown into gear at even a moderate walking pace. The old racer would instantly pitch forward and be revolved face down off the back of it. However, like many things in life, when it came to doing an ECG test there were many ways to skin a cat.

It was virtually impossible to tell the age of a rider as he or she thundered past on track. Liver spots, osteoporosis, arthritis – all invisible as a bike flashed by. However, decrepitude was glaringly obvious when the bike was pulled back into the pits. Many an old rider would sit for a moment to gather himself. Hope that his leg would support him and not crumple when it was swung off the saddle. I had the history of three operations to my right knee. It was an awkward dismount from my F1. Each year I lost a little more bend in the knee and to compensate I would raise the seat height a little. The F1 was becoming tall: not tall in the ridiculous dirt-bike tall category but definitely tall for a road race bike. I needed a dismount device: possibly a manservant: possibly a serf who would drop to all fours and make like a foot stool when I pulled up.

Some riders would use a stick to get to their bike. A tight shuffle was a common gait in a garage, a stiff short limp leaning the upper body forward and hoping the lower half will keep up. Injuries, age and general unwellness could contribute. A walking stick could be used; a Zimmer frame was unacceptable.

If there was one consolation, it was that a seizure may not be the end of the world in a two-stroke engine. However, it could be the end of a rider's world if it happened at a fast stretch of track; a two-stroke rider lived with a finger poised over the clutch lever.

SPRAY 'N' WIPE

The two-stroke race ended and the Castrol blue haze gradually drifted away and up to destroy a bunch of ozone. It was time for the New Era Formula 1300cc race.

There was a quick spray-n-wipe as Andy got a final loving coat of Pledge on his GSXR 1100 before submitting it to the track. He gave the front of his leathers a solid spray too, they could have done with a little dubbin, but that would have to wait. Andy had a towel spread beneath his bike. He could give the soles of his boots a wipe before putting them up on the pegs. Saved the filth from the pit floor sticking to his boots and then getting blown back onto his pristine rear wheel.

'Have a good one, mate,' I said, and gave Andy a clap on the back and sent him out into pit lane. The New Era Formula 1300cc bikes burst forth from their garages like steroid-injected tadpoles emerging from frogspawn. These bikes were too "modern" for the IC class but strangely, even the top spec ones were not putting in quicker laptimes than the IC bikes. Aaron Morris, on an FZR 1000, was cleaning up in the races but his quickest time, 1:39, was still a couple of seconds slower than the quickest IC time.

If you put a Harris F1 Yamaha FJ 1200 motor beside an FZR 1000 and went through them in comparison, inch by inch, it would be interesting. The XJR/FJ engine was a much heavier lump than the FZR; and unsophisticated in its basic air-cooled form. The water-cooled five-valve FZR was sweet but only allowed a little fiddling with before it became likely to explode. You could get it into the 170-180 hp range but it was then something of a grenade.

The UK F1s were reported (rumoured) to be at 150-160 hp. The XJR/FJ could be cut, welded, drilled and ground with industrial zeal. It was robust and while it would remain a heavy lump, it could be a powerful and reliable heavy lump; and reliability was heaven in motor racing.

MY CONFUSION

I was confused as to how the IC bikes, at the pointy end, could be quicker than the more nimble and lighter modern Post Classics. But I sensed the beginnings of understanding, helped along by the creator of the CMR frames, Denis Curtis. Denis informed me that to get the CMR package performing at its best I needed to push it much harder; peddle faster. I weakly endeavoured to explain to Denis that my motor was crap and *it got no pull, baby*.

I was coming to the understanding that my F1 bike and the other Harris and Harris replicas were gran-prix bikes not souped-up road bikes. They were purpose-built for smooth tarmac tracks: rigid, complete prototypes, built from scratch and refined to be weapons on a racetrack; and a racetrack only. I was fortunate to be the owner of a thoroughbred and I was only now beginning to comprehend its glorious potential. It wasn't a struck by lightning instance - as if I had walked a donkey out of the stable one morning and the next, it had turned into Phar Lap - *but it was close*.

I had had something of an epiphany when I tried to compete the F1 in the Bluff Hillclimb at the Burt Munro Challenge. The road up Bluff Hill was notoriously bumpy and I could not get the bike to hook up despite softening the suspension. Every time I tried to get on the throttle it would leap erratically from bump to bump, threatening to tear my arms off and spear into the tee-trees. The F1 was clearly not suitable on that bumpy road; it was a bike bred for the track only. I needed a malleable road bike for that hillclimb.

#24 Neil Howard. Photo: D Begg

CONCERNED AUNTIE FACE

Andy had pedalled a 1:52 in race one. He knew he had pace but if only the other racers were a little more civilized, would give one's bike a little more room. If only they would build an alternative track: or perhaps a 'gentleman's lane'. If the riders each had their own lane they wouldn't have to deal with the muck flung up by others.

The racing line was always the clean line and the one that Andy favoured. To run wide meant getting out amongst the 'marbles': little balls of rubber – the detritus from race tyres that was cast to the outside of the corners. It made running wide treacherous and it was no place for the same extreme lean angles that could be forced beside the inner kerbing of corners where the rubber had been laid down. *Perhaps a horn, or a bell, one could ring when approaching a rider ahead.* A receptive fellow competitor could then move aside to allow one to pass without having to go through any close-quarter action involving fairings, bars, scrapings and general gnashing of teeth. Andy wasn't quite getting his *raceface* on; more a concerned auntie face.

BABY-FACED LIBRARIAN

The flatmates went up to the rooftop viewing area above the pits to catch the action. It was a brilliant perch and gave a panoramic view all the way to Bass Strait. The bikes assembled on the grid, the lights went out and they were off. Michael Dibb (FJR 1200), Dean Oughtred (GSXR 1100) and Aaron Morris (FZR 1000) were immediately at each other like lusty wolves. They pulled the field through T1 and up to the Southern Loop. Out of the loop their clique was already breaking away to form its own feudal battle. Dibbsy and Morris were practically on top of each other as they harried for space through Stoner. Oughtred was snicked in behind and ready to stick it in at the first opening. If you didn't know these fellas your initial reaction after watching them race would be to stay a mile away from them. Obviously nutters, they were scrapping like high-speed demons. Take the helmets off them and you would expect blackened teeth and crazy bleeding eyes. The reality couldn't be further from the truth. Off the bikes they were mild-mannered, quietly spoken gentlemen. Oughtred looked like a 12-year-old librarian. Morris was a redhead choirboy. Dibbsy a vegan ultra-marathon runner. Appearances could be deceptive. What was it about motorcycle racers that caused this transformation? (Okay, Fogerty was different – he was an animal. And … okay, Mick Doohan too. And …). However, the saying that you've got to watch the quiet ones was never truer than in motorcycle racing.

THE UNCLEAN

Andy had qualified 19th with a 1:51. The boys could see him running the outside line - the slower one.

'The boy is still running that wide line,' confirmed Simon grimacing. 'But to be fair it is clear of the shitshow.'

'Eee,' offered Matt, hissing lightly. 'Can tell he's from south of the border. True Tyke would never stray that wide.'

The rooftop viewing was great in that you could watch the start, then scoot across to the other side and see the bikes come up through the Hayshed and over Lukey. Dibbsy had the lead, but Oughtred and Morris were baying at his heels. The rest of the pack came through in a streaming ribbon of bikes. Andy was holding mid-pack and pushed through Hayshed tight: nice, on the apex – but then he held it there too long. This put him on the outside in the run up to Lukey Heights. He was wide, wider than was ideal – out there on the marbles. Then the bike slid from under him and he was down. Andy skated across the tarmac on his side, hit the kitty litter and barrel-rolled a few times.

'He's down. Friggin' 'eck, the man's down!' called Matt.

'He was *wide*,' said Spotty Dave.

'He rides wide,' I called.

'He was just trying to stay clear of the shit-show,' offered Simon. 'Trying to keep his bike clean.' Simon appreciated Andy's hard work to maintain form in a bike.

'Well, she's not so clean now,' added Campbell.

'Stupid eejit,' said Brendan.

'It looked like he just slid off the bike,' I said.

'Yeah, didn't look from here like the front folded,' agreed Spotty Dave.

Andy was slow to get up and then awkwardly stumbled his way across the deep gravel trap to the outside fence. He was bent over holding his right arm with his left hand.

'He looks hurt,' I said.

'Least he's got himself off the track, hasn't stopped the race,' complimented Campbell.

'Very considerate,' agreed Spotty Dave.

'Looks like an arm,' said Brendan. 'Or yer man's collarbone. The eejit.'

'Come on fellas,' I said. 'We better get ready, we're next.'

HOOTER HURRY

The five-minute warning hooter sounded for race two of the IC just as the boys walked back into the pits.

'They've red-flagged the last race,' called Simon. He was looking up at the timing monitor suspended from the ceiling in the garage. 'Andy's bike wasn't moved in time so they've called it. The IC is up now.'

'Shit, the feckers,' muttered Brendan, rushing to get his bike ready. 'Get that *feckin'* doll away!' he screeched, as he saw Chucky perched on his seat pad.

Simon swiped Chucky off Brendan's bike just before the angry little Irishman swung a riding boot at him.

Tyre warmers were dragged off hurriedly, battery chargers uncoupled and the big bikes were jostled out to pitlane. All of them were running total loss charging systems. I liked to do a last-minute air pressure check of my tyres but there was no time for that. At least *I* had a starter motor on my bike. The machines needing roller starting were jostling for position on the rollers out the front of the pits.

I fired the Yamaha and headed down pitlane. Matt was close in attendance, the shorty muffler on his bike made the sound boom off the concrete block pit wall; very cool. Spotty Dave was rolling just ahead of us, standing on his pegs, doing a Rossi impression, pulling the leathers out of his butt, loosening up his joints.

The green pitlane exit flag was waving madly as we approached. The marshal was waving his free hand to urge the riders to get a move on.

Sheesh, I thought. *They're pushing this along, there will be riders not making it out in time.*

Sure enough, Brendan, Campbell and Alex didn't make it out of pitlane – along with a host of riders from other teams – *a cluster fuck*. The red flag was held in front of them in pitlane. They would have to make a mass start from pitlane; that could get messy.

A quick warmup lap and the riders rolled down the straight to their grid marks. The usual grid position confusion was even more frantic than usual due to the number of bikes missing, waiting on the other side of the Armco, for the pitlane start. Even the most intelligent of racers could forget his grid number in the heat of battle.

It did become a little more challenging over the weekend as the assigned spots were fluid: not in the spilt liquid fluid category, but in that the team captain could assign any team member to any grid spot the team had earned. So, if he thought it would help the team to swap some riders around, he could do that. *Good luck trying to sell that to a racer* – he had earned his grid spot by risking his neck in qualifying, he wasn't going to give it up to some numpty who wasn't as quick as him; even if he was a teammate.

As the saying went, 'There's no I in team. But there is me.'

OLD MAN NO PULL

We were off. In culinary terms, I got a medium rare start. Spotty Dave went with me to the outside, forgoing trying to jam it up the inside. He had tried that in the last race but it got a bit hectic and everyone was slowed as a result. My wide line had been a good one in race one and I had been able to make a run on several riders and get the inside line for the Southern Loop. It was an elbows-out move as the pack was tight going through T1 and then needed to flop over onto the other side of the tyre for the Southern Loop.

I fed the F1 subtly into a chink in the samba line of bikes as the pack made an early apex into the Southern Loop and then floated wide, forced there by the speed of the entry and the necessity to go to a neutral throttle until the bikes could be coaxed back to the corner for the second apex and then the winding up to full throttle. You could try and sneak a little more gas in that mid-corner stage but on most of these heavy beasts it just pushed the bike further out. The artistry of cornering and the beauty of the PI track meant that you had a fairly full menu of lines to choose from on many corners.

I went to fourth and wound the Yammy up to 10,000 rpm and shifted to fifth. It certainly didn't get there quickly, even with the downhill run to Stoner. It was like an old man: no pull. I gritted my teeth and held it to the stops, got my knee down and apexed Stoner. *Ha, nice, mate – it can be done. Full throttle through Stoner. Now watch for that braking marker.* At the 150-metre board I went from full throttle to full brake and simultaneously flicked it down three gears. This should have locked the back wheel and caused all sorts of hideous skidding, but it didn't. It either took fine management of the clutch lever, a delicate touch to coerce the back wheel into stability – or, for me, a slipper clutch.

I just about got it pulled up in time and felt through that racing sensory unit (the butt) for that moment of settled space before throwing it hard onto its right for the tight corner. It was all the give and takes of cornering at play. If you missed this apex by a couple of feet then you would be a little too left for Siberia which would put you too early to its apex and hence run you wide, possibly onto the grass, departing Siberia.

And that's just what I did: *dammit*. I didn't want to give up track position to whoever was up my chuff – like every rider out there, I didn't want to get out of the gas unnecessarily. I knew I was too early into Siberia, *dammit*, but stubbornly I tried to stay tight on the corner, pushing the inside bar and forcing the big beast down into the bend – but of course, every bike has a mind of its own – and, this being my bike, it was an obtuse one.

MY THEORY

I was working on a loose thesis based on the concept that race motorcycles and show jumping horses were closely related. Sure, one had a beating heart, but in essence they were both warm-blooded animals. Every horse was different as was every bike. A horse had its own nature that would come out under stress or excitement – like a bike. Example: approaching a jump a horse could shimmy a little – a bike could head shake. A horse could skip sideways a couple of steps before going at the jump; with a bike, under hard braking, the back could step out. A rider had to be firm with the reins to hold the steed back before launching; a rider had to squeeze the front brake lever tight enough to stop the bike as quickly as possible without unsettling it, then lighten the squeeze to allow some trail braking on the lean to the corner. A horse needed grooming and feeding come the end of the day. A bike needed gas and a wipe down.

Mate, are you not pushing the boat out a little far on this theory?

Then there was all the preparation. Grooming the horse, getting the farrier to prepare its hooves and fitting shoes. Then on show day, choosing the correct length of stud for the conditions. Bike: balancing the wheels, choosing the correct tyre for the track conditions. (Ha, like we could afford a Pirelli SC0, SC1, SC2 or a medium wet, or a full wet in either soft or hard compounds). It was either a slick or a wet. *Okay, this is getting a bit wanky*. The horse analogy could be stretching it but there was that saying: The soul travels on horseback. *Wasn't the motorcycle a steel horse? Why was a motorcycle rated in horsepower? The central nervous system of a motorcycle was an iron horse.*

Robert E Fulton (possibly the first man to ride around the world – 1932-33 on a two cylinder Douglas) said a bike and a horse are equivalents: reins-handlebars, stirrups-clutch and brake.

T.E. Lawrence could have the last word: 'A skittish motorbike with a touch of blood in it is better than all the riding animals on earth.'

DAMMIT, DAMMIT

The F1 frame was a thing of beauty but that huge lump of FJ engine (lighter than a CBX 1000, but heavier than a GSX 1100) was deadweight and when I went to the gas it became an anchor dragging the bike across to the outside of the corner. I valiantly tried to stay with increasing the throttle. This was the beginning of the run up to the top of Lukey Heights and I needed every little pony in that engine to work hard. I shifted to third. I knew I was running very close to the outside edge of the track, I also knew that where you look is where you go; conundrum. *Dammit, dammit* – God loves a trier. Ideally, I needed to stay focused on that outside corner before the Hayshed, that slight left – I still had to get my bum across to the right and shift gear again – but now was not the time to be unsettling the bike. If I was about to depart the track, onto the grass, I wanted to know – *needed to know*. Mostly for self-preservation but partly because I needed to update the track plan in my brain which was constantly being updated. Of course, *everyone has a plan, until you get punched in the face.*

I took a quick peek right, not all the way right, just enough to see where the outside edge of the track was – more a straight-ahead peek. Yep, I was online to hit the grass. I got right out of the gas just as the front wheel touched the grass. *The quick action saved the family from the fire and they all lived happily ever after. Brought the bike briefly upright and back onto the track.*

I was a racer and duty-bound by the racer creed to try and win the race, or if that was out of reach, then to try and beat the sucker in front of me: and the next one and the next one. Decisions in the performing of the creed required multiple adjustments during a race and this was yet another one. I sure as hell wasn't going to win the race sliding down the track on my arse.

I slammed the throttle once again to the stops. The bike was not overly happy with this mistreatment and gave a long shudder, but fuck it, needs must. If I had stayed on the throttle I was going quickly sideways on the grass and then it was Frank Sinatra: Fly Me To The Moon.

I gritted my teeth with frustration as two riders took my mistake as a bastard's opportunity to slide up the inside, as I would have done if I were in their shoes.

I got my butt off to the right even though the bike was still turning left, but not a hard left, and went to work settling the big lump. 'There, there, it will be alright, you big hunk of shit – sorry, I mean, you lovely sweet handling pony.'

The bike was confused in that it was being held down into a left-hander by the force of my arms while the man riding it had clearly moved into what was a right-hander body posture. I short shifted to fourth, not ideal, but I needed the bike to be stable when I released it – I also needed to stay at full throttle: and I did. I released the force on the bars and the bike heaved itself quickly onto its right side and went to the apex; it didn't fall over; well technically, it did fall over, but not right over. For all intents and purposes race turns on a motorcycle *are* falling over; the bike was all but on the deck but under a fine line of control. Forward motion kept the bike upright. A sort of crashing – but controlled crashing.

As Jeremy McWilliams would say about his GP racing days: If you didn't feel like you were going to crash at every corner, you weren't pushing hard enough. Imagine how the nerves would be after a day of doing that for a living? And those fellas did that every time they were on the track. And McWilliams was employed at one time to ride the Aprilia RS3 Cube (described by Shakey Byrne as 'an all-out, fire-breathing, tear-your-arms-out-of-their-sockets beast.')

Despite the travel, the relationship woes, the mortgage, the sick puppy, jetlag, general lethargy, illness, the hangover, the professional racer was paid to get his butt on the bike and to try and not blow it up or kill himself, but as near to that as was possible. There was little room for fear or anxiety.

TIKI BAR AT FULL THROTTLE

I stayed on full throttle and drove it hard in fourth, knee down by the kerb, as the revs slowly rose. Short shifting was less than ideal in most situations as you weren't using the full power of the bike but the nuances of this track dictated. It was better to short shift to fourth before Hayshed as it allowed the bike to be stable while on full gas. Trying to shift to fourth, on full throttle, full lean angle, without a quickshifter, could unsettle the bike and that could result in a nasty weave or even an outright tank slapper. There were little accommodations and adjustments as a rider got to know his bike; and himself. Out of MG and into T11 was the other corner for short shifting.

I let the bike drift away from Hayshed on full gas and when it straightened, flicked it down to third and applied a little rear brake to bring it back to the apex up over Lukey Heights, over the crest and back to full throttle briefly before slamming it off, kicking down to second, *gonna marry you slipper clutch*, and pulling as quickly and as much brake lever as I could without the bike doing a forward flip. It was a time for throwing every anchor overboard. Grab that brief moment of stability before chucking it on its right side and getting quickly on the gas.

Drive it as hard as possible on the right side of the tyre then in one smooth rolling motion short shift to third gear and flip it onto the left side. T11 was a deceptive corner and the one I found the most difficult. It was a little like a mini-Southern Loop, although slightly uphill. It was hard to gauge how much throttle you could give it (remember the race one crash where Pridmore looked to be nearly upright when the thing let go). It's a disappearing horizon on the outside of the track so it's very hard to gauge where the edge of the track was. The same with T12: the most favourite corner of MotoGP riders. I engaged fourth midway between T11 and T12, not because I should, it just seemed like the right thing to do – remember, the bike was pulling like a wet tea bag. I had been advised, by who knows who, to go to full throttle when I was abreast of the marshals' gazebo at T12. I didn't really have a clue what a gazebo was, and in the heat haze, the bike at full lean angle, knee down, no view of the outside of the track, knowing I was going ridiculously fast, I was wondering if a gazebo looked like a tiki bar, or perhaps a bus stop – or was it more of a hut? There was no corner on any track in NZ where you could ride your bike at full throttle around the corner. Phillip Island had two – possibly three if you included T12. Stoner, Hayshed and possibly T12 if you were in the legend category.

THE ALIEN WORLD

The Edge... There is no honest way to explain it because the only people who really know where it is are the ones who have gone over. The others-the living-are those who pushed their control as far as they felt they could handle it, and then pulled back, or slowed down, or did whatever they had to when it came time to choose between Now and Later. But the edge is still Out there.

– Hunter S. Thompson

I had been going into T12 in Thursday practice when Jed Metcher and Davo Johnson came under me. They were at full throttle by that stage and their bikes were clearly trying to kill them. Metcher's especially was twisting its modified FJ1200 frame and he was grimly not letting off on the throttle.

I had asked a fellow by the name of John Connor, when I first began racing, about how you found where the limit of grip was. John had replied that you took the bike to where it just crashed, then brought it back a bit. How I had laughed – howled with laughter. So had John. It was only a few months later that I discovered that John wasn't joking.

Mark Marquez still practised that technique. He would crash a couple of times on the Friday of a race weekend searching for that limit of grip and then gradually bring it back a bit for the race. Marquez rode out there in the alien world of The Edge and was even fearless enough to repeatedly take himself over it.

Photo: D Begg

That was insanity to a mere mortal and brought into play some thoughts from the great philosophers.

Albert Einstein: 'The definition of insanity is doing the same thing over and over again and expecting a different result.'

Marquez wasn't insane but he played on the edge of it in racing terms.

I'VE GOT THIS

I hit the bump on the outside of T12 and the bike gave the obligatory headshake; I felt some nip on the sphincter.

The really big slappers, the ones you saw on the telly, must be mind-alteringly terrifying onboard, I thought – but that happened to those in the icon category – of which I was not a member. The front straight was the time for a breather, especially when your bike was as slow as mine. I didn't find Phillip Island to be a particularly tiring track to ride. Many of the corners were lovely, long flowing bends once you got your body position sorted: outside thigh gripping the tank, elbow hooked over the tank and just holding on. NZ, by contrast, had tight little goat tracks that were a lot of work on a big postie bike. Ruapuna was an exhausting track.

I firmed my mind and my wrist and held it on the taps past the 100-metre board. At the 50-board, which appeared alarmingly close to the corner, I went down a gear and gave a light squeeze of the front brake, a-la-Spike, and tipped it into T1 and gradually wound on the throttle. Fine. No worries. I was knee down on the stops going through Doohan corner at more than 200 kph. *What could possibly go wrong?* Nothing. What's more, at the Southern Loop I went deeper this time on the gas and that was tidier, the apex passed under my left knee on the exit and I was well on the gas: way better. I was gaining on the rider in front, Rennie Scaysbrook – one of the guys who had snuck under me when I was doing a little grass tracking on the exit of Siberia. Now was my chance to get that spot back. I held full throttle, top gear, and went around the outside of Scaysbrook through Stoner. I glanced quickly across to the left to spot the 150m braking marker – it read 100. *Mmmn, I thought, that's curious. That would mean I've missed the 150-board; that would be 50 metres back. Whoops.*

I shut it down and went as full on the front brake as I could while desperately kicking down three gears. The slipper brake did its thing but there was only so much it could do; it wasn't a miracle worker. The rear wheel skidded and skipped left, right, left, right.

I've got this, I've got this, I prayed.

I DIDN'T GOT THIS

What had Kevin Schwantz said on his legendary passing move on Wayne Rainey? 'I waited till I saw God, then I braked.'

Racers loved to dwell on braking exploits and the craziness involved.

Alex Phillis had been telling me one, just that

morning. Alex had been at Eastern Creek (SMP) the year before on the XR69. He had just gone through T6, right before the overbridge. 'I've got this, I've got this …' only Alex, at this stage, was only connected to the bike by his hands. The rear had stepped out and given him a wee flick. His feet were now above his head which was above the clocks. He didn't *got it* and binned the lovely XR.

STOMP DEM FLAMES

I desperately needed that moment of stability, just a wee moment, to settle it down: a mere couple of seconds of the bike settling on its suspension, the front wheel and back wheel harmoniously getting into line.

Was it too much to ask? ('Just a wafer-thin mint, monsieur'. 'No, fuck off, I'm full.' 'But it's only a tiny little thin one.')

I could wait no longer: it was either try and make the corner or run straight ahead up the slip road, like many had done before. But, dammit, I had just got that place back from Scaysbrook. I held my breath and threw it onto its right side to make the turn.

Not this time, sonny, said the F1. The front wheel tucked and I departed my bike, or more accurately, my bike departed me and slid gracefully away; Marquez would have saved it. I slid behind the bike, there wasn't even a bump as we parted ways. It was beautiful if you could find such an emotion in this moment: I could. I strangely enjoyed crashing. I loved the way everything slowed down and a cocoon enveloped you. I wondered if death felt like that. It was dreamy; just for that split second. It gave you a different perspective on things. Then things could get ugly, like the unmistakable desperate scraping sound of a bike grinding across tarmac. It was a common sound around motorcycle racing and usually accompanied by the cry: 'Someone's down'.

This crash instead was a gentle low-side and the gentlest of those. I got to my feet when the sliding had nearly ceased. I had learnt some number of crashes before that it wasn't wise for one to arise onto one's feet too early. It could feel like you were barely moving at 50 kph especially after you've just gone through Stoner at 240 kph but even Usain Bolt can't run at 50 kph: that would be 44.25 kph to be exact.

My bike was 20-metres away when I stopped sliding. I got to it just before the marshals. I noticed the grass beside the exhaust was on fire. Some spilt fuel had ignited. Victoria was in such a dry state at that time of year, bushfires were common. I stamped around on the flames in what could have appeared to be a feeble rain dance. Fortunately, it worked. It didn't rain, but the stomping did put the flames out and the marshals didn't have to dump a canister of foam all over my precious toy. They helped me heft it back onto its wheels. The bike was barely scuffed so gentle had been the spill. I mounted up, fired it up, and departed down the exit at Dunlop, back to the pits.

TANT PIS

'How's Andy?' were my first words, as Poppa Smurf helped me put the bike back on its stands.

Poppa Smurf fitted the rear tyre warmer. 'Not good, he's driven himself to the hospital.'

'Driven *himself*?' I queried, fitting the front tyre warmer.

'Yeah, said he was going to the hospital, borrowed a car, and gone.' Poppa Smurf straightened up and grinned. 'Fair to say, he was a bit grumpy. Didn't want anyone with him.'

'Where's his bike?' I asked, plugging in the battery charger.

'Next door.'

'And?'

'Not bad, just a bit scuffed.' Poppa Smurf frowned. 'You know, the usual. Broken clutch lever, left peg a lot shorter,' he laughed. 'It slid for a while on that peg. Probably saved much more damage.'

'At least it was the left side – didn't do the muffler,' I agreed. 'A grumpy Yorkshireman, eh. *Tant pis*, as the French would say.'

'Don't know that one,' said Poppa Smurf. 'But piss, yeah, he was pissed off.' He flicked a thumb at my bike. 'What's wrong with your bike, why are you back?'

'Very gentle low side at Miller,' I replied, giving my bike the once over. 'She's sweet as. Just a bit of spit and polish.'

Poppa Smurf held valiantly onto my sleeve to help as an anchor as I shrugged and twisted to get the race leathers off. I changed quickly into some shorts and a T-shirt and went up on top to watch the last couple of laps of the race.

A WEE LIE DOWN AT MILLER

Aussie Davo Johnson led McWilliams over the line, both of them clocking best laps of 1:37.5. They were both riding Harris XR69 frames but McWilliams had the big Yammy 1250 FJ engine while Davo had the long-suffering GSX 1100.

Troy Corser, Aussie legend, came in third – also on a Harris frame. His was powered by a Honda CB 1100R taken out to 1150cc – part of the fabulous T Rex stable put out by ex-footie player Rex Wolfenden. So that was Harris, first, second and third and all with different flavoured donks. An impressive showing by the English frame makers. In fact, eight of the top 10 bikes were framed by Harris or the CMR copy. The other two were a McIntosh and a Katana. The McIntosh was made by Kiwi Ken McIntosh and ridden by Irishman Paul Byrne. The Katana was a chrome-moly copy made by Trevor Birrell and Dale Gilbert -of drag racing fame. Steve Martin was riding that and one of the tricks of the frame was that it had quick release engine mounts; very handy when regularly blowing motors.

Spotty Dave rode a solid race and came in 24th, just dipping into the 1:47's. He was a happy camper; *he looked half his age*. Brendan was down into the 1:44's and 21st. He was getting to know his newish XR69 and his laptimes showed it. Only 29 bikes, of the 36 starters, finished the race. Matt came in 28th with a best of 1:51 and Campbell was next with a 1:54; his was the only two-valve in the field that finished. Campbell was already making plans for next year and they involved

T Rex Harris Honda. Photo: D Begg

more firepower. Roger, one of the Aussie/Kiwis, had blown yet another engine. He had none left but would go on the scrounge. He wasn't hopeful as the GSX 1100 engine was as rare as a goose's golden egg.

'Fockin' slow, mate,' said Matt, as I held his bike. I didn't dare attempt to put it back on its stands; it was a complicated affair, Matt's stands, and best left to the inventor; who was particular.

'Ah, wouldn't worry, mate,' I said. 'Your times are improving every race.' I grinned, 'Perhaps you should try for a rolling start.'

'A what?'

'A rolling start,' I enthused. 'No one would see you down at the back of the field. Just roll in behind the safety car then hammer it when the lights go on. Should get you up to mid-pack before turn one.'

'Thanks, pal. Very helpful,' said Matt sarcastically. '*I went past you* when you were having your wee lie-down at Miller. What happened there?' 'Oh, you know.' I nodded my head. 'Ambition outweighed my talent.'

Spotty Dave joined us. He had a grin from ear to ear; he was well chuffed.

'You found some speed, eh, I'm guessing,' I suggested.

Spotty Dave chuckled. 'Yep, I reckon. Nearly got it about right. I was definitely up for it and didn't take any prisoners.'

'So, your mirror trick,' I said, leaning in close so those nearby couldn't overhear. 'It's worked.'

'*Yes* it has. I did have a couple of anxious moments going through Stoner and again into MG, so maybe I just need to give it one more tweak.'

I was curious. 'What age do you reckon you're at?'

'I'm thinking …. I saw myself in an RNZ Air Force uniform this morning – in the mirrors. It looked like an entry uniform: certainly an NCO. The tie was a little out of shape, but I never could tie the bloody things. So, that would make me about 19; a nervy 19.'

'Well, 19-year-olds have anxiety,' I offered, reflecting.

I couldn't remember being anxious. Nervous yes, but that was more excitement than worry. Anxiety seemed to be a modern norm for the young person. They were full of it. Couldn't go to school some days. Some couldn't even get out of the house with worry.

I was convinced helicopter parents were a major part of it: children no longer had the chance to explore, take risks, adventure, fight, get the edges knocked off them. They couldn't get cold, or too hot. Certainly couldn't get hungry. It was all about comfort. Everything was about safety. Health and safety. *Unhealthy and too safe,* to my way of thinking. How were you ever going to make yourself, build yourself into someone; your unique being?

As it said on the back of my sweatshirt. *'True crazy is attempting to limit risk to the point where a kind of living death occurs'.*

Perhaps, instead of a device – like a phone – being shoved into a 10-year-old's hand, a motorcycle throttle was placed inside his/her grip – children would have a much better chance of avoiding anxiety. *And don't stress, a throttle goes both ways, baby.*

I refocused. 'Actually, not. Can't remember me being anxious. But then I'm not that smart – certainly not as smart as you, Spotty Dave. No smoke and mirrors with me.'

Spotty Dave twinkled. 'I reckon if I can get it up a couple more years it will be sweet.'

We set about sorting our bikes for the next day's racing. I went to the Pirelli tent and bought a new SC1 for the rear – the front would be fine.

COULD HAVE BEEN WORSE

Andy reappeared in the pits just as we were finishing up. He had his left arm in a sling and looked very sorry for himself; which wasn't far off his usual look.

'At least it's not your wanking arm,' commented Campbell, always one to look on the bright side of life.

Andy frowned. 'Thanks for that.'

'Come on,' I said. 'Let's get to the van. You can tell us all about it.' I gathered up some loose gear and grabbed my bag. 'You driving Andy?'

'Ha, fockin' ha. Everyone's a comedian with all your chelpin.' Andy's mood was in the slums. Another racing weekend ruined. 'Simon can drive. He's got chuff all else to do.'

'Hey, steady on, brother,' reacted Simon. 'The Chuckster and I have been busy.'

A stony silence greeted that sentence.

I nodded to Matt. 'Come on, looks like you're still the driving man, Matt,' and picked up Andy's bag with my free hand. 'Collarbone Andy?'

'Yes,' replied Andy, stoically falling in beside me.

'Ribs?'

'No, just collarbone.'

'Could have been worse,' I said, then pausing a moment. 'Have you even considered that you may have brittle bone disease? You seem to shatter any time you fall off a bike.' I chuckled, 'Perhaps you spent too long underground, in the coal mines; not enough sunlight. You're lacking photosynthesis.'

Andy grunted. 'That's a man's world down there – in the pit – *you* wouldn't even survive.' He phlegmatically trudged on. 'Anyway, *I'm* fair t'middlin, but *how's* me bike, I can't bear to look,' he groaned.

'Not bad.'

'You would race it tomorrow, if yer man were any sort of man,' declared Brendan, scooting in first as we piled into the van. Andy got the front seat, automatic now, due to his injury.

'If it's any consolation,' said Brendan, shuffling busily to the back seat. 'You, yer man, looked good going down the front straight today. Way better. You weren't doing your feckin (Brendan mimicked Andy's head going up and down) noddy up and down head – reading your book thingy.'

'Yeah, true that,' agreed Campbell, taking the middle bench seat. 'You were stretched out nice on your bike. Very professional. You even had your bum over the back off the seat, even slid up onto the tailpiece. Very streamlined. Even for a big fella.'

'Yer man was actually using the windscreen to look through, not over. You know that's why they are made clear,' added Brendan, unnecessarily.

'Impressive,' I agreed. 'Probably gave you another 20 k an hour slid back on your bike like that.'

'Yeah, well, that was the fockin problem,' mumbled Andy, awkwardly trying to clip the seatbelt, then giving up. 'I *was* slid back off the thing. I couldn't stay on.'

'What do you mean?' I asked.

'That's why I crashed at Lukey.'

'Yeah, you were a bit wide. Probably out on the marbles.'

'I was wide, yes. *I'm always wide* - if there's bikes about. Never know what they'll do. And all that crap they throw up, sticks like buggery to the bike.' Andy paused and gazed out the side window. Then he swivelled his head around towards me. 'No, it wasn't that. I slid off the bloody thing.' He coughed awkwardly. 'I think I put too much Pledge on it.'

This brought a moment of silent consternation. Then a loud snort of laughter from someone in the van.

'And I Pledged my suit,' added Andy. 'That made it all the worse.' He gave a small chuckle and looked out the side window again.

'Really?' said Matt, pausing before putting the van into gear. 'You *slid* off it?'

'It was tarrah. I couldn't stay on the focker. I may as well have been off for a snek lifter. I was sliding all over it.' Andy grinned at Matt. 'You should have seen me trying to brake at Miller Corner.'

'Oh, aye.'

'I slid up onto the tank. Ee ba gum, I must have looked like the arse end of a donkey.' Andy guffawed. 'I only didn't go over the front of the bike because my knees hit the bars.'

'You're kidding now,' said Matt, chuckling.

'No, I'm not. And I'll tell you something for free. It was quite steady in that position. The bike was quite stable. It may be a new way to brake.'

'So what happened at Lukey?'

Andy looked again out the side window, reliving the slippery ride. 'I came through Hayshed – did you know, there's a lot of muck lying on the track there.'

'Yes, yes, yes,' a chorus from the back.

'I looked like one of them, boarders, is that what you call them? Them fellas out fillin thi boits in the waves.'

'Boogie boarders,' said Spotty Dave. 'They're called boogie boarders.'

'Aye, them boogiers,' continued Andy. 'That's what I looked like. Slid off to the left, only hanging on with my knee hooked on the tailpiece. Then when I tipped in tub to'left, well, off I slid to'right and I sailed roight off.'

AN ACQUIRED TASTE

Saturday night was posh dinner night back at the track. The flatmates scrubbed up and we put on our black and grey team shirts: Team NZ IC Phillip Island. Andy decided to stay home and nurse his wounds. Simon decided to keep him company for a while, then he and Rastus, and Chucky, had a mission to carry out.

A huge marquee was set up on the grass beside the front straight, directly opposite the pits. The flatmates got past security as we were legal; the event was free for IC riders.

All you could drink and eat. Boags beer was the only beer available, then there was red and white wine. Boags was Tasmanian and an acquired taste; which was acquired quickly if you had a free ticket.

The Kiwi tables were off to the side of the stage. The Aussies were directly in front and the other teams were spread about. Me, being Kiwi team captain, knew I would be called at some stage to say something. I nervously went for another Boags.

I contemplated repeating the seven commandments I'd recently heard:
- Drink water. I am not Lawrence of Arabia's camel
- 100 pretzels is not a meal

DC preaching to the converted.

- If I start thinking about penguins, I am too cold
- If I start thinking about hell, I am too hot
- Too much coffee has made lab rabbits explode
- If I find myself reading the Wikipedia entry for Death, step away from the internet
- I am the only zoo animal currently living who has the key to my own cage. Open it and go outside

I decided the commandments may be a little too deep and meaningful for this crowd.

The host for the evening was none other than Alan Cathcart. Sir Alan Cathcart as he was honourably known in motorcycle circles. He was a brilliant host and a font of knowledge on classic and post classic bikes. Giacomo Agostini was at the meeting doing parade laps a couple of times a day on his 500 MV Augusta.

That would have to be one of the loudest bikes on the planet. I reckon that Ago must be deaf as a post by now.

Agostini still had his movie star good looks and debonair ways despite being well north of 70. Sir Alan quizzed him on his race career and, of course, being Italian, the answers were given in delightful Itanglese with accompanying extravagant hand signals.

Dinner was then served. Each table was called to steer itself along the smorgasbord.

Sir Alan waited until the mains were nearly consumed and called Jeremy McWilliams to the stage. He was up there for the UK team, but of course had an Irish accent. Troy Corser was hauled up for the Aussies. Colin Edwards for the Yanks. Paul Byrne for the Irish.

Each one was a famous rider with multiple titles. Then I was called up. *Gulp*.

I did notice that for once in my life I was the big guy. Byrney had a bit of size but the former GP racers were smaller and slighter than me at only five-foot nine.

I was handed the mic. I took a gulp of amateur air; I made no pretences about being any good. I said the Kiwis were the donkeys of the meeting and the boys had to be at work on Monday; we were normal working-class blokes. I said we felt fortunate to be invited and that most of the Kiwi lads in fact were lucky to even own a race bike.

I explained to the audience that it was a tough gig in NZ owning a race bike. Kiwi women were a strong breed and most had little tolerance for the silliness of bike racing; little did they know the sheer cost of the silliness. Hence a Kiwi racer had a bike in his shed, *but no*, it wasn't actually his. It was his mate Bob's. Bob couldn't tell his missus as she would go berserk if he had a race bike. So he, being a good mate, was looking after it. And fettling it. And taking it to the track on race day. Of course Bob was spinning the same story to his wife about the race bike in his shed which wasn't his, but belonged to Bruce. Bruce's missus would go berserk if he had a race bike.

THE ESCAPADE

Meanwhile, Rastus and Simon – and Chucky – were in a van heading for the western end of Phillip Island and a meeting with a chap named Shaggy, about a couple of 20-litre methanol cans that had fallen off the back of a truck. Simon had the directions in his pocket, it was at Sealers Cove.

He wasn't pleased at having to ride shotgun on this mission; he was displeased he didn't have a shotgun. Shaggy came from a long line of sealers dating back a couple of hundred years. Simon didn't know what kind of inbred mutant the man could be but he suspected it could be an ugly one. He was slightly consoled by the fact Rastus was likely to be unfazed by whatever was thrown their way; this rooster Shaggy couldn't be worse than some of the specimens found in shanties around Bluff, NZ.

A weather-blown hut came into view. As they drew closer it manifested into a cragged hutch pegged to a rock that never knew sunshine. It was by itself and perched on the exposed coastal cliff of the peninsula, out in the maw of the night. Alas, there was no neatly trimmed front lawn out here in the eternal glum. This was an area of tussock grassland and dune scrub. Trees were twisted like witches fingers and gouty knobs splayed ragged branches. A full moon was back-lighting the property and the high barbed wire fence around it in full definition black and white like a scene from The Great Escape. It was Stalag Luft 111 and any moment now, Steve McQueen was going to fly his Triumph TR6 over the wire.

Simon dug the note of paper out of his pocket. 'There's no house number on it, surprise, surprise. It just says to go down Back Beach Road. When it comes to a T intersection, go straight ahead on the track which leads to Flynns Beach. It's the first house you come to. Looks like the only house,' observed Simon. 'Geez, mate, I don't know.' Simon grimaced: 'Is this a good idea?'

'Any idea is a good one,' enthused Rastus. 'How else are you going to have adventures in life? It does look kind of creepy though.' He chortled. 'Like something out of Hansel and Gretel.'

'Or a Steven King film,' sniffed Simon. He turned to Rastus, 'Surely there must be some other gas you can use, mate. What about Avgas?'

'Nah, mate, no chance.'

'Premium?'

Simon didn't fully understand the volatile nuances of fuels and didn't want to. He carefully put a 50/50 mix of Avgas and premium unleaded in his tank as he was instructed to by his mechanic; as did most of the fellas in the Kiwi team. You got the benefit of the lead in Avgas giving cooler running and protection and then the long burn of the unleaded. There were higher octane racing fuels available but they were very expensive and the average pleb racer would have found more benefit spending an hour a week in the gym or taking a big dump before hopping on his bike.

Rastus laughed. 'Nah, mate. My bike is set up for methanol and won't run on anything else. It gives it a great kick up the arse down the straights but it's a bastard all the same. Sucks moisture like a sponge and you're forever draining the stuff out and flushing your system to keep it clean.'

Rastus sprung the van door and turned to Simon with a devilish grin. 'Let's go meet the wicked witch, hee hee.' He slid from the van, then leaned back in toward Simon. 'Better bring Chucky just in case.'

Simon moaned. *I could be on the couch with a coldy, just me and the Chuckster hanging out. Yet here I am on some godforsaken island about to go into who knows what.*

There was a high gate made of rusty gridded steel bar, like a design you would find in a prison.

'Should we knock or something?' asked Simon.

Rastus grinned. 'On what?'

'Or make a noise, give a shout.'

'Nah, mate. She'll be right,' said Rastus. 'Besides, this prick is expecting us.'

He boldly pushed the gate open, which of course screeched like a rusty bastard. Rastus took a step inside the compound. 'Come on, mate, no worries,' he encouraged Simon, who resignedly caught him up and they shuffled forward towards the shack.

The hovel had seen some weather. It was bare of paint and the weatherboards were scoured close on the grain. The windows still contained their glazing but a few had cracks through them.

A sharp crashing of undergrowth caught them off guard as a large dog of the pitbull/mastiff variety burst into view. It paused briefly, took one delicious look at them and charged.

'Oh shit!' barked Rastus.

Simon gripped Rastus's arm and let out a long, whistling fart and made a little wee.

They took an involuntary step back as the brute came on.

When confronted by a grizzly it's important to remain calm. To look it in the eye.

Or, to not look it in the eye. To stand stock still. Or, to run like crazy. Once it's on you, it's important that you play dead. Or, to try and poke its eyes out.

This was the time to run – but no, too late. They both had simultaneously done the math; as you do in these situations. The brain was a wonderful vessel in computing time/distance/and velocity in a split second. They were racers, this was automatic. The math said they wouldn't make the gate before the hound was on them.

'Back up, back up,' grunted Rastus. His go to wrestling move was the leg drop but this brute had four of them; two more than Rastus had trained for.

Simon farted again, and had another little wee. He attempted to slip in slightly behind Rastus, a similar move to the one you would make if scuba diving with a buddy and a great white appeared. Stab your buddy and swim like a bastard.

The dog was still coming and unless it was a bluff charge, they were going to have to take it on. It was nearly on them.

Simon by now had got himself half in behind Rastus. Suddenly he had an idea. He thrust Chucky out in front of them – thrust it right in the face of the berserk hound – like the doll was some kind of crucifix: a vampire move.

The pitbull cross went eye to eye with Chucky's withering death stare and hit the anchors. Its paws went from full forward to full slide lockup, then full reverse all within the space of seconds. It yelped in terror and tore away around the back of the shanty.

Rastus and Simon stood frozen in the moonlight. Two grown men, one with a doll held at full stretch – and a small damp patch in his shorts.

'Sheeeiitt,' said Simon.

'Shit indeed,' agreed Rastus. 'That was close. *There's* your adventure, pal. Come on, let's get this over.'

Simon snorted, 'Yippee-ki-yay motherfucker.'

They went up to the door and Rastus hammered loudly on it.

It opened almost immediately. A rangy, dreadlocked dude leant a skeletal slouch against the door frame. 'Greetings gentlemen.'

'Good evening,' reciprocated Rastus. 'You must be Shaggy.'

'Yes indeed. Did you meet Jester?'

'Would that be the puppy?' asked Rastus, trying to regain some of his jocundity.

'Aye, he's a beaut, isn't he?'

'He is at that,' agreed Rastus, then chuckled. 'A little bit of a scaredy cat though.'

'Oh,' said Shaggy, somewhat affronted; definitely puzzled.

'Big dog like that being afraid of a little doll like this, said Rastus, indicating Chucky.

Shaggy considered Chucky, who was now cradled in Simon's arm like a baby. He went to say something, glanced up at Simon and then thought better of it.

'Mmmn, you are a couple of gentlemen indeed.'

Shaggy didn't have the methanol at his property. He said it was close and they should take the van. He would come with them.

It was only a couple of kilometres to Summerland Beach. Shaggy led them along the observation boardwalk where more than 700,000 tourists a year visited to see the little penguins Phillip Island was famous for. The island had the largest Little penguin colony in the world and at dusk 4,000 of the 32,000 living in the waters around PI, would make their way beneath this boardwalk to their burrows.

And it was here, partway along the boardwalk, that Shaggy slipped between the railings and dropped to the sand just below.

'C'mon,' he commanded.

Simon and Rastus dutifully slipped down to the sand. There were thousands of little webbed footprints in all directions. Shaggy strode through them and ducked beneath a section of boardwalk.

'In here, this is my little burrow,' he laughed. 'My wee storage depot.

Who would know, eh?'

There was a setback well into the sand face and what looked like driftwood piled all higgledy-piggledy was in fact a door. Shaggy went to all fours and crawled inside. After a brief scuffle he withdrew dragging two 20-litre cans.

'This'll be what you're after,' he sniggered.

Rastus unscrewed the lid of one can and took an indirect whiff. It had the faint but distinctly candied smell of methanol.

'Beauty, mate.'

Cash was exchanged. They dropped Shaggy back at his hootch and drove hurriedly home. Rastus was by now fully energised. Simon was fully exhausted and needing new undies.

PART FOUR
THE HEAT GOES ON

WHO'S YOUR DADDY

I stepped out into a thin light for my morning walk. It was said that a morning walk could help lower the risk of heart disease, stroke and certain types of cancer. It made the bones stronger. It could clear the mind, lower the blood pressure, increase the energy. Even improve the memory and stave off dementia. Maybe boost emotional and mental health. I reckoned all of that was probably bullshit; but I was awake, so I might as well walk.

It was the last day of the meeting and I was feeling it in my bones – and my arms, legs, and … everywhere. My fitness regimen wasn't perhaps ideal. I rode a pushbike a bit and walked the dog. Maisie, the dog, liked her walks and especially liked them when I would reluctantly propel myself from a trudge to a form of brisk stumble. Maisie, being a smart dog who knew a thing, noted that my legs weren't the longest and hence I was never going to stretch the pace.

I would occasionally throw a stick. Maisie duly returned it as the idiot obviously wanted it back.

'Who's a good dog? Who's a good dog?' I chanted.

Maisie knew these inane questions were rhetorical garbage. *Wait for it!*

'You're a good dog. You're a good dog.'

Maisie was only three years old yet I treated her like a hard-of-hearing geriatric.

'Who's your daddy now? Who's your daddy?'

NO DYLAN FAN

Chucky was perched on the washing machine when I entered the laundry. He said nothing. Neither did I. I recovered my clothes from the drier. I gave Chucky the hairy eyeball but the little bugger appeared completely unfazed. In fact, if anything, he gave it back with even more hair on it. *What was I thinking?* You weren't going to out-eyeball crazy doll.

I slunk out of the laundry feeling a little undone and headed for my room.

Were there fewer mirrors in the hall? I stopped and backed up to take another gander. There definitely appeared to be fewer mirrors.

Campbell was over the stove, working a frypan.

'Whatever you're doing Campbell, it's working with that bike of yours,' I said, as we got our breakfasts sorted.

Matt was bent over his muesli. 'It's that tutty a cow he eats in the morning.'

'Bacon and eggs,' corrected Campbell, and awkwardly cracked an egg on the side of the pan. He had working man's hands and was conscious of the delicate eggshell. 'Bacon comes from a pig, eggs from a chook … even where you're from.'

'Well, whatever the fock it is, your bike hasn't missed a beat.'

'You should know,' laughed Campbell. 'You're right there with me.'

'Yeah, slow as fock.'

'Hey, steady on.'

Matt put his hands up. 'No, pal – sorry, I didn't mean you. Your bike is slow as fock. It's me, I'm slow as fock.'

'Today's the day,' I announced, digging into some muesli and canned peaches. 'Time to leave it all out there. Don't pull any punches. Don't drop the ball. The ball's in your court. Time to answer the bell.'

'On any Sunday,' added Campbell, setting his plate of fry on the table.

'Now, there's a movie,' chimed in Simon, comfortably immersed in the couch. 'One of the greats.' Simon had assigned himself a pozzie on the couch early in the vacation. He had indented it to his mass. The couch was the mould, he was the filler.

'What do you reckon, Andy?' I asked.

Andy, eyes bloodshot with tiredness, was slumped awkwardly on the couch near Simon, trying to get his slinged arm comfortable. 'Theerz nowt s'queer as folk.'

'I reckon, Andy,' I said, with a dry chuckle. 'You should have to make a *Pledge* to us.'

'Ha, fockin' ha,' said Andy. 'Clowns to the left of me, jokers to the right, stuck in the middle with you.'

'Didn't take you for a Dylan fan,' chortled Simon. 'More a Leonard Cohen man. "I caught the darkness, it was drinking from your cup, I caught the darkness, drinking from your cup, I said, Is this contagious? You said, drink it up".'

This actually got a smile from Andy. 'I would clap. But as you can see,' he said, lifting his sling. 'I'm a one-armed paper hanger.'

'How did you sleep, brother?' asked Simon.

'Sitting up,' grimaced Andy, reflecting on his night. *Hanging on in quiet desperation is the English way.* 'Was fockin' uncomfortable, I can tell you. 'Fockin' motorbikes.'

'Amen to that. F'in' motorbikes,' agreed Simon. 'What do you reckon, Chucky, *hee-hee-hee*.' Simon waggled Chucky endearingly in his hand. Chucky's cold blue eyes bounced around the room.

'You, yer man, keep that little fecker away from my bike today,' warned Brendan, from the dining table. 'Don't know what you were *thinkin* bringing dat doll.'

'You guys need to relax,' Simon chuckled, clearly enjoying our unease. 'The Chuckster wouldn't hurt a fly. Would you little man?' He bounced Chucky up and down on his knee.

I dragged my eyes away from the evil doll. 'Well, I reckon if it wasn't for bad luck, we wouldn't have any luck. We need some good luck today.'

'You're starting to sound more like an Irishman,' laughed Brendan. 'We'll make one out of yer man yet. Soon you'll be saying, "may the devil fly off with your worries". Ha.'

GREMLINS

'I have something for you fellas,' smiled Campbell mischievously. 'With all the talk of luck, mainly bad luck, I've got *something* that might help.' Campbell departed his breakfast half-finished and clunked a brown paper bag on the bench. From it he pulled a bunch of tiny black felt bags and went around the room handing them out to those who were still in the IC hunt. That was everyone bar Simon. Andy was in the P6 class – well, used to be.

'What the hell?' questioned Matt.

'Gremlin bells,' answered Campbell. 'Or guardian bells, or spirit bells if you want. They bring good luck. I call them gremlin bells.'

'What, do we hang them from yer man's ears?' asked Brendan, tinkling his bell busily by his ear.

'No dude, you hang them from your bike,' answered Campbell, taking his place back at his plate. 'The ringing is said to ward off gremlins. You know, electrical faults, fuel issues. All the things that happen to us.'

'Well, *lord knows* we could use anything,' I laughed. 'Thanks, mate. You are special.'

'Amen to that,' endorsed Simon. 'You're from Christchurch so there's no doubt you're special.'

The Gremlin Bell story: road goblins were evil little creatures that left obstacles in a rider's path:

Photo: D Begg

like old mufflers, pieces of rubber, boxes, diesel fuel and unexplained objects that could cause a tyre flat or something to break. The goblins also chased animals onto the road in front of riders.

Their sole purpose was to make riders crash or break down. One night a lone rider had been riding in the hills. A bunch of goblins threw their whole package of nasty tricks at him and brought him down. They then closed in for the kill. The rider was in a bad way from the crash but wasn't going down without a fight. He lay in the ditch, barely able to move and threw whatever he had at them. They kept on coming. The last thing he could grab was a small bell and he rang it in fury; *at least I will go out to music.* The sound of the bell confused the goblins. It was also heard by some resting riders nearby who went to investigate and rescued the fallen rider.

Since then, the bells had been carried by those who suspect gremlins were out to get them. They're very popular with those who ride Harleys.

MIRROR TIME / ASYLUM STREET SPANKERS

Spotty Dave came into the kitchen from the hallway. He was munching a piece of toast spread liberally with Vegemite.

The flatmates gazed expectantly at him.

'Well? Yer man got anything to say?' voiced Brendan.

Spotty Dave munched contentedly on his toast and grinned. 'I think I've got it bang on. Little bit of twiddling with the knobs, not that there are any, but you know what I mean.'

'You've got a lot less mirrors in the hall,' I noted. 'Have you given it away: your experiment?'

'Yeah, *what's with that?*' echoed Campbell. 'When I get up in the dark for a leak I have to try not to smack into the bloody things, on the way to the john. This morning I didn't even notice them. Thought I'd woken up in the wrong house for a moment.' Campbell giggled. 'Haven't done that for a while. The missus wasn't happy.'

Spotty Dave grinned happily and nodded. 'I've managed to cut down the number of mirrors that I need to get the job done.'

'I've been thinking,' interrupted Matt, frowning. 'How do you know your reflection hasn't skipped a mirror? I tell you summat, one could be slightly off. Aye, it could be refracting.'

This seemed a reasonable question to those assembled.

'Aha, but you are mixing your refs,' said Spotty Dave. 'Reflection and refraction. Refraction happens because the speed of light is different in different materials. But my mirrors are made of the same material and I've kept the distance and angle constant. I have pure reflection.'

'Yes,' said Matt. 'But doesn't the jump in age distort the older you get?'

This seemed a perfectly reasonable question to the boys.

'I'm not bending light rays, I am bouncing them back.'

The boys were following. Bounce light rays back and you had reflection.

Seemed reasonable. *How hard could that be?*

'I've decided to use the tachyonic particle to speed things up.'

'Hang on, hang on,' intoned Matt, arching an eyebrow. 'The tachyonic particle is bollocks. It's as much use as a fireman with a wooden leg.'

He arched his other eyebrow. 'Aye well, it's just a theory.'

Spotty Dave appeared greatly amused by this. 'Yes, but doesn't everything start with a theory?' he laughed. 'Then it's just a matter of proving it.'

'True!' cried Brendan. 'Theory: we believe yer man Andy spends too much time with the Pledge on his bike. Proof: he slides off the bugger at Lukey.'

'Ha, fockin' ha,' muttered Andy.

'Theory: yer man Matt won't twist the throttle full on. Result: he's feckin' slow.' Brendan smiled, well pleased with his work; an Irishman giving it to those Poms.

'You're a roight comedian, you are,' protested Matt; slightly amused.

'So, you're working with a hypothesis in that hallway?' I asked.

'Well, it was a hypothesis, but now it's a reality,' replied Spotty Dave.

'Mother of Mercy, man!' shouted Brendan. 'You believe you've made a time machine in the hallway of a holiday house in Cowes, Australia!' He guffawed. *'Now I've heard it all!'*

'Hang on. Aye you were working with normal reflections in the mirror,' settled Matt, 'and the time it takes for each reflection to travel back in time – which obviously magnified. Now you're using an imaginary particle to speed up the reflection.' Matt vigorously scratched his beard. 'That's nae even possible. And if it were, it would be uncontrollable. *Wouldn't it?'*

Dave smiled. 'A tachyonic particle travels faster than light and so I can get back in time quicker than using normal speed-of-light particles. I've got it down to only five mirrors.' Spotty Dave looked very pleased. 'I reckon I can get it down to three. Makes it much simpler. Could get away with only one suitcase.'

'By gum, yes it would,' agreed Matt, laughing heartily. 'That is, if faster-than-light particles *existed*. A tachyonic particle cannot exist because it's inconsistent with the laws of physics.'

'And who wrote those laws?' asked Spotty Dave.

'Scientists.'

'People.'

'No, scientists,' said Matt.

'Scientists are people too,' offered Campbell.

'Yes, they are,' agreed Spotty Dave. 'So, the laws can be re-written.'

Matt folded his arms and sat back in his chair. Spotty Dave had a point; even though it was dubious whether it was tenable.

Simon, Campbell, Andy, Me and Brendan resembled the laughing clown head ball game at a circus: mouths wide open, heads swivelling back and forth. This magic was beyond us.

Matt sat forward again, he had another idea. 'If a tachyonic particle did exist, according to the theory of relativity, it would violate causality. And you know where that could end up.'

'Agreed,' said Spotty Dave. 'A potential slippery slope, my friend.'

Matt looked concerned. 'You're playing on the edge of the grandfather paradox. That's a very deep rabbit hole … and one you may not return from.'

'Hold the bus!' I cried. 'You've lost us totally. Grandfather paradox.

What the hell?'

Matt laughed. 'Yep, my brethren. It being Sunday, Spotty Dave is giving us a sermon on going back in time at such a speed that potentially he could be alive before his grandfather. The grandfather paradox.'

'I know that one,' said Campbell.

All heads swivelled to look at Campbell. Campbell was a quiet man; but a man of many surprises. *But really: the grandfather paradox?*

'It's a song by the Asylum Street Spankers,' laughed Campbell. 'Loosely, it reads like this: Matt was 23, married to a widow who had a grown-up daughter. Matt's father married the grown-up daughter. This made his dad his son-in-law. Now, Matt's daughter was his mother, coz she was his father's wife. Matt's wife had a baby boy. The boy became a brother-in-law to his dad. So, he became Matt's uncle – which also made him the brother of the grown-up daughter, who was, of course, Matt's stepmother. His dad's wife then had a son and he became Matt's grandchild, because he was his daughter's son. Matt's wife was now his mother's mother and because she was his wife, she was his grandmother too. So, if Matt's wife was his grandmother, then he was her grandchild. And as the husband of his grandmother, Matt became his own grandpa.'

Silence. Then exhaling of held breath. A shocked hush hung like a nebulous cloud: it slowly reformed and reshaped itself into a moment of stunned admiration. This was becoming quite the Sunday morning. None of these fellas were religious but the Church of the Motorcycle was fully attended this morning.

Campbell spent a lot of time alone in the cab of his truck, stuck in traffic. His mind had a lot of time to wander – who knew what depths were in it?

'Oookaay,' said Brendan, with grand understatement. 'I'm glad we got that out of the way. Where did you say yer man was from?'

'Christchurch,' answered Campbell, merrily.

'Thank you for including me in your little poem … song, or whatever the fock that was,' said Matt. 'The real grandfather paradox would arise if a person travelled to a time before their grandfather had children, and kills him – this would make their own birth impossible.

The term, 'blow your minds' was created for this moment. The boys, our senses befuddled, withdrew our minds into our own little spaces, our own little clocks; *our own little cuckoo clocks*.

Matt looked to the ceiling and whistled. 'The paradox indicates a cause can be eliminated by its own effect. Basically it becomes reverse causation.' He frowned at Spotty Dave. 'I think we need to keep an eye on you Spotty Dave! From the little I know, superluminal speeds – that tachyonic particles would travel at – are either imaginary; or very dangerous.' Matt scrunched his brow. '*Who knows where our Spotty Dave could end up!*'

THAT OLD CHESTNUT

Simon had taken over the driving duties. He didn't have anything else to do, besides terrify people with Chucky – who had adopted a perch on the dashboard.

The pit garages were a lovely thing first thing in the morning. Horsepower lying mute. The roller doors were wound up and behold, there was a plethora of motorcycles ready to be let rip into the tempest. But at that moment all was quiet up and down pitlane: no engines to be fired up until 9am. To the uninitiated the garages were just smudge-floored concrete bunkers filled with old motorcycles exuding stinky odorants. To the racer they were garages of mean potential, strong elixirs, to be inhaled. Weapons ready and amping to be taken to battle. *Valhalla?*

I got the tyre warmers onto my F1 and plugged in the battery charger. I flipped the fuel tank cap and stuck in the piece of doweling rod I used as a fuel gauge. The 50/50 mix hadn't evaporated overnight. I knew it wouldn't have but these were the checks you made on a race bike. I then went over the bike with a rag and some Pledge; not to the depth Andy would. Cleaning the bike not only gave one the chance to make it look nice, it also was the time to check for anything loose: bolts, nuts, tie-wire, cable ties. Cable ties weren't attached to bikes from the factory. However, all of my bikes had at least a couple somewhere on them. That hoary old chestnut: form or function. I liked a good-looking bike; but not too good-looking. I liked a bike that you could chuck down the road and not feel too bad about scratching the paint; hell, that's racing.

MOTORCYCLE MAN

I had seen men become emotionally attached to their bikes to the point where the prettier the bike was the more risk-averse they became. It could be argued that Simon and Andy's bikes were in that category. They were works of art and it would be sacrilege to throw them at the scenery. Brendan turned out gorgeous kit too but he was an Irish racer: the Irish only knew full gas.

The difference between a modern sportsbike and a classic one was in the character of the beast. A modern bike was like a modern car – *yawn*, it did everything well and was ultra-reliable: *boring*. A classic always had foibles and those became a part of the makeup of the machine. Even two modern bikes of the same make and model weren't identical. However, classic bikes were world's apart from each other even if they were brothers from the same mother; they were *very* individual. The classic bike was strong yet fickle. It occasionally hesitated, it broke, it was often nervous – all of those traits seemingly human. *Classic bikes were folk too*. You could have a relationship with your old bike and that wasn't necessarily unhealthy. You probably wouldn't talk about it in too fuzzy a terms; you needed to be careful on speaking too emotionally about your bike. That could get a wrinkled brow and a sideways look from your mate.

Old guys didn't sell their old bikes, even if they'd stopped racing them some years before. You didn't sell your best mate. That bike had become part of the fabric of who you were; it was your history. *It had become family*. So what if it was worth a small fortune. *You sell your soul, what do you have left?*

I had gone the pretty bike route once in my racing career. It was a
GSXR 1100 painted white with shark teeth on the nose emulating the P-40 fighter planes of the 1940s. It looked menacing. I had gone to some trouble with stickering it up and getting the race numbers just so. I crashed it fairly heavily at the first meeting after it was tarted up. Many thought I was a wanker for trashing my lovely bike. I thought I was a wanker too, but mostly because I'd spent too much time and money on making it look pretty.

The F1 I had at PI was of course, to all intents and purposes, a new bike. I had crashed it on its first run at Manfield, just a low-side slide. I had used a front tyre given to me with the words: 'It's barely been used.' I only used my own tyres after that.

BLACK BRIGHT DOG

I stood back and decided my bike was ready to race. I had it going about as good as it could considering its gaping flaw: the head needed an expert rebuild; read: some money spent. The funny thing with building race engines is that trying to extract that last bit of performance is costly. Faster = more danger = more adrenalin. Speed is King. True or false but getting the ultimate out of your engine (whilst keeping reliability) is a driving force. That's what keeps motorcycle wackos fettling late at night in their cold, musty sheds. I probably had more fun when I first started racing and knew nothing. I was swapping engines and frames and even doing mad experiments like running a front 120 slick on a rear 4.5" rim on a CBR600. It was all a little 'run what you brung' but it was pure fun. And cheap. But that's the nature of motorsport: you want to go faster - to win. Nirvana is to realise the potential of your machine and that costs.

We had a 10-minute warmup-cum-tyre-scrub session first thing for those that wanted it. I liked to do the scrub sessions as it got the head in the game early; and offered another chance to check the bike.

I went next door to see how Andy's bike was and if the Yorkshireman needed a hand. He really needed his wife, Mel, to look after him. Mel would likely wish to be anywhere but at the track but she was long suffering. She had to be. Andy took 30 seconds each morning in kissing her goodbye. He reckoned that's how long they used to kiss when they were first dating so anything less would mean she didn't love him anymore.

Andy was standing back from his bike, looking at it. He had his hands on his hips. More accurately, he had his hand on his hip. The other was resting in its sling. 'The dog is black bright, look at the state of him!'

Andy was viewing the good side of the bike; the side that hadn't been down the road. There wasn't a scratch on that side as the bike had slid only on the left. It *was* dirty though.

'Have you seen the other side?' I asked.

'There isn't another side,' replied Andy evenly.

'No, I mean the left side.'

'*I know what you mean,*' muttered Andy, shaking his head. 'The state of it. Filth everywhere.'

It was true. There was a fair amount of dirt on it. Kitty litter was sprinkled on the ground, having fallen out of the belly pan.

'Come on, gis a hand,' said Andy. 'We'll put it out back of pit and I'll set to with Pledge.'

Andy took the rear stand while I manoeuvred the bike back and forth to get it out of the corner of the garage. Being a street bike once-upon-a-time it had a decent steering lock. On my bike, with a pure GP frame, the steering lock was negligible. Maneuvering it, was like trying to turn a donkey in a milk crate. I had noticed on the telly that with MotoGP bikes, when they came to the pits, the back wheel was pulled onto a low dolly enabling the bike to be whisked quickly into the garage without all the back-and-forth shenanigans that I had to go through.

THE LITTLE FOCKER

Brendan had his sweet XR69 ticking over, building up heat, as I walked back into our pit. The wired Irishman, who liked to stay busy, was doing double-duty in that he was also racing in the Unlimited Forgotten Era class; a truly magnificent title. It evoked images. Vintage colosseum fighting with no rules.

The flatmates went up onto the roof to watch the action. The tarred surface of the roof with its elbow high walls provided a good perch to take in the vista. Brendan had qualified on the second row. He got a good start as the pack thundered away to Doohan Corner.

Brendan was in fifth place, pushing for fourth, as they came over Lukey for the first time. A Moto Martin Suzuki 1100 was just in front of him.

'He's on his game, the little focker,' said Matt, summing it up neatly. Brendan was one of three brothers, all originally from Cork in Ireland, and all fast racers. There was Brendan, Derek, and the other one. One of them was seen drinking from a dog bowl at festivities the year before. None of them would own up to it; not even the other one.

By the second lap Brendan had moved up to fourth, having overtaken the Moto Martin. However, the pilot of the Moto Martin fancied himself and decided to dive bomb a pass on Brendan as the bikes plummeted down to MG Corner; a classic place to overtake.

We held our collective breath as it was a bold move, potentially a reckless one. The Moto Martin got parallel with Brendan's bike but even from distance you could tell it was carrying too much speed and with only two-pot Lockheeds to pull it

Brendan hunting #76 Scott Webster, #29 Barrett Long and #5 Colin Edwards. Photo: D Begg

up, it was probably going to be too big of an ask. *And it was.* The front of the Moto Martin folded and the bike slid sideways under Brendan giving him a fair shunt in the side.

'He's got it, he's got it!' shouted Andy, as Brendan's bike was propelled off the track and onto the grass.

'The wanker,' said Simon, echoing our communal thoughts on the desperate move by the pilot of the Moto Martin.

'Brendan looks okay,' said Campbell.

Brendan had stayed upright but was 20 metres from the track.

'Yeah, but he's lost a ton of places,' replied Andy.

Brendan slowly rolled along the grass infield. He finally came to a stop, then fell over. He made no attempt to put his leg out to steady himself.

'Silly bugger,' said Simon. 'What's he playing at?'

In reality, Brendan had attempted to put his leg out to catch the bike, only, his leg wouldn't work. The Moto Martin had impacted directly onto his leg, pinning it between both bikes. Brendan lay with his bike, like he was still in riding position, but in a horizontal manner. He was making no attempt to get up.

MOVE ON, SON

Yellow flags were waving at the marshal station and these then changed to red. The flatmates filed down the steps back to the pits to get ready for the IC warm-up session. We did what racers do, compartmentalize a situation and move on; we were becoming experts at it. Big engines were being fired up down the length of the pits, a truly magnificent sound early on a morning. There wouldn't be anything like that come the electric motorcycle age. A Tesla didn't quite do it beside a 72 Holden Monaro GTS with a 350 big-block Chev.

THE CHUCKSTER

Chucky was standing on Brendan's tool trolley as we filed our IC bikes back into the pits after a two-lap warmup, his icy stare greeting our safe return. Brendan had the first space at the back of the garage, so each rider had to file past that empty zone to get to their respective spot.

I got myself and my bike sorted; unfortunately the horsepower fairy hadn't called during the night – it was still a gutless wonder. I walked over to Brendan's area and considered Chucky, perched on Brendan's tool trolley. I gazed hard at the doll. 'Don't s'pose that little bugger had anything to do with Brendan's crash?'

'The Chuckster,' said Simon, looking affronted. 'Chucky boy is our friend.

He liked Brendan.'

I sucked in some air. *Hang on.* 'Why do you talk in the past tense?'

'What do you mean?'

'You said, "liked"!'

'I meant, like.'

'You clearly said, "He liked Brendan". Is that another job done, move onto the next?' I was angry. It was tough enough trying to herd the bunch of cats who made up the Kiwi team, keeping them informed that their next race was such and such and which grid spot they were in, wiping their noses, patting them on the bottom, 'Get up there, boy.' And because they weren't in reality all Kiwis in the Kiwi team, they were spread all over the pit garages. It was quite a walk to get the upcoming IC race information to them all. I didn't need the extra exercise. I certainly didn't need a doll from hell making it more difficult.

What I needed was a moment to think – some clarity. *How many riders did we have left to make up the Kiwi team?* We had started with 11. Of the four Aussies, three were out: Roger out of engines. Glen, dropped valve. Damien, the head gasket was shot. Brendan was done. Simon was done; and pleased about it.

I exhaled through my teeth. 'Perhaps you could take Chucky for a walk.' I gave Simon a stern glance. 'There's a nice lake in the middle of the course. Perhaps you could take him for a swim in it.'

Simon was a master of the hurt Labrador look. 'Come on Chuckster, the
Kiwi captain is in a grumpy mood.'

BEWARE THE GUST

There was a fair wind gusting down the front straight. The temperature was climbing steadily: it was already in the 30s. A fully faired bike could become a sail if a gust caught it just so. Wind was a common consideration when racing on the island. The wind had been blowing off Bass Strait the year before. A gust had caught me as I had come over Lukey Heights pushing me from the inside kerbing to the outside, all in one smooth motion. There wasn't anything I could do about it; it was out of my control; it had felt scary, surreal and beautiful all in one. The front wheel had been shifted sideways by an invisible hand and it was done with a gentle touch. Grip was regained on the very inside of the track and I had serenely ridden that line down to MG.

The tailwind this year was from the opposite direction and would push my speed up going down the front straight; that was a bonus with my bike lacking top speed. The yin to the yang is that it would also push everyone else's up so no real benefit to be gained. It would give us a headwind through Stoner to Dunlop and the climb from Siberia to Lukey would be a bastard. That was definitely what I didn't need with my gutless wonder.

ANDY A FEATHER DUSTER

Andy had found a rainbow feather duster from somewhere and was beginning the cleaning of his bike from the top down. He had the bike outside of our pit garage, on the infield. A large Yorkshireman with an arm in a sling and the other attached to a feather duster: not something one saw every day. A small group of onlookers watched him work. They were all stood on the left-hand side of his bike so they weren't really watching him clean. They were looking with bemusement at the damage that had been done in the slide off the track. Such a shame for such a pretty bike. The fairing had long scratches in it like an eagle had taken its claws to it. The screen was cracked and a piece was missing.

Andy ignored their gawking and muttered comments. The side he was tidying was still perfect – whatever they were looking at was an aberration. Andy was originally from a small mining town called Clowne, in Derbyshire. Derbyshire wasn't technically part of Yorkshire, although it might as well have been. Clowne had originally been called the Celtic Clun: which meant spring, or river. Then called Clune, Clon, Clouen. Some wag had then renamed it Clowne. Hilarious fun until you visited the former pit village and found it wasn't quite the light, fluffy land of entertainment you might have imagined. The circus *did not* come to town in Clowne. Andy had spent the first 13 years of his working life underground in a coal mine in Yorkshire – he did go home at nights. He had the sticker of a clown face on the tank of his GSXR in honour of his birth town.

I found it curious that the bike had been a beautiful thing just a few days before but it had now become a clown of a more sinister nature:

The Joker. In the Batman movie, half of the Joker's face had been horrifically disfigured when he fell into a vat of chemical waste. Half of Andy's bike had been mutilated. I might make that comparative observation to Andy at a later time; *this was not that time.*

A BIG SHAKER

I went for a leak. You often found yourself beside a legend while taking a leak in the mid-pits concrete toilet block. They may have been or still were one of the best riders on the planet, but there was no such thing as a legend bladder.

I held the bathroom outer door for Corser to exit. Then I lined up on the wide urinal beside Colin Edwards. McWilliams was further along. Even the greats needed to take a nervous one before racing. I shook the last drops out, I wasn't a big shaker, and zipped up. A hand gripped my shoulder and turned me around. It was Bo. The American captain used his other hand to give me a come hither indicating of the finger and guided me into a toilet cubicle. Bo shut the door behind us and locked it. He reached behind me and flipped the toilet seat down. He then put downwards pressure on my shoulder lowering me onto the toilet. Bo leant back against the toilet door and folded his arms, a big smile on his face. He reached behind to his jean pocket.

'Here, pardner, take a swig,' he said, sliding a hip flask out of his pocket. 'Jack's finest.'

I was uncomfortable perched on the potty with the big American hovering over me. *Who wouldn't be?* 'Thanks, but no thanks. I'm out in the next IC race.'

'Yes, well about that, pardner.' Bo took a long pull on the flask and smacked his lips. 'God dang, that's good. Jack, ether and burnt rubber in the morning … the smells of victory. I tell you, son, Nam might not have been good for most, but for me, it was liberation. We pretty much ran the place – sure the Gooks didn't like us, but it was Club Med for a certain type of freak.'

'Aha, was it,' I said, limply. 'I didn't know you were in Vietnam – didn't think you were that old.'

'I ain't.' Bo grinned and produced a tired, half-

Jimi Mac (on the right) doing the Rollie Free.

smoked cigar from his Western shirt pocket. He rolled it in his fingers to straighten it then stuck it in the corner of his mouth. He pulled a packet of matches from the same pocket and lit the cigar, rotating it slowly to get an even fire.

'Is there some reason we are in here?' I asked reasonably.

'Speaking of freaks,' said Bo, removing his Stetson and wiping some sweat away with his sleeve. 'There's a bit of dissension in the ranks. There's a bit of clucking about but I can't find the nest. Some of the other team captains are banging on about our bikes. Saying they're illegal and we have gone too far. God dang, they don't know what going too far even smells like!' snarled Bo. 'They've never had a gang of Latinos selling them bad shit, and knowing they're selling you bad shit – and *you know* it's bad shit – and *they know that you know*, that it's bad shit.' Bo was gesticulating wildly. His cigar caught me on the ear. There was the brief smell of burnt flesh.

'Ouch,' I yelped, grabbing my ear.

'Sorry 'bout that, son. Got excited.' Bo snickered. 'You need a lot of sun after bad drugs … and melatonin. A lot of melatonin. Liquid form if you can get it. Hawaii's the place. The Samoans down there can help you.' Bo was on some kind of a flashback. 'Anyway, son, what do you think? Are our bikes illegal? I mean, this is motor racing isn't it? Some of these roosters we're up against are more slippery than a pocketful of pudding.'

'Jimi Mac's bike does have a whole GSXR front end,' I offered. 'It's off a K9, if I'm not mistaken.'

'You're probably not,' allowed Bo, taking a long pull on the hip flask. 'Could be a K8. There is a bit of dawg about Jimi Mac, I'll grant you that. Fast! He can blow out the lamp and jump into bed before it gets dark. It wouldn't surprise me if that boy isn't part coyote, if you know what I mean.' Bo cackled and puffed effusively a couple of times. A cloud of rich, blue smoke rose over the toilet door.

A long, drawn-out fart, like a siren, sounded

CLASSIC MOTORCYCLE MADNESS

from the cubicle next door. Bo hesitated, he indicated to the next cubicle with his thumb. 'A lot of people can't handle it, this racing. Their stomachs are flipping like bad meat at a Mexican barbecue. Pre-race nerves, son. The trick is to get a belly full of cheap beer the night before. Hold it down with some canned spaghetti and you're good to go.' Bo chuckled, 'You can have that tip for free.'

I attempted to rise from the toilet. 'I probably should go get ready.' It was race time and I really didn't need this dissolute American bearing down on me. Hell, Bo's brain had shorted a long time ago; drink, drugs and depraved behaviour had sent it haywire.

Bo gently pushed me back down. 'There's a reason Merica is the greatest country in the world. We lead it. If it wasn't for the good ole US of A we wouldn't be on the moon. Now, this event is fine with all the old bikes and what have you. But some of these old boys are so country they think a seven-course meal is a possum and a six-pack. If we want to move it forward there has to be a leader.'

I considered that it was possible Bo was about to talk some sense; *there was* a stagnant intelligence within the man. I settled, I didn't have much time, but if the American captain could just give me something useful, maybe I could go into bat for him; at least briefly. I pulled a length of toilet paper off the roll to wipe the sweat from my eyes. It was single ply and thin as an old lady's eyelid. It simply dissolved in my hands and clung between my fingers. It was like trying to dry my eyes with snot.

'I've been keeping a bike back, pardner. Hid away. In the tall cotton,' said Bo, he leaned forward, taking his weight off the toilet door. 'It's still in the crate. Dude, between you and me, it's *special*,' he said, putting emphasis on the word, special.

'What's special about it?'

'It's running on Nitro. It's faster than a sneeze through the screen door.'

'What?'

'Nitro, baby. Nitrous oxide.'

'Okay, Bo. This may be a step too far.' I couldn't help smiling. I had to laugh a bit. Bo was outrageous but this was new heights even for him. 'Are you serious? Nitrous.'

'Yep. I love the smell in the morning. Pardner, it's the smell of victory.'

'You stole that from Apocalypse Now,' I said, grinning despite the situation I found myself in – this big American lunk leaning over me in a toilet cubicle at Phillip Island racetrack. *You couldn't make this stuff up.*

There was another long fart from next door.

Bo banged on the skinny divider: 'Quiet down in there, arsehole. We are in a meeting here.'

There was a muttered reply that we couldn't make out.

'Running nitro is definitely going to be obvious,' I said. 'Won't it?'

'No smell, baby,' smiled Bo. 'This stuff is fresh. I've just tried a wee … shall we say, sample. It's the good stuff.' Bo touched the side of his nose for emphasis. 'It's fast. And, I feel the need for speed.'

'The nitrous bottle will stick out like a sore thumb,' I declared.

'No bottle, dude. It's all in the frame.' Bo laughed. 'We've got it all in the frame. It's hidden like hen's teeth. You can't see any of it.'

Bo appeared to be covering his bases.

'Who's going to run it? Can't believe Colin will agree to that.'

'Not Cole.' Bo paused, removed his Stetson once again and rubbed the sweat off his forehead with his sleeve. He took another slake of the Jack. 'Between you and me, Cole hasn't been that quick. I mean, he's kind of up there but he seems to be hanging in country where the buses don't run.

He's not gelling with that bike; plus they've had a few mechanicals.'

'Okay, so who's your rider?'

'Jimi Mac. He's the man, if Jimi can't do it, nobody can.' Bo chuckled. 'Jimi Mac loves technology in a motorcycle … and a woman, come to that. He embraces a Betty with a rebuilt front - if you'll excuse the pun.'

Bo squinted, as if going through a mental checklist. 'Besides which, he's a fireman, so, you know, if anything were to go wrong; which it won't.'

'Okay,' I said. 'I mean, not okay. But I do like excitement and you bring no shortage of that. And I do like Jimi Mac. But please don't tell anyone you told me. Remember, I'm the Kiwi; the good guy.'

Another fart sounded.

'Hey shithead, keep it down!' called Bo, banging his fist on the divider again. 'It's people like you that give speed a bad name. Goddam hippy!' Bo turned his attention back to me. 'Listen. Pre-race diarrhoea is nothing to be ashamed of. There's plenty of dudes in this paddock that have it. You get on that spag and cheap beer and you'll be fine. Take it from Bo.' He inclined his head towards me. 'But I just need to know that you are batting for the right side, boy.'

I shook my head and smiled. I raised my arms in the, I give up, sign.

'What about a little line, pardner, that'll help you out there.' Bo pulled a small plastic bag from his jean pocket. 'Little shakey, it helps, out there when the hammer's down.'

I shook my head, smiling. 'I'll be fine. We better go.'

We emerged from the cubicle just as John McGuinness walked out from the one next door.

BREAKAGES

'Looking good,' I said to Andy, as I arrived at the back of our garage. Andy had ditched the duster and was back onto the Pledge. He was still tidying the undamaged side of the bike. It was a little awkward with his broken wing. 'Are you going to do the other side?'

'Fock off,' said Andy.

The five-minute hooter sounded. Timing was everything. Simon was loitering around Brendan's bike, which was back in the pits. Chucky wasn't with Simon. The XR69 was fine – it had been a very gentle lay down on the grass; Brendan's leg had been a good cushion.

'Any word on Brendan?' I asked, squeezing myself into my leathers.

'Yep, broken leg.' Simon's brow knitted with concern. 'And ankle.'

Andy wrecked.

'Ouch.'

'Yep, not good. It's a worry out there. Too easy to get smashed up. He's gone to Dandenong Hospital.'

I looked closely at Simon. 'Where's Chucky?'

'Down the pits somewhere, not quite sure.' Simon glanced nervously at me. 'Must go and find him.'

'Give us a hand to get going, first' I said, indicating my bike.

'Sure, brother. No worries.'

SLIM PICKINGS

Alex Phillis had a going machine again. Twelve riders had started the weekend for the NZ team. We were now down to six. A team was scored on the finishes of your top five. Even Campbell could be scoring points – if he finished.

Spotty Dave was already on his way, cruising down pitlane, his Harris looking spotty – his leathers looking spotty. Matt was telling some helpful chap not to touch his stands and that he had it under control – basically to F off. Campbell had Poppa Smurf lowering his bike to the ground. Four out of the seven flatmates were still running. Rastus' bike was also being lowered to the ground. Kevin was helping Rastus: two Invercargill boys doing their thing.

All of the Kiwis still running made the outlap, with no one stuck doing a pitlane start. That was a good beginning to proceedings. Riders went

Campbell. Photo: D Begg

through their usual pre-race rituals. Everyone had their own way of settling in. Valentino Rossi would stand on his pegs, no hands on the bars and pull his leathers out of his crack, both front and rear. Marc Marquez liked to lean way forward over the nose of his bike, then way back, then flex each leg out as wide as it would go. In the classic racing world, there were no such conventions. Most riders were just happy to make it onto their bikes without falling over.

The field was decidedly smaller that morning compared with the day before. Missing teammates starting spots could be occupied by fellow team members. This kept the grid tight, but it was probably only two-thirds the size of Saturday's grid. I had promoted myself just ahead of Spotty Dave: one row forward. Bragging rights would be important come the end of the day so it was good to give oneself a fighting chance. I didn't know what age Spotty Dave was that day but he appeared very confident, as young people do. An old body, but one with a youthful bold mind: he had an edge.

AN ABSOLUTE FLIER

The red light went out and I got an absolute flier – very unlike me. I shot past the two rows in front of me and ran inside for a gap tight on the apex – a very different line to my other starts but one had to be reactive. It was like *I* was running on nitrous, *ha*. It had been an outstanding start. *I hope I didn't jump the start.*

No time to worry about that – besides, I couldn't change that now. I was already in third gear, so no need for that awkward change down while diving into the Southern Loop. I went in deep and applied some small subtle front brake and went to a neutral throttle. I could feel the F1 drifting a little wider than I wanted and eased on some rear brake. The bike liked this and squatted the back a smidge which brought it back towards the apex. I gave a little more rear brake and a click of throttle. The bike didn't dislike this so I gave it a little more throttle – it was holding its line.

How sweet is this. I drove the bike forward and hard out of the corner. I was somewhere in the front third of the field; *insane*. I was certainly up there with some of the big boys. The riders around me had names on the back of their leathers: McGuinness, Edwards, Spike (Edwards). *Come on mate, mind on the job – you're not reading a race programme.* I shifted to fourth and already I could feel that strong wind hitting my left shoulder. I shifted to fifth, not knowing whether that was the right thing to do or not – the wind would be hitting me through Stoner. Leon Haslam had been blown off the track onto the grass on this corner during a round of WSBK. Miguel Oliveira had been blown off T1 by a tailwind during MotoGP. I tried to recall cautionary words about the wind, on that corner.

I got my butt off the inside of the seat and my knee out early, full throttle, and forced the big bike onto its side to hit the apex tight, this was no place to be running wide. There was a marshals' hut before the apex. A heavy gust of wind hit me big time as I came out the other side of the hut. The wind got under the belly pan fairing and finely unweighted the front of the bike. The front tyre lost its edge grip and began sliding. I felt this happening in slow motion; because it was slow, in relative terms.

However, as slowly as the bike was drifting sideways, the forward motion was north of 200 kph. I wondered if this was how my life ended: good things didn't usually happen when you departed a motorcycle at over 200 kph; *I had experience of this*. My brain contacted my wrist and said, dude, shut off the throttle. I didn't do this consciously; I was just along for the ride. The shutting of the throttle shifted some weight off the back of the bike and transferred it to the front and, more importantly, to the front tyre – it regained a contact patch with the track. It gripped, gripped again and held a line – all be it, a line that didn't have tarmac ahead.

I instinctively pulled the bike upright, just as it hit the grass. The move saved me from crashing however I was now more passenger than rider, and found myself still travelling at around 200 kph but this time on the grass, parallel to the track.

I enjoyed my trail riding. My main weapon was a KTM 300 EXC. I wasn't sure how fast the two-stroke enduro bike could go, but probably not much more than 100 kph. It had big knobbly tyres, perfect for grass. Slicks weren't ideal. I knew enough – I'd done enough off-track excursions in my race career – to know, don't touch any controls and don't, for heaven's sake, try to turn the bike.

Make sure you were heading straight and then make a plan, *quickly*.

I went down a couple of gears and prayed the slipper clutch would play ball. *Please do not lock the back wheel.* That worked. I then eased a feather of rear brake on and worked the pressure. The front brake did not exist in the plan.

Fine, so far. I was well aware that, though my speed was gradually falling, I had to cross the track when it came back at the Dunlop hairpin; I wasn't going to get the bike stopped before it. I chanced a glance over my left shoulder – and yes, God was looking after me, and the other riders: there was a big gap before the next gaggle of bikes. I got off the rear brake and let the bike run, bounce briefly on the edge of the track, and shoot across it to the grass on the other side. I now had acres of room to stop before the tyre wall.

I got my bike back to the pits and put it on its stands. I put the tyre warmers back on and plugged them in – made sure they were working. I plugged in the battery charger. I removed my helmet and gloves and carefully placed them on the seat of my bike. I then went for a walk away, outside. A time to breathe big breaths. In, 1-2-3-4, out 1-2-3-4: it was a lovely day to be alive.

THE STATS

Davo Johnson pipped Jeremy McWilliams for the win. Davo was the only rider in the 37s. His top speed was 276 kph. Jeremy was fastest at 283 kph and he was in the 38s. The next nine riders were also in the 38s, a little off the pace due to the high heat in the track. Troy Corser was eighth but the Honda Harris F1 was a little off song. Colin Edwards was 10th.

Alex Phillis would have been the first Kiwi but his bike expired in the last lap. It started making a rattle and Alex got the clutch in quick and shut it down. The cam chain tensioner had snapped. His crew were hoping for little damage. Whip the rocker cover off, have a look around and if it was all hunky dory, put it back together with a new cam chain tensioner; a rare thing if it was only that simple.

That meant only four Kiwis finished race

three. Matt, Rastus, Spotty Dave and Campbell. Campbell did score points for the team.

I had done my calming walk. I hadn't needed to change undies, although my sphincter had definitely tightened during the terrifying grass-tracking. My pelvic floors were tight and taught.

Spotty Dave had finished in 22nd and was well pleased. Rastus was 26th and excited. Poppa Smurf was excited too and bouncing. He had been watching the monitor in the pits and saw Rastus top speed: 291 kph: the first time a 290-plus speed had been reached at the Island Classic.

'*Did you see, did you see?*' he exclaimed.

'No, you muppet, I was on track,' I said.

'*291!*' sang Poppa Smurf, gleefully.

Rastus had his helmet off and was grinning expansively.

'Someone will be asking questions,' I cautioned. 'Have you hidden your M&M's well away.'

'No worries, sunshine,' confirmed Rastus, laughing. 'Don't worry be happy. I've put them where the sun don't shine.'

Okay, I thought. *That could mean anything.*

Campbell had also benefitted from the strong tailwind down the chute and upped his top speed to 234 kph. He finished one back from Rastus in 27th.

Matt had come in 28th and last. He had slowed in the last couple of laps, worried at the excessive air and track temperature. He was an engineer and raced with the image of a working engine going round in his head; the expansion of moving parts at high revolution in the heat. Valve stems being stretched and valve faces being hammered against their seats. Conrods being tortured on the up-stroke then blitzed back down at 10,000 revolutions per minute. Piston rings overheating and losing their tension. Big-end bearings turning

#3 Davo Johnson. #22 Jed Metcher. Photo: D Begg

blue with exhaustion. Main bearings threatening to spin out of their caps.

The conditions, combined with his natural tendency to worry, saw him ease the throttle; it may have been a judicious move.

COME TO THE BOIL NICELY

I found Matt crouched down by his engine. 'Check this out,' he said, pointing at his fuel filter.

I squatted beside him. The fuel filter was a merry little kettle, petrol bubbling away.

'That's come to the boil nicely,' I appreciated. 'Anyone for tea.'

'Aye, son. She's maftin out there,' said Matt, smiling grimly. He put his finger to the fuel filter glass and swore as his finger was unsurprisingly burnt. His poor air-cooled engine was being asked to perform stunts in the 45-degree heat that even a coal stoker would shy away from.

The rules did allow for oil coolers to be fitted to the old engines. That saved many of them in that heat. But when the track temp was in the 50s and the air temp was in the 40s there was little air cooling to be had. None of the big four-strokes had water-cooling until the later 1980s.

'Fock me, and we've got another race.' Matt grimaced and stood up. 'It's not really roight.'

'No, it's not,' I agreed. 'But we do have another race.'

I had a team captains' meeting to attend. No doubt the heat would be a talking point.

GEEZ, COBBER

Wally arrived at the Kiwi pits just as I was walking out.

'Just a quick word, cobber,' he said, quietly moving me to a shaded spot under the steps to the upper deck. 'Now, I'm not one to complain, as you know, but I've heard a whisper.' Wally cracked a smile, slightly reptilian – slightly crocodile. *No, that would be Troy Corser: The Crocodile.* 'The Yanks have some super-duper bike they're going to run in the last race. Something that could win it. They're right there, on the points; it could be crucial!'

'Is that right?' I said, scrunching my eyebrows and thinking, here we go, more fuel for the conspiracy fire.

'Yeah. The word is that Jimmy Mac's going to ride it. He hasn't even been riding in the IC! He's been doing the New Era Formula 1300 on a Gixxer 1100.'

'Well, he can't use that,' I said, needlessly.

'No, agreed. He'll be running this new super-duper that no one's seen.' Wally breathed out heavily. 'Geez, mate, it's getting harder every year. Now, I'm not one to whinge, but we need to find out more about this.'

Wally looked closely at me. 'Cobber, have you heard anything about it?'

'Me?' I squeaked. 'Umm, let me think.' I rubbed my chin, folded my arms and looked skywards. 'No. No, I don't think I have.'

Wally was giving me a hard stare.

I took this opportunity to slip in a touché move. 'There's rumours about, mate – like flies.

You wouldn't have any little secrets of your own, would you Wally?'

'What! Me?' Wally looked aghast at me. *How could he, a man who's soul was whiter than snow, be accused of anything.* He pulled the peak of his Duckhams cap a little lower.

'A little birdy told me something,' I pursued. 'Something about a swingarm. You have a swingarm with a difference.'

'Moi?' Wally's French wasn't very good. His acting lessons also needed sharpening.

'Come on, mate,' I grinned. 'A little carbon in the swingarm. In fact, only a little alloy in the swingarm, and I hear, that's only in the paint.'

'Geez, cobber, you listen to some funny things.' Wally removed his cap and ruefully scratched his scalp. He put it firmly back on and pulled me further under the steps, closer to the wall. 'Look, I'm not one to moan and I don't want to spit the dummy, but sometimes if you can't beat 'em, you've got to join 'em.'

These side games to the main event had a stress of their own but they were proving entertaining. 'What's going on, Wally?'

Wally coughed and bowed his head lightly. 'We are trying a little experiment on the FJ.'

I didn't exactly feel righteous, but I couldn't help but feel a little virtuous. 'Would that be the FJ with the illegal headstock?'

'Geez, mate.' Wally made a wry face. 'You've been hanging about with bad people. Sounds like people with too much time on their hands.'

'That FJ?'

'Yes, that FJ,' conceded Wally. 'It's nothing, just a little experiment.'

'What swingarm are you using?'

'Well, cobber, one of the boys got friendly with the director of race technology at BMW.' Wally

Katanas await. Photo: D Begg

whistled softly. 'Believe me, you wouldn't believe half the stuff they've got going on. Anyway, they had a couple of carbon swingarms laying about off the S1000 RR, the race HP4.'

'Laying about,' I chuckled.

'Yeah, well, not quite laying about,' laughed Wally. 'But you know what I mean. What a beaut. He gave one to my man.'

'Gave?'

'Yeah, I know. Sounds unlikely – but that's what he did. No dramas. And you wanna know what else?'

'No. But yes.'

'It looks remarkedly close to the braced ones the Birrell boys make for the Katanas. A little skinnier but similar to the ones they make from alloy … so of course, we had to make this one look like alloy. That's where you get the silver paintjob.'

'So, Wally. If I was to run a key along the swingarm of your trusty FJ, I would find a nice sliver of silver paint coming off. And carbon beneath it?'

Wally winced. 'For Pete's sake, *please* don't do that. But yes, you would find something like that.'

'Sounds like quite a big secret,' I said.

'Look, it's really nothing.' Wally cocked an eye. 'It's nothing compared to what those Yanks are planning, with that Bullet Train.'

'There are a lot of rumours flying about, as you well know, Wally,' I soothed. 'What makes you think this Yank bike is not just a rumour?'

Wally winked. 'One of the Yank girls told me they have a secret weapon.'

'Are you sure she wasn't saying that *she* had a secret weapon,' I chortled. 'It can be confusing when an attractive woman starts talking mechanical.'

'It can be that, cobber,' agreed Wally, laughing. 'Look, we better get to this meeting. But I'm gonna bring it up – this Yank bike. So, I just need to know, that I've got you onside. We are batting for the same side.' He looked again at me.

I nodded, convincingly. Well, enough to convince myself that I looked convincing. Wally came from a land founded by criminals so it wasn't an easy country to be pulling the wool over the collective eyes. *You can't fib a fibber.*

ISLAND CLASSIC – CAPTAINS' MEETING 3

Captains: USA-Bo, Ireland-Pog, NZ-DC, UK-Arthur, Australia-Wally

Agenda: Items
3. Water cooling 4. Fork size

The captains' meeting got underway just before midday. It was in an air-conditioned boardroom which pleased everyone. The Poms and Irish were especially doing it hard in the extreme temperatures.

'Good morning, gentleman,' began the chair. 'Very warm conditions. A little different to Friday but that's Phillip Island for you.' He smiled around the table, watching carefully, warily for any change in species. He wasn't going to get caught out by that fish hallucination again – or any other distortion. He'd taken a couple of Valium an hour earlier to chill off any further weird jaunts into another world; to calm himself. But he had to admit that

Loading some mojo. Photo: D Begg

he was now feeling a little drowsy. He propped his hand under his chin to keep his head up. *Yawn, perhaps a wee nap might be in … So hard to keep the eyes open.*

He probably should have only taken one Valium. He must stay alert. *Fall asleep and these captains could turn into killing machines and tear my throat out.* A line of drool escaped from the corner of his mouth. *What the…?* The chairman snapped himself awake. A small pool of saliva had formed on page one of his notes. The chairman placed a discreet hand over it and glanced up to see if anyone had noticed.

Pog had an obtuse eye on him.

'Righto,' said the chair, with a shake of his head. 'I had a quick look at the points before I came over. It's tight; looks like it's all on the last race.' He read from a sheet of paper. 'Australia 585 points, USA 575, the UK 570, Ireland 490 and the Kiwis …' Damn, the drool had landed right on the Kiwi score. 'The Kiwis are … can't quite read it.' He smiled weakly. 'The Kiwis are in possibly the 300s. Bit of a smudge on my notes.' He smiled apologetically. 'Anyway, they're last.'

'Well done, Mr Chairman,' endorsed Wally. 'Now before we get started, I'm not one for having a whinge…'

The table to a man chuckled its greeting to this statement.

'What?' said Wally. He smiled self-consciously and tugged the peak of his cap. 'Yeah, right. Fair dinkum, I know when to pull my head in. But, there is a matter been brought to my attention which I feel duty-bound to bring to all of youse.'

'Is that youse, or ewes – of the baa-baa kind?' asked Pog.

More chuckling.

'Because I tink the good gentlemen assembled here need to know if we've gone agri-aquarian with the conversing of.'

Wally frowned deeply. 'Strewth, you blokes are harder to talk to than the Wagga Wagga Motorcycle Club.' He put his hands up in a plea for a moment of silence. 'I have it, on good authority, that the Yanks are planning to run a … special bike in the last race.'

All eyes turned to Bo.

'Bo, is there something you need to tell us?' asked the chairman.

Bo was slid back comfortably reclined in his chair. He had his long legs crossed under the table, with his worn cowboy boots, one on top of the other. Despite the heat, he was wearing a black Western shirt with silver embroidery above the pockets. His black Stetson was low on his brow and the ever-present cigar was in the corner of his mouth. Johnny Cash would have been proud.

Bo languidly removed the cigar and rolled it in his fingers. He smiled a mischievous grin. 'Now, you gentlemen seem to be a bit het up. You know you shouldn't go round listening to the rumour mill. Some rumours are so crooked they have to unscrew their britches at night. Never know, what you might hear.' He smiled reasonably and moved his eyes around the table. 'I've heard, from a reliable source, that the Aussies are running an FJ with a frame that's been cut and re-welded, in, what shall we say, a different geometry: more like one you would find on a modern R1.'

There were murmurs around the table; and they weren't in disagreement.

'And we shouldn't probably get started again on the Irving Vincent. No need now. Unfortunately, that rare mustang is no longer in the stables. Gentlemen, pigs get fat; hogs get slaughtered.'

Bo paused as the murmurs took on a new tone.

'The story continues that our good friends over in Limeyland are possibly running a six-speed Nova box in their quickest bike. And possibly that bike has some cubic capacity confusion problem. That acronym would be CCCP; and we know the trouble we've had with the commies in the past.'

All eyes swivelled to look at Arthur. Arthur began to push his chair out from the table to rise.

'Sit down, pardner,' commanded Bo. 'We don't need you climbing on that high horse again.'

Arthur paused mid-rise, re-considered and lowered himself.

Bo continued: 'And our good friends, the Irish, where many of my fellow countrymen came from – not so much down my way though. There's a rumour the Irish are running their bikes on a form of ethanol – a fuel they've made themselves.'

All eyes swivelled to Pog. His bushy eyebrows pulled down a notch but otherwise Pog's face remained expressionless. The Irish had had centuries of accusations laid on them; they knew how to absorb; and wait.

'Seems to me,' continued Bo. 'That the only team who is squeaky clean, is the Kiwi one. If I say a Kiwi dips snuff, you could look under its wing for the can.'

'So that would make us the winners!' I declared, with delight. 'You are all disqualified.'

Bo laughed. 'Ha, not quite, my little feathered cowboy. On the contrary, that would be why you are coming last.' He chuckled with slight condescension. 'We are motor racers, hombres, and there's a fair bit of tickling goes on in the nether regions in racing. Always has been. It's a part of the business. It seems that *we've all* got bones buried in the yard, wouldn't you agree? Now, we could start digging for them but how's that going to look to the general public? Wouldn't it be smarter to leave those bones buried than have them in piles on top of the ground for all the meddlesome vultures to get their beaks into? That's all I'm saying … *if you get my drift.*'

There was a moment's silence. The fellows around the table were mentally checking on how close to the transgression line they were walking. It would have been a grand time for Johnny Cash to come over the speaker: *I keep a close watch on this heart of mine, I keep my eyes wide open all the time, … because you're mine, I walk the line.*

Damn, motor racing was all about the fine line, about chicanery and guilefulness. About pulling a trick because sure as hell, your competitor was up to mischief. Cooling fuel to near freezing so it would shrink and therefore you could put more in the tank, so to speak – great for endurance racing, fewer stops. Or running a three-metre, *large*, fuel line so you could carry more fuel.

The chair coughed. 'So, you're not running a hot rod, Bo?'

'Nothing special.'

'Right, glad we cleared that up,' stated the chair. He looked about the room and gave a sickly smile, one that had a breath of despair about it. *Crikey, he was just trying for some clarification of the rules; snake handler would be a better description for his job.* 'Our first item today, gentlemen, is whether we should allow water cooling.'

'And turbo's,' I contributed. I wasn't serious but it seemed like a good time to stir the nest even further. I was basically there for the entertainment. The Kiwis weren't on the same field in the cheaty game as the rest of the teams. Sure, we were using avgas and methanol but those were legal in NZ. It had all gotten so far-fetched I was having trouble believing it.

The Irish were running bikes on ethanol, which was probably a grey area, but *they were* fuel injecting which was definitely a no-no. The Americans were about to run some kind of hot rod which sounded about as illegal as you could get. Some sort of hopped-up freak machine on steroids. The Aussies had a bit more going on than I knew for certain. I suspected that chopping a frame dramatically was borderline cheating. Running a BMW S1000RR World Superbike swingarm was way out there. King Rat was British captain Arthur and he could loosely be blamed for getting us into this mess by inconspicuously getting the class rules changed. The engine he'd put in McWilliams' bike was likely over the allowed specs. It was running a six-speed box and that wasn't available back in the day … or was it? So many grey areas. He was running McGuinness' bike with an electric gadget tucked into the tail, designed to screw up the ignition system of any bike that got too close.

I was having trouble believing the carry on. All the teams were cheating and I had the inside scoop on it all due to the confidence the captains' had taken with me. I had become their confidant, their Andorra, their Swiss bank, their Vatican. I was pope and father confessor for their dirty little secrets. I held this information tight within myself like four days of constipation.

This was unchartered country I had entered and how easily I had stepped into this strange land. And disturbingly, if I was really going to get into a bit of self-analysis, how easily I had become the door that led down this garden path. Each captain had come unbidden to my door and turned my handle. Did I have a choice? Was I born as the conduit for people's kinkiness to find an alternative way?

I may have been the ear for these team captains to lean into, and the soul for Spotty Dave to cast his weird mirror spell on, but I now felt quite independent of these goings-on. I hadn't started them but they now had a will of their own and were lunging forward of their own accord.

Classic racing began as a way to run older bikes and to have a simple, low-budget form of motorsport. Running a classic bike was now *way* more expensive than running a modern. This race meeting was ample evidence of that.

'Here we go,' lamented Wally. 'Turbos. If it's not bad enough already, we don't need artificially aspirated engines in the mix – and I'm not usually one to complain. This isn't drag racing.'

'Ha, your fastest bikes are built by drag racers,' I retorted. 'The Birrell and Gilbert show comes to town on those Katanas Giles and Martin are running.'

Wally looked a little hurt. He thought I was his comrade. *Fellow Anzacs.* Truth was, the Kiwis often felt a little like Anzac biscuits: chewed up and spat out.

The chair endeavoured to stay on issue. 'We decided last year to once again discuss the possibility of introducing water-cooled engines. The current engines aren't getting any younger.'

Arthur took this as his invitation to speak. He rose to his feet and adjusted his tie, making sure the knot was correctly in place. 'I am somewhat concerned at the direction this discussion is taking. Perhaps, good fellows, we should be looking to history for our answers. We mustn't forget the war.'

This silenced the murmuring. *What war?*

I had a fair idea that Arthur was meaning WW2. Pog thought Arthur was meaning the Confederate Wars between the Protestant settlers and the Catholics – a time of little trust. Even the King and parliament, seeking to quell the Irish Rebellion, wouldn't trust each other with control of the army.

Bo, too, thought Arthur was speaking on the Confederate War: but the

American Civil War fought between the Union states and the southern Confederate states. (This war was a couple of hundred years after Pog's war).

Wally was flashing back to the war with his last wife, Tracy. Cyclone Tracy. There's something beautiful about the creative destruction of a woman's wrath. Wally smiled wryly at the memory. Sitting in his gruds in a deckchair on the porch while Tracy went to war. She said the bubble had burst. Wally put it down to a nasty allergy she had to Hondas. He had a secret nickname for her: The Grenade.

The song, Miss Birmingham Small Arms (BSA) had surely been written for her: Why this woman's got a built-in destruction button with my face on it. Can't kickstart her, can't jumpstart her, can't bumpstart her. My girl is a BSA.

Wally had sat back, beer in hand as Cyclone Tracy/ The Grenade exploded his house. The pictures off the wall first, the table last. It went through the window. Nothing was left standing or hanging. She even pulled the fridge over.

Cyclone Tracy left him completely unharmed: 'Honey, you've got to live with whatever batshit is inside your head and that's a far worse punishment than anything I can do to you.'

In his defence, Wally would claim he was blinded by the blackness of her soul. Last Wally heard, she was president of the Roaring 40's motorcycle gang; no Hondas in that club.

'What war?' asked the chair, much to the relief of all gathered.

'Why, the World Wars, my good chap,' exclaimed Arthur. 'Are you not paying attention? The dirty Hun was up to no good, I can tell you. As a result, they didn't make any motorbicycles worth a damn. Then the Orientals came into it, late in the piece, not as late as America, eh what,' chortled Arthur. 'Somehow, we are using their engines now. I am just saying, good sirs, that perhaps we should look to the empire for some steadying, some temperance of the outlandishness coming on display at this show. Perhaps we should only race British.'

'Hate to tell you this, pardner,' drawled Bo, 'but it was a German who invented the first motorcycle.'

Arthur looked aghast, 'Impossible.'

'Possible, probable, and happened. Mr Daimler. He was a German. As am I – a few generations back. As is any Texan worth his weight.'

'I would have thought it would be Lord Snowdon, or his father,' huffed Arthur.

'*Water-cooling*,' encouraged the chair, despairingly. 'Can we please stick to the point.'

'Aye, the water wheel,' endorsed Pog. 'Twas, grand times at the Derry when the water-wheeled mill ground the harvest for the baking. Terry from the Derry, the very man his-self, tinked to send an idea up to the loft he called his brainchild. He found a new friend in Karl Benz – of the German nation Mr Bo's egg was formed from – who taking it upon his-self, brought the first velocipede to Ireland's fair shores. It was totally unsuited for the roads of good Ireland: which were extinct in that they had yet to be built. Said bike could only rock back and forth on a muddy patch, much as Bo's grannie would rock his daddy.' Pog hee-hawed. 'Twas the thermal siphon turned the internal combustion world asunder.

Hot air always rises – I give yer man Arthur, as the prime example. So too, hot water. Fortune smiled on us in not giving us a Christmas box full of the cast iron wonder of the thermal siphon. Imagine the weight; giddy up.'

Pog chuckled heartily. 'I tink it would likely take us till Christmas to get the wonder of the thermal siphon from Siberia to Lukey Heights. Yer man Mr Stevens of Dublin was the first to make the race velocipede in Ireland. He built it on the North Quays, near O'Connell Street, by the butchers, and it did indeed win the races in Phoenix Park.'

'Ummm, thanks, Pog,' said the chair, doubtfully. 'Yes, well, …'

'If we let water-cooling in, where does it end?' interjected Wally. 'Fair dinkum. Now, I'm not one to spit the dummy, but a GSXR 1100 is only oil-cooled, but it is a lot lighter than a GSX engine – and it can make more power, with a little fettling. Next, you'll have our American friends running Panigale engines in their old Dukes.'

'The Ducati 851 was the first water-cooled Duke, I think,' I said. 'Then you have the Kwaka. The GPZ 900 Top Gun bike was water-cooled. The Gixxer, like you mentioned, Wally, became water-cooled. There are a few choices. It will make the show a lot more complicated.'

The captains absorbed my words with consternation. Being a team captain wasn't a privilege; it was a lot of work.

'Look,' I continued, placatingly. 'We're here to race bikes, have a few beers and a good time. Not to have to play peeping Toms around the pits seeing who's doing this and who's doing that. This is supposed to be retirement racing.'

'Funny you should raise this, pardner,' said Bo. 'This meeting perhaps should be where fine bikes and riders are put out to pasture. But we now have these young guns piloting them. They don't know nothing about pasture … maybe jumping the fence.'

This brought laughter.

'What say we have a turbo class?' joked Bo. 'And these young cowboys can ride those. The GPZ Turbo is a lovely pony – we have a few of those in the back paddocks in the US of A. The CX500 Turbo. The Suzuki XN85 Turbo. That one is even air-cooled.'

The meeting as usual had descended into silliness.

Croz, Robbie and slumdogs.

PART FIVE

THE BUSINESS END

THINNING CROWD

Race four, the final race of the IC, was held mid-afternoon, before the crowd started thinning. People had a long way to drive home in Australia.

Alex was back on the grid after the replacement of the cam chain tensioner. He was keen to show what he could do. The rest of the Kiwi team were down the back of the grid; our accustomed patches. Spotty Dave and I were side by side. Matt,

Peter Hickman gets a flier. Photo: D Fitzgerald

Rastus and Campbell were a bit further back. It was the same six in the Kiwi team that started race three. The air temperature was 45 degrees Celsius. The track temperature, well, no one was brave enough to check that.

This race would decide the winning International Challenge team. It was close between the Americans, British and the Aussies and the tension was palpable. We weren't racing for a world championship; no sheep stations on the line. In effect, we were racing for jellybeans. But the front few rows were filled by fellas that had won world championships, Macau, Isle of Man TT's, Suzuka 8-Hours and other significant meetings. They were professional racers; *it was always about winning.*

Thirty-nine IC bikes had started on the grid on Saturday morning. Twenty-nine were all that were left running by Sunday afternoon; some of them not well.

The front row had the usual suspects: Jeremy McWilliams (UK), Davo Johnson (Aus), Jed Metcher (Aus). Second row: Peter Hickman (UK), Colin Edwards (USA), Alex Phillis (NZ). Third row: Jake Zemke (USA), Troy Corser (Aus), Steve Martin (Aus). Fourth row: John McGuinness (UK), Paul Byrne (Ire), Jimi Mac (USA).

A YOUNG MAN'S MOVE

I didn't get a flier this time. I saw no gaps to slide into so reverted to the outside line. Spotty Dave made a steady start and disappeared into the middle of the first corner melee. I spied him again as the bikes jostled and swooped into the Southern Loop – *how could you not, with all those spots.* He was a couple of bikes ahead of me. Half a gap opened on the inside and Spotty Dave stuck his front wheel into it, standing up the startled rider beside him. A young man's move, I grinned, ruefully – a Marc Marquez signature move. Get the front wheel inside the rider ahead on the corner and push it into his knee. The automatic reaction was self-defence: stand the bike up and Marquez would squeeze through.

All of the bikes made it safely through the Southern Loop for the first time that weekend – probably on account of there being fewer bikes on track. Usually a couple got flung out wide like frisbees.

I took it all the way to the redline in fourth gear before banging it down to fifth. No quick shifters on these bikes and it was all the way out of the gas and all the way back to full gas on the throttle. It sounds like a long journey of the wrist but it was instinctually quick and cost miniscule time; *but it was time lost.* PI was an ideal track for a quick shifter.

The Mikuni RS38 flatslide carbs were an agricultural squirter of petrol. At idle they sounded like an idiot playing on his teeth with a wooden hammer. The big slides couldn't be trusted to close on their own, wind pressure and vacuum could combine to cause sticking. Big springs were mounted on the throttle shaft to help snap them closed. Push and pull cables were fitted and these were assisted by yet more springs. This combination made for a throttle that was so hard to twist you needed to be Popeye to work it. I suffered arm-pump terribly, always had. A CV carb was what I really liked but they didn't have the brutal effectiveness of a flatslide. *Still, it couldn't be as bad as a TZ750 could it? Four cables running to the throttle body!*

Paul Byrne leads the field. Photo: D Fitzgerald

I had noticed, during my sauntering around the UK pits, that McWilliams was also running Mikuni RS38's. That made me feel good that the quickest guy had gone the same way as me. But I bet the Poms had found a way to make the throttle less of a workout. The RS38 worked best when it was either on or off; it wasn't one for subtlety.

I wound it firmly to the stop and held on. I owned Stoner now, *haha*, and I held it tight inside which gave me a nice choice of lines for the next corner. There was the inevitable inside dive bombing at Miller Corner from a couple of wannabees but I had got my braking spot-on and came back under them through the tight hairpin leading to Siberia.

I could see Spotty Dave ahead, working over another poor sucker – riding like he was in a World Supersport race.

I had my line for Siberia sorted, apexed late, then worked my way up the climb through Hayshed to Lukey – muttering under my breath about my gutless wonder; *couldn't pull the skin off a banana*.

There was a bike down on the outside of the track just after MG – a curious place to fall. Hickman was trudging off to the side of the track.

He had been running in first before slapping himself to the ground. Johnson and McWilliams had been up his chuff and had done very well to avoid hitting him, however, the avoiding actions had cost McWilliams a few places and he was now third. Johnson had swerved onto the grass in his evasion and was still trying to get back to the track. Phillis used the disruption to shoot into first and Irishman Byrne slotted in on his tail. Byrne was appreciating the bonus of his high-compression ethanol-injected bike and it was now coming into its own. On paper his bike was not as quick as Phillis's but the conditions were optimum for the potato propellant and he now was at least on parity.

Corser was running a close fourth and latched onto McWilliams's rear.

CLASSIC MOTORCYCLE MADNESS   165

NITRO BABY

> *Live out where the real winds blow—to sleep late, have fun, get wild, drink whisky, and drive fast on empty streets with nothing in mind except falling in love and not getting arrested . . . Res ipsa loquitur. Let the good times roll.*
>
> – Hunter S. Thompson

Jimi Mac had made a clean start. It was always a bunfight for the rows just back from the leaders. No one wanted to give an inch: an inch given in early combat was many yards lost after a few corners. Jimi Mac had the fortune of being behind a couple of messy skirmishes and took some fractured openings with an eager grin.

He may not have had the race cred of those ahead *but he had nitro, baby*! He also had a bike that only weighed 150 kg. The CMR frame was made of steel, but very thin steel. The CMR swingarm was now gone, it was too heavy. Bo had a man, who knew a man, make a swingarm out of magnesium. The triple clamps were carbon fibre. Every bolt on the bike was made from titanium. The fairings were carbon.

The bike was running a K9 upside-down front end but with Ohlins carbon fibre fork tubes. It ran carbon ceramic rotors that were 50 per cent lighter than the steel ones. BST carbon fibre wheels ran inside Pirelli SCX, WSBK tyres.

Corser was on his second bike by now: a hybrid FJ1200. He could ride anything, that fella. Put him on a scooter and he would still be competitive; a true motor racer: he just loved to race. Corser knew the FJ didn't have quite the mumbo of the Harris Honda F1 he had been peddling but still, it wasn't that slow. What it did have, was braking and turning stability thanks to the modifications of the headstock and the fitting of the carbon fibre swingarm. Not only was the carbon swingarm significantly lighter than the standard but it gave three-dimensional stiffness due to the engineering of the carbon fibres.

But, hang on, what the Devil was that? Corser couldn't stop his jaw dropping as a flash of stars and stripes rocketed by!

The nitrous oxide was perfect in the heat that day, introducing extra oxygen into the intake charge. Jimi Mac's illegal IC bike was already a highly-strung bird: it had run 180hp at the wheel on the dyno back in Texas. This was before they filled its frame with nitro. Because the nitro was stored as liquid, the evaporation of it in the carb manifolds helped drop the intake charge temperature. This cooling caused a denser charge, reducing detonation while increasing power.

Jimi Mac came out of T12 turned the throttle to full, put his head down behind the screen, cackled eagerly and shifted his hovering thumb to the red nitro button. At 320 kph he blew by McWilliams as they went over the start/finish line. He hadn't raced this bike before. He knew it could stop like all hell with its light weight and the braking mods. But he also knew he was travelling way faster than he did on his P6 bike; *hell's bells – way faster than he'd ever gone*!

A FIREMAN AND A NUTTER

Jimi Mac was a fireman and a nutter. Calculating risk and reward was a daily occupation. He hit the picks at the 100-metre board and went down a couple of gears; he too was running the Nova 6-speed box.

McWilliams was nothing if not brave. He wasn't exactly sure what had just happened, but he did know that some turkey (a very fast turkey) had just flown by him – *wasn't his supposed to be the fastest bike in the IC?* The British rider left his braking to a startling 30 metres and pushed himself up the inside of Jimi Mac. He then used his lifetime of racing skills and got his head down but it still took another two laps to work back up to Byrne and Phillis.

Jimi Mac tried to hook in and shadow McWilliams, but the Irish legend had too much talent and gapped him. Jimi Mac was on a steep learning curve to try and match his skill level with the level of the bike under him; he was but a club racer but a very brave one.

He decided to brake for Miller at the 50-metre mark, which was ridiculous. The crazier thing was that the bike nearly pulled it off. If Jimi Mac had been a couple of pies lighter it may have pulled up. But he wasn't and the pit exit road proved a godsend in that he could keep the bike upright and on tarmac. There was a small

escape path which went hard right and led back to the track. Jimi Mac took this and re-joined the chase.

Corser, Metcher and Johnson went past while he was doing his self-inflicted long lap penalty. *But he was learning.*

THE BLOOD TRAIL

The race was six laps long. Jimi Mac and his new best buddy, Nitro, caught and passed Johnson and Metcher on Gardner Straight on the fourth lap. A rush of wind was all they felt. Corser was on the anchors at the 150 into Miller on lap five. Jimi Mac went past and hit the picks at the 100 and easily pulled up using the carbon brakes to good effect. He was improving and worked his way through the back of the circuit quicker than he had ever done before. By the time he got through T12 he could see McWilliams, Byrne and Phillis a few hundred metres ahead.

The white last lap flag was horizontal in the wind and by the end of the straight he was on them. Jimi Mac pulled into line behind

McWilliams and waited – like a mako. He fell behind through the Southern Loop and wasn't as skilled as the fellas in front through Stoner. But he caught up on the brakes into Miller; he now owned that corner.

Out of Siberia he once again found himself being gapped but a brief squirt of nitro mumbo pulled him back up through Hayshed to Lukey.

This bad shark was now on the blood trail. He did the best he could through MG and T11 but he was 50 metres back as they filed into T12. The three ahead were practically biting on one another's back wheels as they gave nine-tenths of throttle to get the best run to the flag. The slipstream effect on these bikes was negligible and it was all about the drive. McWilliams got the best drive and pulled level with Byrne as he pulled level with Phillis. Three abreast they bore down on the finish line. Who would win? Bar to bar, hunched low under the screens, mano a mano, no inch to be given.

Jimi Mac got abreast of the marshals' hut, hit the red button and let loose the nitro hounds. The big bike lit up and hurtled forward with all its power and glory to take the checkered flag.

The three guns hit the line and sat up with disbelief. *What the hell had just happened?* Like sprinters in the Tour de France, each one of them was sure he had won: by a tyre width - on the line… *yeah/nah!* They had been done like a dog's dinner. It was only by inches but pants down, bum shellac'd, by a stars and striped mutant. *Unbelievable*!

STOP MAN

Jimi Mac stayed hard on the gas. To all and sundry it looked as if he was still racing. *Hadn't he seen the checkered flag?* He braked at the 50 for Doohan and tore around, knee down, still in full combat mode. He went through Stoner nearly on the stops. Jimi

Mac barely braked at Miller and instead of trying to turn he shot straight ahead to the infield track exit. He slowed to twice the posted speed and hurried up the road to the back of the USA pit garages, rode up a ramp and into the back of a box truck. The roller door came down behind him and he jumped off the bike.

Jimi Mac then exited a side door of the box body and leapt down the steps, two at a time. A replica of the bike he'd just ridden was inside the American pits being warmed up. It wasn't quite a replica as this one was completely legal under the IC rules, such as they were, but at a distance it looked identical to the rocketship, especially the outlandish stars n stripes paintjob.

He rode out of the pits, onto pitlane and down to the front of the control tower where the other front runners from the race were gathering.

THAT'S ALL SHE WROTE

McGuinness had finished in eighth place. All but on top of him were Colin Edwards, Martin, Zemke and Spike Edwards. McGuinness was the slowest of that gaggle but every time one of them made a run on him their bike would splutter and drop a coil. It was a sight to behold. McGuinness was like a bear beating back her cubs. One of them would make a run to pass him, hesitate, then fall to the back of the group, then re-muster and run again like a mindless salmon.

Colin Edwards finished a disappointing 12th, never having got on well with the bike. The misfiring on trying to pass McGuinness was the final nail in the coffin. Colin Edwards wouldn't be back to race at the island.

Spotty Dave overtook riders consistently in the race and finished in 13th. His youthful inner-self helped in the last two laps where older riders were beginning to fade. There was no slowing him down and he whooped across the finish line.

I was running steady until the last lap when I heard a not unfamiliar rattle coming from the engine. I pulled the clutch and moved the bike off the racing line and to the inside of the track just before Miller. The extreme temperature had been too much for the XJR/FJ and it had popped a valve shim. The head of that valve departed its stem and had a merry old time tap dancing on top of the piston. Hard to say which happened first but the end result was a scarred combustion chamber and bits of metal embedded in the top of the piston. And another DNF.

Matt's bike had also overheated and dropped a valve on lap four. He and I got to share the same pick-up trailer on the ride back to the pits.

Rastus's bike was running great due to the cooling effect of the methanol. Campbell came in last again but full dues as his bike had finished every race of the meeting – only 19 bikes finished the final race so it was no mean feat. He also scored valiant points for NZ in what had become a submarine of a team. Campbell's GS 1000 tortoise beat many hares. Hopefully Wes Cooley was gazing down with a smile.

FREE BEER IS GOOD BEER

It was pack-up time. The quicker you got your bike and gear crated, the quicker you could have a beer. The heat was intense and sweat ran in the eyes as we packed. Some had fancy bike boxes they'd blagged from the MotoGP paddock but most used the crates that new bikes were delivered in to dealers. Get the bike into the chocks, strap it down. Shove tyres, toolboxes and spares all around it. As close as possible to what was on your carnet list. Then cling-wrap the whole lot or fit plywood sides. When the job was done it was time for a beer; and that first one tasted so good.

Prizegiving was held upstairs in a large airy room. All the windows were open but at 42 degrees it made no difference. AC was the only salvation and it wasn't on offer.

The beer was free. The staff were on a constant trot back and forth between the chilly bins and the serving table. You could get a six-pack of Boag's; and everyone was. Free beer was good beer.

'Brother, I've just drunk six of these suckers and I feel nothing,' said Simon, his sweated shirt clinging tightly. 'It's so hot, I'm drinking them as fast as I can and nothing's happening.'

'Me too,' I agreed, sweat dripping off my nose. 'I think it's the heat. They're 20 per-cent evaporated by the time you get them to your mouth and you lose another 20 before they reach the throat. It's hot, mate.'

Simon nodded wildly and broke another Boag's from the plastic holder of a six-pack. 'Don't think I've ever been so hot. Even on cricket trips to Oz.'

I went for another beer; I was no drinker but I was feeling heroic. One beer was a frantic thirst quencher, two and I was in the zone; my brain had sped up – my brain and the *Engliahs* language had locked together like foreign dogs on a cold beach. Three beers and *theires* warning signs. Four beers and I was convinced and so *stubbone anf oreceful* that MY answers had to be put down in the pub

Kiwis at play.

quizz. Five, and I'm shedding the *Enlgish* language: too boring. I was now speaking *Spankish ore parleyvoo Francois*. Six, and grunts and swearing were replacing words and every beer thereafter meant more grunts and more swearing. The next morning I would endeavour to find out who I'd been with the evening before and ring them to apologise for what I couldn't remember.

BEDLAM

The prize giving was the usual bedlam. Bracksie, the commentator, was trying to keep the process under some form of control while also trying to keep the sweat out of his eyes. He had a towel to mop himself. He was a pro and knew the show must go on. The individual awards were lost in the sound of the blokes at the back of the room nattering away like old fishermen.

'Come on, you mongrels, fair suck of the sav,' intoned Bracksie, again.

'Keep it down.'

'Yeah, a little respect,' a voice called, from the front of the room.

The hum of sound dropped by half, then gradually crept back up. There was no stopping this roller coaster from building up its carriages full of drunks.

The Kiwi team had won some kind of award that I had never heard of.

The FIM Oceania Historic Road Race Cup. We had beaten the Aussies. It looked like it had been won by the two-strokes. Bloody hell. Jock Woodley went up with the other Kiwi strokers and got a cup and some medals. This contest was run on a level playing field and the Kiwis had won it! We had won it fair and square! *Bloody hell*!

Then it was time for the International Challenge winning team awards.

The Kiwi team had come last; not a huge surprise. I was called to the stage. I stumbled to the front – perhaps the beer *was* having an effect.

'Sheep shagger,' a voice cried. 'Baa-baa,' some others.

I tried to make a brilliant speech but I was never good off the cuff. On seeing a video later, I realised I was slurring – a lot.

Pog was next on stage. The Irish were magnanimous in defeat. They would celebrate anyway. Pog gave a quick speech which got lost in interpretation and noise. There were cries of 'potato' from some in the crowd. Pog paused grimly: 'Stoning by potato for yee. Yer mother looks like a potato.'

This caused a great eruption of delight amongst the crowd. The key to respect from a mob of Aussies: *Give it back to them*.

Bo slid through the crowd to the stage. He was high as a kite. I noticed the bulge of a pistol stuck down his butt, under his shirt.

'You dawgs quiet down,' he said, grabbing the mic from Bracksie. He did gain some quiet. Put a tall man with a Stetson on stage and most people would give a moment.

'Winners are grinners. *Right*, Jimi Mac. Y'all keep that image of the last race in your heads. We may not have won this war but we ain't quitters. No sir, we'll be back … and we'll be armed!'

The crowd were not going to be bullied by this cowboy. 'Go home Yank'.

'Next time Buckaroo.'

Bo glared out at the crowd and took a swig from a small brown bottle. He wiped his mouth and reached behind himself.

Kiwi team. Photo: D Begg

Uh-oh, I thought.

Bo paused then withdrew his hand. Some spark of sensibility must have ignited in his brain. Instead, he waved his arm in a dragging motion. 'Where's my team? Get up here, you good old boys.'

The Americans gathered on stage wearing their white T shirts pasted with a large number 1 on the front in the colours of the stars and stripes. They had prematurely popped the cork so to speak. They looked a little bewildered. They were eight points off the win – but that was only third place. Second loser.

'Wrong number,' some wag called out from the crowd.

Jeremy McWilliams fronted on stage for the UK team. They were second by two points. There was no way the skipper, Arthur, would confront this rabble: the monarchy would be horrified at the state of the empire. McWilliams was nominated. McWilliams was from Belfast and this crowd were mere pansies to him. He took the microphone and waited; the Irish knew how to wait. Eventually the mob hushed.

McWilliams smiled thinly at us. 'See youse next year and g'luck to ya.

Oh, and go feck yerselves.'

Wally was waiting in the wings and couldn't wait to get on stage. The Aussies had won. He began winding up for a long one and it was evident he was going to thank everyone he'd ever known, including his mother, before his speech was out.

A MILLION DOLLARS

Most people headed for the doors. It was time to disband and get back to their hotels, houses and holes to wash up and celebrate. Get downtown as soon as they were showered. Maintain impetus. If you stopped moving, it would be nigh on impossible to get going again. My flatmates and I were dedicated followers of the tradition of going out to celebrate the event.

The flatmates piled into the van for the ride back to the rental. Spotty Dave hadn't attended the prize giving.

Matt said Spotty Dave had jacked a ride before the awards ceremony and would catch us later. He had swerved away from Matt in a state of hazy euphoria: his last words were: 'No point *me* going to prize giving. *I* already feel like I won a million dollars.'

The lads piled out of the van in merry spirits. The warm Boags was left in the van and we hurried to the kitchen for more beer: cold beer.

'What's happened in the hallway?' asked Campbell, entering the kitchen after having gone for a pee. 'There's broken mirror all over the carpet.'

The boys crowded into the hallway. Sure enough, shards of mirror were spread along the floor like a shattered mosaic.

'What's that smell?' asked Simon. 'Exhaust?'

'Some sort of combustible hydrocarbon smell,' said Matt, sniffing abundantly.

'Smells like burnt benzine to me,' said Andy, also nose in the air and snuffling deeply.

Campbell checked the bunkroom. 'No sign of Spotty Dave. His suitcases are still there and his clothes are there.'

We stood loosely, considering the mirror fragments and the charred odour.

'You don't suppose …,' I suggested.

HEALTH AND SAFETY

It was a two stubby walk to town. I took a small weaving detour across a lawn to peer through a house window at the tennis on the telly. It was the men's final of the Australian Open. Nadal was a set up on Federer. The people in the house heard a noise and looked around to see me leaning on their windowsill. Fortunately, they were also motorcycle racers.

The bars were heaving with drunk motorcyclists. Spectators, friends, family, fans and racers in a mash of beer and bodies. The Aussies were triumphantly passing the trophy around. It was full of bourbon and waves of it spilled on the crowd. The Yanks were beginning to loosen up and get into it: there was still some shock factor that the mightiest nation hadn't won. Jimi Mac was gleefully howling, celebrating his victory in the last race, like a one-eyed man in the kingdom of the blind. The Irish were causing havoc, looking for a scrap or a kiss. They were pissed and lushing themselves in slack-lipped displays of emotion. They had either won or lost, but they had had a time. The English were trying to chin up. They weren't great losers and were terrible winners. The trick unit in the tail of McGuinness' bike had backfired. He hadn't been quite fast enough to get to the pointy end and cause havoc. Instead, it had slowed more Poms down than anyone else. The Kiwis were friends to all and up for any boisterous goings on. There had never been the expectation of winning in the NZ camp but we had given our all.

Randy Scott, an Irishman from NZ, was drinking whisky with Troy Corser. He shoved one into my mitt. 'Get that down you, son.'

Brendan would have had a ball, shame he was laid up in a hospital bed in Berwick. Still, someone was looking after him. The surgeon at the hospital, while inspecting him, had asked: 'So what bike were you riding?'

'Yer man rides a classic bike.'

'Type?'

'It's not a well-known model by yer average man. But she's got a Suzuki heart.'

'Model?'

'XR69.'

'Ah, like Croz used to ride.'

Brendan was in the right hospital.

On the far side of the pub, Simon had McGuinness's mechanic, Big Dave, up against the wall. Two heavyweights but face to face as friends. Simon was interested in buying a Padgetts superbike, the HM Plant one that McGuinness raced at the IOM. He figured Big Dave could work on Clive Padgett for him. Simon had immediately sold his XR 69 to Rastus after it blew up and now, using his stable logic, this meant he had stall space for another bike. Simon needed a superbike like he needed a hole in the head, *but whadayagannado?* He was an addict.

Big Dave was searching for a way to escape Simon's shopping embrace.

Andy and Matt were towering over fellow Yorkshireman Spike Edwards. The two 'Kiwis' had somehow scored pints of bitter and were back with like brethren and ramming themselves full of the Yorkie.

Campbell had Maria Costello cornered and was grinning like a Cheshire Cat. He had his t-shirt hoisted up and was hounding her to autograph his belly. He beamed and waved across to me. I looked closer; my eyesight was already getting bleary. It wasn't really Maria Costello – but she was a platinum blonde. I didn't have the heart to go and tell Campbell the truth – I just gave the thumbs up.

There was a scuffle in the corner. I watched idly. Bo was in the middle of it and being wrestled by members of his team. I intercepted an American heading for the bathroom.

'What's going on?'

'Ah, Bo tried to knife somebody.'

'What?! That's not like him,' I said. I reconsidered – maybe it *was* like him – but he would need just cause. 'Why?'

'The dude told Bo he was a health and safety officer.'

'Oh,' I considered. Definitely the wrong guy to be making that confession to. 'What the hell's a guy like that doing around motorcycle racers?'

The American laughed, 'Must have got the wrong barn dance. Health and safety. *Ha*, do any of us look healthy or safe?'

The American and I gazed about at the sea of boozed faces, flushed and hectic with post-race intoxication. People in mindless hazes clinging to each other and their beer cans.

Bo attempted another lunge at the H & S officer but his crew held onto him and headed him for the door.

He shouted back, over his shoulder, '*Hey asshole*, next time I'll flick you across the room and you'll land in your own pile of poo!'

Bo gave me an expansive wink as he was hustled by and out the door onto the footpath.

'Yee-haa,' guffawed the American beside me and stumbled away to the men's room.

CRAZY SHIT

Simon appeared at my side, 'Crazy shit, eh? Another year where it's gone nuts at PI.'

I considered: it had been nuts. More nuts than other years? Certainly more carnage in the team. *Do I really need the stress of trying to maintain this cageful of monkeys called the NZ team? Maybe medication to help get through the week on the island? Valium, ether, morphine – or something illegal. Cocaine. What about Viagra? That was supposed to get you up. Could it also keep your spirit and energy up? And in what dose? It was so tricky to get the timing right.* I recalled a recent conversation with my doctor.

'This one you need to take an hour before … you do it.'

'So, what you're saying is that I would need to be on a promise? Or at least very hopeful.'

The doctor had glanced at me dubiously, 'If you take the whole pill you can feel quite light-headed. The blood has gone to … that area, and there can be less in your head. You can just take half a pill. You have to experiment a bit with … doing it.'

I had noted that the doctor couldn't actually put a name to doing it. Shouldn't a medical doctor, of all people, be able to find a suitable name for shagging?

Steve Dobson. Photo: D Begg

The doctor had still been reeling a little from my confession that I'd been suffering Long Covid for 20 years. Lack of libido, brain fog, sore joints, headaches, lethargy, lack of motivation, cramps, night sweats, flashbacks: all symptoms that I recognised.

'There is another pill which lasts for 36 hours,' the doctor had offered hopefully. 'It costs $78 for two pills. So, you can do it whenever you're ready.'

I had thought for a moment. 'So, it would be a little like stalking then. You, being the predator, would have 36 hours to carry out your strike.

You just need to find the prey.'

The consultation hadn't ended well, as usual. I wondered why the doctor kept me on the list. Her final words were: 'Watch your blood pressure. Oh, and don't eat grapefruit.'

Out of 11 starters for the Kiwi IC team, only four had finished: Alex, Spotty Dave, Rastus and Campbell. Nine engines had blown up. Four failures with electrical problems, which had been fixed. Three crashes (plus Andy). One in hospital (plus Andy).

Chucky not only didn't terrorise the other teams, which was Plan A, he had torn the Kiwi team a brand new one. *Chucky was a psychopathic, pathological, salty little spittoon.*

Would I be up to doing this gig next year? I needed to mitigate. Restitution was necessary. An exorcism of some form. I sucked a large breath of air then let it hiss out through my clenched teeth with a sound like Alka Setzer hitting water. Yes, I could do it. I was Motorcycle Man, after all.

I leaned close to Simon's ear. 'Where's Chucky?'

THE END

www.ingramcontent.com/pod-product-compliance
Lightning Source LLC
Chambersburg PA
CBHW041158290426
44109CB00002B/52